the
SOVIET
UNION

Opposing Viewpoints®

Other Books of Related Interest in the Opposing Viewpoints Series:

American Foreign Policy
The Arms Race
Central America
Latin America and US Foreign Policy
The Middle East
Nuclear War
Problems of Africa
The Vietnam War
Terrorism

Additional Books in the Opposing Viewpoints Series:

Abortion
AIDS
American Government
The American Military
American Values
America's Prisons
Biomedical Ethics
Censorship
Chemical Dependency
Constructing a Life Philosophy
Crime & Criminals
Criminal Justice
Death and Dying
The Death Penalty
Drug Abuse
Economics in America
The Environmental Crisis
Male/Female Roles
The Mass Media
The Political Spectrum
Sexual Values
Social Justice
War and Human Nature

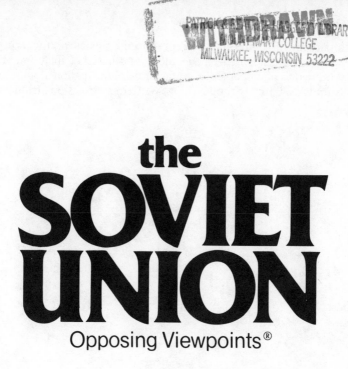

the
SOVIET
UNION

Opposing Viewpoints®

David L. Bender & Bruno Leone, *Series Editors*

Neal Bernards, Janelle Rohr, Karin Swisher & Bonnie Szumski, *Book Editors*

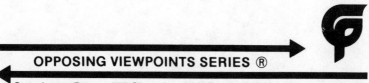

OPPOSING VIEWPOINTS SERIES ®

Greenhaven Press   577 Shoreview Park Road   St. Paul, Minnesota 55126

Library of Congress Cataloging-in-Publication Data

The Soviet Union : opposing viewpoints.

  (Opposing viewpoints series)
  Bibliography: p.
  Includes index.
  1. Soviet Union—Politics and government—1982-
2. Soviet Union—Foreign relations—1975-
3. Soviet Union—Economic conditions—1976-
4. Human rights—Soviet Union. 5. Soviet Union—
Foreign relations—Europe, Eastern. 6. Europe,
Eastern—Foreign relations—Soviet Union.
I. Bernards, Neal, 1963-   .II. Series.
DK289.S687 1988   320.947   87-25523
ISBN 0-89908-404-4 (pbk.)
ISBN 0-89908-429-X (lib. bdg.)

"Congress shall make no law... abridging the freedom of speech, or of the press."

First Amendment to the US Constitution

The basic foundation of our democracy is the first amendment guarantee of freedom of expression. The *Opposing Viewpoints Series* is dedicated to the concept of this basic freedom and the idea that it is more important to practice it than to enshrine it.

Contents

Page

Why Consider Opposing Viewpoints?   9
Introduction   13
Chapter 1: Does the Soviet Union Seek
            World Domination?
    Chapter Preface   16
    1. The Soviet Union Seeks World Domination   17
        Harold Rood
    2. The Soviet Union Does Not Seek World Domination   25
        Vladimir Zamkovi
    3. Soviet International Involvement Is Purely   32
       Humanitarian
        Nikolai Sedov
    4. Soviet International Involvement Is Self-Serving   36
        Richard N. Perle
    5. Soviet Influence Is Expanding in Latin America   42
        Timothy Ashby
    6. Soviet Influence Is Not Expanding in Latin America   50
        The Center for Defense Information
    A Critical Thinking Activity: Recognizing Ethnocentrism   58
    Periodical Bibliography   60
Chapter 2: Does the Soviet Union Guarantee
            Human Rights?
    Chapter Preface   62
    1. The Soviet System Guarantees Basic Human Rights   63
        Leonid Kazinov & Yaroslav Renkas
    2. Soviet Human Rights Are Undermined by Corruption   70
        Konstantin Simis
    3. Soviet Human Rights Violations Must Be Tolerated   79
        Theodore H. Von Laue
    4. Soviet Human Rights Violations Should Remain   86
       a Concern
        Mikhail Tsypkin
    5. Soviet Women Have Full Equality   93
        *Galina Sukhoruchenkova,
        interviewed by Lyudmila Zabavskaya*

6. Soviet Women Do Not Have Full Equality   97
   David K. Willis

7. Soviet Jews Are Repressed   101
   Roger Pilon

8. Soviet Jews Are Not Repressed   108
   Florence Fox

A Critical Thinking Activity: Recognizing Deceptive   115
   Arguments

Periodical Bibliography   117

Chapter 3: How Strong Is the Soviet Economy?

Chapter Preface   120

1. The Soviet Economy Is Healthy   122
   Gennady Kobyakov

2. The Soviet Economy Is in Crisis   128
   Aleksandr Solzhenitsyn

3. The Soviet Economy Is Improving   134
   Abel Aganbegian

4. The Soviet Economy Is Not Improving   140
   Paul Kennedy

5. The Soviet Economy Is Undergoing Economic   147
   Reform
   Mikhail Gorbachev

6. Soviet Economic Reform Is a Myth   154
   Lawrence Minard, Peter Brimelow & Seweryn Bialer

A Critical Thinking Activity: Distinguishing Between   160
   Fact and Opinion

Periodical Bibliography   162

Chapter 4: What Is the Soviet Union's Role in Eastern Europe?

Chapter Preface   164

1. The Soviet Union Has Been a Model for   165
   Eastern Europe
   Marian Orzechowski

2. The Soviet Union Has Stifled Eastern Europe   171
   Ladislav Hejdánek

3. Soviet Domination Harms Eastern Europe's   176
   Economies
   Herbert J. Ellison

4. The Soviets Do Not Dominate Eastern Europe's   184
   Economies
   Vyacheslav Sychev, interviewed by Vladimir Ganin

5. The Soviets Have Destroyed Polish Freedom   192
   Timothy Garton Ash

6. The Soviets Have Protected Polish Freedom   199
   Mike Davidow

A Critical Thinking Activity: Evaluating Sources of 206
   Information

Periodical Bibliography   208

Chapter 5: Is Glasnost Genuine?

Chapter Preface   210

1. The Soviet System Embraces Glasnost   211
   Mikhail Gorbachev

2. The Soviet System Will Not Allow Glasnost   218
   Robert L. Pfaltzgraff Jr.

3. Glasnost Is a Public Relations Ploy   225
   Vladimir Bukovsky

4. Glasnost Is Not a Public Relations Ploy   231
   Julius Jacobson

A Critical Thinking Activity: Recognizing Statements 237
   That Are Provable

Periodical Bibliography   239

Organizations To Contact   240
Bibliography of Books   244
Appendix of Periodicals   247
Index   248

Why Consider Opposing Viewpoints?

"It is better to debate a question without settling it than to settle a question without debating it."

Joseph Joubert (1754-1824)

The Importance of Examining Opposing Viewpoints

The purpose of the Opposing Viewpoints Series, and this book in particular, is to present balanced, and often difficult to find, opposing points of view on complex and sensitive issues.

Probably the best way to become informed is to analyze the positions of those who are regarded as experts and well studied on issues. It is important to consider every variety of opinion in an attempt to determine the truth. Opinions from the mainstream of society should be examined. But also important are opinions that are considered radical, reactionary, or minority as well as those stigmatized by some other uncomplimentary label. An important lesson of history is the eventual acceptance of many unpopular and even despised opinions. The ideas of Socrates, Jesus, and Galileo are good examples of this.

Readers will approach this book with their own opinions on the issues debated within it. However, to have a good grasp of one's own viewpoint, it is necessary to understand the arguments of those with whom one disagrees. It can be said that those who do not completely understand their adversary's point of view do not fully understand their own.

A persuasive case for considering opposing viewpoints has been presented by John Stuart Mill in his work *On Liberty*. When examining controversial issues it may be helpful to reflect on this suggestion:

> The only way in which a human being can make some approach to knowing the whole of a subject, is by hearing what can be said about it by persons of every variety of opinion, and studying all modes in which it can be looked at by every character of mind. No wise man ever acquired his wisdom in any mode but this.

Analyzing Sources of Information

The Opposing Viewpoints Series includes diverse materials taken from magazines, journals, books, and newspapers, as well as statements and position papers from a wide range of individuals, organizations and governments. This broad spectrum of sources helps to develop patterns of thinking which are open to the consideration of a variety of opinions.

Pitfalls To Avoid

A pitfall to avoid in considering opposing points of view is that of regarding one's own opinion as being common sense and the most rational stance and the point of view of others as being only opinion and naturally wrong. It may be that another's opinion is correct and one's own is in error.

Another pitfall to avoid is that of closing one's mind to the opinions of those with whom one disagrees. The best way to approach a dialogue is to make one's primary purpose that of understanding the mind and arguments of the other person and not that of enlightening him or her with one's own solutions. More can be learned by listening than speaking.

It is my hope that after reading this book the reader will have a deeper understanding of the issues debated and will appreciate the complexity of even seemingly simple issues on which good and honest people disagree. This awareness is particularly important in a democratic society such as ours where people enter into public debate to determine the common good. Those with whom one disagrees should not necessarily be regarded as enemies, but perhaps simply as people who suggest different paths to a common goal.

Developing Basic Reading and Thinking Skills

In this book, carefully edited opposing viewpoints are purposely placed back to back to create a running debate; each viewpoint is preceded by a short quotation that best expresses the author's main argument. This format instantly plunges the reader into the midst of a controversial issue and greatly aids that reader in mastering the basic skill of recognizing an author's point of view.

A number of basic skills for critical thinking are practiced in the activities that appear throughout the books in the series. Some of the skills are:

Evaluating Sources of Information   The ability to choose from among alternative sources the most reliable and accurate source in relation to a given subject.

Separating Fact from Opinion   The ability to make the basic distinction between factual statements (those that can be demonstrated or verified empirically) and statements of opinion (those that are beliefs or attitudes that cannot be proved).

Identifying Stereotypes   The ability to identify oversimplified, exaggerated descriptions (favorable or unfavorable) about people and insulting statements about racial, religious or national groups, based upon misinformation or lack of information.

Recognizing Ethnocentrism   The ability to recognize attitudes or opinions that express the view that one's own race, culture, or group is inherently superior, or those attitudes that judge another culture or group in terms of one's own.

It is important to consider opposing viewpoints and equally important to be able to critically analyze those viewpoints. The activities in this book are designed to help the reader master these thinking skills. Statements are taken from the book's viewpoints and the reader is asked to analyze them. This technique aids the reader in developing skills that not only can be applied to the viewpoints in this book, but also to situations where opinionated spokespersons comment on controversial issues. Although the activities are helpful to the solitary reader, they are most useful when the reader can benefit from the interaction of group discussion.

Using this book and others in the series should help readers develop basic reading and thinking skills. These skills should improve the reader's ability to understand what they read. Readers should be better able to separate fact from opinion, substance from rhetoric and become better consumers of information in our media-centered culture.

This volume of the Opposing Viewpoints Series does not advocate a particular point of view. Quite the contrary! The very nature of the book leaves it to the reader to formulate the opinions he or she finds most suitable. My purpose as publisher is to see that this is made possible by offering a wide range of viewpoints which are fairly presented.

David L. Bender
Publisher

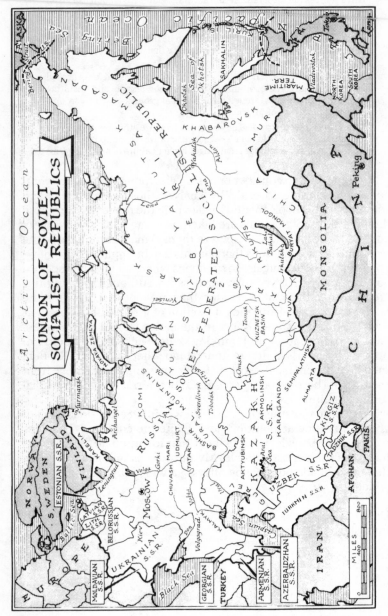

UNION OF SOVIET SOCIALIST REPUBLICS

Reprinted with permission from *Current History* magazine.

Introduction

"Russia. . . is a riddle wrapped in a mystery inside an enigma."

—Winston Churchill, 1939

The source of the Soviet Union's power has long perplexed Western observers. Why does this nation, which is undergoing massive bureaucratic reform, which is plagued by food shortages, and which is mired in a costly war in Afghanistan, continue to be viewed as one of the two major world powers?

A central factor is the Soviet Union's military strength. Soviet leaders invest fifteen percent of the nation's gross national product in military affairs. Two-thirds of all Soviet industry provide goods for the five branches of the military. The emphasis on military research and development has led to the creation of an immense and sophisticated nuclear arsenal. This awesome nuclear capability worries many military analysts because Soviet leaders traditionally have been secretive when discussing nuclear strategy, the destructive potential of their missiles, and, until recently, arms control. It is these same leaders and their US counterparts who govern the destiny of humanity by how well they handle their nations' nuclear weapons.

The Soviet Union's power is also strikingly evident in the political and economic influence it wields in Eastern Europe and many Third World nations. The Warsaw Pact countries, including Czechoslovakia, Poland, East Germany, and others, look to the USSR for advanced technology, agricultural imports, and military aid. In addition, the Soviets provide humanitarian aid and a military presence to revolutionary governments in countries such as Angola, Afghanistan, and the People's Republic of Yemen.

The Soviet Union also lends political, military, and moral support to existing Marxist nations such as Mongolia and Mozambique which are struggling to succeed with communist societies based on the Soviet example. Thus, the Soviet system remains a model for countries like Cuba and Nicaragua whose citizens have suffered under unjust feudal economies and dictatorial capitalists.

Understanding the Soviet Union is a necessary prerequisite to comprehending the dynamics of international relations. The authors in this book attempt to demystify the Soviet Union and explain the motivations that drive this Eastern superpower. The authors include prominent Soviet dissidents, foreign policy experts, Soviet leaders, and American political commentators. The five topics covered in *The Soviet Union: Opposing Viewpoints* are: Does the Soviet Union Seek World Domination? Does the Soviet Union Guarantee Human Rights? How Strong Is the Soviet Economy? What Is the Soviet Union's Role in Eastern Europe? and Is Glasnost Genuine? By reading the diverse viewpoints in this book, readers may come to a greater understanding of this vast, puzzling superpower.

Does the Soviet Union Seek World Domination?

the SOVIET UNION

Chapter Preface

Is the Soviet Union an expansionist power, and do its leaders have world domination as their goal? Many US officials would answer in the affirmative, citing the takeover of Eastern European countries like Czechoslovakia and Poland and the war in Afghanistan as examples of overt expansionism. They would also cite covert actions, such as military and economic aid to Angola, Cuba, Nicaragua, and Vietnam, as examples of the USSR's continual efforts to defeat the West.

Many others would disagree with this assessment, arguing that the accusation of Soviet expansionism is Cold War propaganda. Even if the Soviets were expansionist, these critics argue, they have neither the resources nor the willpower to achieve world domination. While the Soviet Union will support revolutionary movements to cause the US and Western Europe to expend military and economic assistance, the spectre of nuclear war makes it virtually impossible that the Soviets could pose a real threat to the democratic nations.

Whether or not Soviet policy is expansionist has an impact on efforts to improve Soviet foreign relations with the West. The authors in the following chapter debate the implications of Soviet intervention.

"Every action that ends by granting some strategic advantage to the Soviet Union. . . is a step intended to contribute to the defeat of the West."

The Soviet Union Seeks World Domination

Harold Rood

Both the US and the USSR compete in the economic, political, and military spheres, and each nation accuses one another of attempting to gain superiority. In the following viewpoint, Harold Rood argues that the Soviet Union's actions are clear and decisive attempts to gain superiority and eventually defeat the US. Rood holds the Keck Foundation Chair of International Strategic Studies of Government at Claremont McKenna College in California.

As you read, consider the following questions:

1. Why does the author argue that the Soviet Union is dominating Asia?
2. The author argues that the West acts naively about Soviet preparations for war. Why?
3. Do you think the author is right about the Soviet Union? Why or why not?

Harold Rood, "Soviet Strategy and the Defense of the West," *Global Affairs*, Summer 1987. Reprinted with permission.

It flies in the face of fashionable theories of international politics and comfortable views of the nature and capabilities of the regime that rules the Soviet Union to suggest that there is a competent, coherent strategy aimed at defeating the Western alliance. To accept that Soviet foreign policy aims daily at facilitating Soviet strategy against the West is to confront the prospect of general war, for strategy has to do with the winning of wars.

What a nation intends to do in the international sphere can be understood both by what its leaders say and by the manner in which the elements of its national power are developed and employed. No action that costs money, requires the investment of resources, and is troublesome to take lacks purpose or reason behind it. When money is spent, troops, ships and aircraft are accumulated and deployed, diplomacy and propaganda exercised, it can be expected that policy is at work....

Preparing for War

If any other nation in the world had undertaken the material military measures that the Soviet Union has over the past decades, one might reasonably suggest that such a nation was preparing for war. The continuing increase in the size and capabilities of the Soviet armed forces and those of their allies, to a point where they enjoy superiority over the forces that can be easily brought against them, is preparation for war. The accumulation, step-by-step, of a series of strategic positions, the fostering of alliances such as those with India, Libya, Syria, Vietnam, Cuba, and North Korea, suggest the existence of a coherent strategy aimed at the decisive defeat of the Western alliance.

Soviet officers, generals, and admirals studying Marxist-Leninist teachings are given the following instructions on war:

> The essence of war is the continuation of politics by means of armed force. That is the main characteristic of war. Therefore, this definition of the essence of war does not include many of the important ways that are used to secure victory...notably economic, diplomatic and other forms of struggle. The definition of the content of war and that of the forms holding and expressing this content are much more all-embracing. These definitions include a wide range of processes...attending the armed struggle, are concerned with it and serve to achieve the political aims of the war, the aim of gaining victory.

As Marshal V. W. Sokolovsky observed in 1975,

> The more effectively a country uses the forces and means accumulated before the war, the greater the results it will achieve at the very beginning of the war, and the more rapidly victory will be achieved.

The marshal wrote in *Soviet Military Strategy,* "The acceptance of war as a tool of politics also determines the interrelation of military strategy and politics, which is based on the principle of the full dependence of the former on the latter."

Locked in Struggle

At the meeting of the Communist Party's Central Committee in June 1983, Yuri Andropov, the party first secretary, said the two competing social systems of the East and West are locked in a momentous struggle, upon which the future of mankind depends. He had said earlier, when he was head of the KGB, "Marxism-Leninism is the textbook for achieving Socialist world revolution and the building of a new society in every country of the world."

Pravda, the Communist Party newspaper, put it more boldly still: "The struggle between the world proletariat and the bourgeoisie will continue until the final victory of communism on a world scale."

Ceaseless Preparation for War

There *is* a larger story of Soviet bloc plans, and from time to time it must be told. You may call it a Soviet program. You may call it a blueprint if you like, but it makes more sense to speak of a common program which is well understood and does not often require commitment to paper. The program is one of territorial expansion and enhancement of political, economic, and military power. Its agencies are those of the Soviet Union and its allies in accord with the oft-reiterated principles of proletarian internationalism. It is directed at the destruction of the Free World, that is to say "imperialism," which is to say the great democracies.

I do not say there is a timetable. I do not say the Soviets want war, though it would be foolish to say that what they want is peace. What I will argue is that the evidence of many years indicates, first, that the Soviets ceaselessly prepare for war, and second, that long-term Soviet bloc designs are being instituted as opportunity permits in the military, political, and economic arenas by Marxist-Leninist organizations and governments. They are succeeding more often than failing. And the free peoples of the world, while not always fully conscious of these plans, are very much the worse for them.

Jim Courter, speech delivered before The Committee for the Free World, May 2, 1987.

In a briefing given his staff on June 4, 1975, a Soviet consul in Japan cast some light on the operation of Soviet strategy:

What I consider the most joyous occasion at this time is the reopening of the Suez Canal for the first time in eight years. What it means is that the great sacrifices made by the Soviet Union from the time it supported Israel's war of independence to the cease-fire when it supported Egypt are finally being rewarded with the re-opening of the Suez Canal. The long-cherished ambition

19

of advancing southward by the Soviet people is finally materializing after more than fifty years since the founding of the U.S.S.R. What the Soviet Union expects to realize through the use of the Suez Canal is to secure command of the sea in order to carry out its security concepts in Europe and Asia. The use of the Suez Canal will permit the Baltic Fleet, Northern Fleet, Mediterranean Expeditionary Fleet and Black Sea Fleet to link with the Pacific Fleet and the Indian Ocean Expeditionary Fleet in the Indian Ocean.

Recalling the great material assistance lent by the Soviet Union and its allies to North Vietnam in the course of its conquest of South Vietnam, Laos, and Cambodia, the consul said,

As a post-Vietnam measure, the Soviet Union's concept is to establish a third state in the Indo-China peninsula. The federation will be made up of Laos, Cambodia and Vietnam . . . . In order to establish the Indochina Socialist Republic as a pro-Soviet state, the Soviet Union intends to exert its efforts to the build-up of a certain group of the Cambodian Unification Front.

Vietnam as a Pro-Soviet State

On July 5, 1975, the government of the People's Republic of China accused the Soviet Union of trying to fill the vacuum created in Southeast Asia after the United States abandoned South Vietnam. By September 1975, it was clear that Vietnam was, in fact, a pro-Soviet state and that steps had already been taken to deploy Soviet forces into Indochina.

Soviet naval and air units are now stationed in Indochina and Vietnamese forces have been considerably expanded. In 1970, when the United States had a half-million men in South Vietnam, North Vietnam had an army of 470,000 men with about four hundred tanks. By 1982, nine years after U.S. forces had been withdrawn and seven years after the fall of Saigon, the Vietnamese army numbered over a million men with two thousand tanks.

It cannot be mere coincidence that the Soviet Union and its allies, having supported North Vietnam to defeat the United States and conquer all of Indochina should end by possessing air and naval bases there today and should have seen to the buildup of Vietnam's armed forces. Nor is it coincidence that Vietnam with its Soviet bases should be only eight hundred miles from the Philippines, where a Communist-led insurgency is fighting the government and where the U.S. naval base at Subic Bay and Clark Air Force base, the only two U.S. bases south of the Ryukyus until one reaches Diego Garcia in the Indian Ocean, are located.

A Plan To Dominate Asia

At least the government of the People's Republic of China does not consider such things to be curious coincidences:

The Soviet *strategy* in Asia is to lay down a strategic cordon around the continent, stretching from the Mediterranean, the Red

Steve Benson. Reprinted by permission: Tribune Media Services.

Sea, the Indian Ocean and up to Haishenwei (Vladivostok), and using the "Cuba of Asia" as its hatchetman to seize the whole of Indo-China to dominate Southeast Asia and South Asia....

So the Soviet Union started a large flanking move to encircle Western Europe with the main object of seizing sources of strategic materials...controlling the major sea routes linking Western Europe and the United States and those linking the two with Africa and Asia.

If the Chinese view is correct, then every action that ends by granting some strategic advantage to the Soviet Union, however slight it might seem, is a step intended to contribute to the defeat of the West. To suppose otherwise is to misunderstand how those who rule the Soviet Union view such matters.

In April 1967, Leonid Brezhnev explained to a Communist Party conference the meaning of the war in Vietnam in relation to the situation in Europe:

Even today the struggle for peace in Europe pins down the aggressive forces of the imperialists...and prevents them taking part in suppressing the liberation movements in other parts of the world....[D]espite stubborn efforts the United States has not managed to attract its NATO...allies into the Vietnam adventure, as occurred during the Korean War....To tie down the forces of imperialism in Europe...is important in itself, but is also to deal it a defeat which would have effects elsewhere.

From this it can be seen that there is some strategic relationship between where operations undertaken to gain a favorable outcome in war take place and those operations elsewhere intended to contribute to that outcome.

That relationship is described by Admiral Gorshkov in his book, *Seapower and the State* (1976),

> To achieve superiority of forces over the enemy in the main sector and *pin him down* in the secondary sectors. . . [is] to create such a situation that the enemy will be paralyzed or constrained in his operations, or weakened and thereby hampered from interfering with our operations. . . .

Waging a Successful War

It seems evident that there are, among those who rule the Soviet Union, some who understand the nature of strategy. If they see an unremitting struggle between East and West and conceive of winning that struggle, then what the Soviet Union does abroad must be viewed in the light of its strategic significance for the outcome of that struggle. Policies and actions that are strategically directed are intended to bear directly on the ability to wage successful war. . . .

Under the North Korean-Soviet alliance, in return for the Soviet right to overfly North Korea, to use North Korean air bases, and to use ports on both the east and west coast of North Korea, the Soviet Union gave North Korea fifty new MiG-23 fighter aircraft.

It is, of course, obvious that a Korea unified by force from the north constitutes a severe strategic threat to Japan. Just as the United States was able to support the defense of South Korea in the Korean War with air operations from Japan, so could Soviet and North Korean air forces conduct air operations from South Korea against Japan. What one must always ask when an adversary takes what appears to be a strategic step is how that step will facilitate his strategy. What would possession of South Korea let the Soviet Union do that it could not otherwise do or that it could not do so inexpensively?

The great concentrations of population and industry in Japan are now within range of Soviet long-range air forces based around Vladivostok and on Sakhalin. From bases in South Korea, Soviet ground-attack aviation would be within range of the most important targets in Japan, and it is evident that lack of adequate air defense is a major vulnerability of Japan.

The use of ground attack aircraft to support an attack on Japan from Korea and from the Soviet islands north of Japan would free Soviet long-range aviation for more strategic and long-range operations over the North Pacific.

The Korea and Tsushima straits, now in Western hands, are obstacles to the war-time deployment of the Soviet Pacific fleet southward. Soviet naval forces based on the west coast of Korea avoid those obstacles just as Soviet possession and defenses in the Kuriles would permit Soviet naval deployment into the Northern Pacific.

With Japan, the Ryukyus, and the Philippines neutralized or in the hands of the Eastern alliance, Soviet naval forces would enjoy freedom of action to operate across the Pacific as well as southward to connect with Soviet naval forces based on the fringes of the Indian Ocean and in the Middle East.

Soviet Expansionism Through Military Might

The U.S.S.R. is the first world power in history whose ambitions can avail themselves of nothing except military force. The Soviet empire is hardly a model in the economic or technological domain, in its political institutions or in its lifestyle.

The two trump cards of hegemony are power and prestige. The Soviet Union has lost the latter. If it loses the former, its global role is finished. Its leaders know that—which is why we must never forget that we are not negotiating a purely technical matter. We also are dealing with expansionism, the vital principle of the Soviets' national policy and the only means they have to extend their influence in the world.

Jean-François Revel, *World Press Review,* November 1986.

For the Western alliance, it would mean denial of bases from which to operate against the Soviet homeland. But the pushing eastward of Soviet military, naval, and air forces is not merely defensive. The Soviet Pacific fleet and eastern air forces are targets worth destroying, but an attack on Siberia by Western forces, even if they had the capability, which they do not, would not defeat the Soviet Union. The heart of Soviet power lies to the west of the Urals, and that is where the defeat of the Soviet Union would have to take place.

The Pacific, therefore, has some other value in Soviet strategy beyond the defense of the Soviet homeland, if there is a comprehensive strategy at work....

What Kind of Strategy?

If Soviet strategy is indeed global in its compass, then it cannot be expected that a Warsaw Pact attack on NATO Europe will find Soviet, North Korean, and Vietnamese forces assuming the stance of neutrals, any more than a war in the Far East would leave Warsaw Pact forces without something to do in Europe.

Here then is the problem for the West in considering its defense. Does Soviet strategy aim at the eventual occupation of Western Europe and the conquest of the free countries in Asia or does it aim at the thorough defeat of the United States within the Western Hemisphere?

If Soviet strategists have done their homework, they understand that if the United States is rendered powerless, all else—NATO Europe, Japan, South Korea, and the rest—will fall by the wayside. That is because the United States is the center of power of the Western alliance.

Or does the Soviet Union, as a Eurasian power, only have a continental outlook despite its global strategy? Does that strategy aim only at the absorption of the countries on its immediate periphery, leaving the United States intact even if defeated abroad?

Do Soviet operations in the Gulf of Mexico, the Caribbean, and Central America constitute the erection of a secondary theater of operations to pin U.S. forces down while the Soviet Union and its allies seek decisive operations elsewhere? Or are the forces of the East bloc aiming at a war on four fronts against the United States itself? The four fronts include the Atlantic, the Pacific, the Gulf, and Caribbean, as well as that to be mounted through the skies by Soviet strategic nuclear forces.

The Soviet Union is clearly prepared for war and its preparations both material and strategic continue apace. The West is not prepared for war but contemplates any prospect of war with distaste and even horror. Yet each strategic step taken by the Soviet Union before war starts is intended to encompass the defeat of the West, as cheaply as possible for the Soviet Union. When war comes the West will be surprised just as France, though at war with Germany for nine months, was surprised on May 10, 1940. . . .

A Discernible Logic

Based on observation, logic, and reasoning, it is possible to discern the relationship between events, to grasp the significance of the relationship, and to understand where a chain of events can lead. But it is not possible to demonstrate what will happen until after it has happened, when it may be too late to avoid the penalty of inaction or wrong action.

In strategic matters and the conduct of successful war, there is an inherent and discernible logic. Events connected with such matters may be reasoned through as rigorously as any of the correct proofs of Euclid's propositions. That is because strategy and war deal with physical objects and material events in time and space. And the physical universe has its own inherent and immutable logic that is subject neither to human preference nor to sentiment.

"The Soviet Union is in the vanguard of the peace-loving forces of the world."

The Soviet Union Does Not Seek World Domination

Vladimir Zamkovi

Vladimir Zamkovi is the author of *The Philosophy of Aggression,* a pamphlet published by the Soviet press. In the following viewpoint, Zamkovi argues that contrary to US propaganda, the Soviet Union is a peace-loving nation. The USSR is forced to act in an aggressive fashion because of the relentless provocations of the US.

As you read, consider the following questions:

1. Why, according to the author, does the US accuse the USSR of military aggressiveness?
2. The author cites a key philosophy behind US worldwide intervention. What is it?
3. Why is the US philosophy of anti-communism counterproductive, according to the author?

Vladimir Zamkovi, *The Philosophy of Aggression.* Moscow: Novosti Press Agency Publishing House, 1987.

Mankind is approaching the 21st century amid a truly dramatic struggle between the forces of progress, socialism and peace, on the one hand, and the forces of imperialism, reaction and war, on the other.

The confrontation of the two world systems—socialism and capitalism—is taking place at a time when there exist large stockpiles of weapons of mass destruction. This is a characteristic feature of the present stage of historical development. Therefore, the problem of war and peace, taken together with other global problems of our time, such as the ecological, energy and demographic problems, is becoming particularly urgent and acute....

The Soviet Union is in the vanguard of the peace-loving forces of the world. Its consistent efforts in the postwar years have made it possible to resolve many crisis situations that were fraught with the danger of a nuclear catastrophe, and to curb those forces that count on a world war as a means of attaining their selfish aims.

The peace-loving forces, which express the interests and desires of all peoples of our planet, are being opposed by influential forces of war represented by monopoly capital and its military-industrial complex. This determines the intricate dialectics of their confrontation.

Practically throughout the 1970s the process of detente and of a restructuring of international relations on the principle of peaceful coexistence of states with different social and state systems was under way. But the early 1980s saw a revival of "cold war" practices and a deterioration of the international situation through the fault of the reactionary and aggressive forces of modern capitalism, above all of the US ruling circles. The danger of war has sharply increased. It is no exaggeration to say that mankind now stands at the brink of a nuclear catastrophe.

US Aggressive Actions

Special responsibility for this situation rests with the current US administration under President Reagan, which is taking drastic large-scale actions aimed at upsetting the existing military-strategic balance in the world and attaining military superiority over the Soviet Union. The approval of huge military budgets; the development of new types and systems of weapons of mass destruction; the deployment of medium-range ballistic missiles in Western Europe in close proximity to the borders of the socialist community countries; the course of militarization of outer space; the buildup of the US military presence in the "hot spots" of the world; direct interference in the affairs of other states—such is a far from complete list of the US administration's actions which have seriously aggravated the international situation and increased the danger of the outbreak of war. This foreign policy course is a result, above all, of mounting pressure by the US military-industrial complex, an atmosphere of war hysteria, anticommunist psychosis and of blind faith in the impunity of "muscle flexing" in politics, all of which are so characteristic of the entire ideological climate in the United States.

The current foreign policy of the United States is countered by the consistently peaceful policy of the USSR. In the last few years the Soviet government has advanced a number of new initiatives for strengthening peace, preserving the existing military-strategic parity and ensuring equal security. These include the Soviet Union's unilateral renunciation of the first use of nuclear weapons and proposals on demilitarization of outer space, on the adoption of a code

Ollie Harrington for the *Daily World*.

of conduct governing the relationships between the nuclear powers, and on freezing the existing arsenals of nuclear-missile weapons. . . .

The peace initiatives of the Soviet Union are in full conformity with its peaceful policy. "We are not pursuing a Metternich-like policy of 'balance of forces', setting one state against another, knocking together blocs and counterblocs, creating 'axes' or 'triangles', but a policy of worldwide detente, strengthening world security and developing universal international cooperation," said General Secretary of the CPSU [Communist Party of the Soviet Union] Central Committee Mikhail Gorbachev. . . .

US Imperialism: Sources of Aggression

Today a reliable yardstick for determining the degree of progressiveness and humaneness of the two opposing systems, socialism and capitalism, and of the social forces, ideologists and statesmen representing them, is the attitude to the problem of war and peace.

The ideology of socialism is oriented to peace and social progress. It is based on the firm conviction that a global war can be prevented. This conviction underlies the peaceful foreign policy of the socialist countries.

The imperialist powers, on the other hand, owing to the very nature of monopoly capitalism, are fundamentally opposed to the ideals of peace and progress. The history of the last decades has shown that the ideology of imperialism is aimed at justifying a continued arms race and substantiating the idea of inevitability of wars, including a global nuclear catastrophe.

The ideologists of imperialism have advanced many theories which have gained currency and which directly or indirectly serve this inhumane purpose.

They seek to promote the aggressive policy of US imperialism and to provide arguments of a philosophical nature for backing up the idea that war cataclysms are inevitable.

The powerful and influential military-industrial complex in the United States sets down the principles, tasks and objectives of the global strategy of US imperialism at the present stage of historical development.

A Global Strategy

The first task of the global strategy of US imperialism is to upset the existing balance of military forces in the world, which is based on the generally recognized parity of the nuclear-missile power of the United States and the Soviet Union, and to secure unilateral military advantages in order to be able to dictate its will to the socialist countries and subject other states to political blackmail.

The second task of the global strategy of US imperialism is to make use of various forms and methods of neocolonialism in order to establish its control over the economic and raw-material resources

28

of the Third World countries, above all those possessing rich sources of oil and non-ferrous metals.

The third task is to coordinate the actions of the three main centres of present-day imperialism—the United States itself, capitalist Western Europe, which is in the process of economic, political and military integration, and imperialist Japan with its well-developed industrial and technological potential.

US imperialism seeks to draw all other capitalist countries into the zone of influence of these centres by means of a ramified network of political and military blocs.

The USSR Is Not Expansionist

The Soviet Union has no great-power, hegemonistic or expansionist ambitions. To claim, as Franz Josef Strauss did in Munich that the Soviet Union "has as its strategic object the preparation of a worldwide communist revolution and imperialist expansion" is to reveal one's total ignorance of the fundamentals of Soviet policy. The Kremlin does not aspire to the role of a supreme arbiter in international affairs or seek to order the destinies of all humanity as the White House does, overestimating the role and possibilities of the U.S. The Soviet leader has described the Soviet Union's role in the international arena thus: "A world without threats must and can be built, a world of good-neighbourship, a world in which each nation would occupy a worthy place respected by the others. The Soviet Union is working towards precisely such a world, wants to be part of it.". . .The U.S.S.R. does not divide the world into zones, into spheres of influence or of "vital interests."

Vladlen Kuznetsov, *New Times*, no. 12, March 31, 1986.

Finally, the fourth task of the global strategy of US imperialism is to undermine the might and the unity of the countries of the socialist community and of the entire world communist and working-class movement without running the risk of direct military confrontation. This is attempted through an elaborate system of political, ideological, and psychological subversive actions.

Imperialism's Strategy

These tasks and objectives of US imperialism's global strategy are mutually complementing and form a single complex. In implementing them the US ruling circles extensively use various forms of overt and covert violence, subversion, terror, conspiracy, infiltration, and military presence in the hot spots of the world.

This strategy, dictated by the interests of the transnational monopolies, is built on ideological premises deriving from certain specific features of the United States' historical development.

The ambitious claims of US imperialism for a dominant place in the world and for the role of supreme arbiter in international relations, and its desire to dictate its will to other states and to lay down rules concerning how other nations should live are rooted in the ideology of the American bourgeoisie, which is closely linked with the history of the formation of the United States and its emergence as the most powerful country in the capitalist world.

Militant Expansionism

The ancestors of present-day Americans who colonized the portion of the continent where the United States was to be founded were full of the spirit of militant expansionism which was peculiarly blended with a faith in their messianic destiny.

From this spiritual leaven grew the ideology of one of the most militant contingents of modern imperialism. An analysis of this problem shows that the most important components of the ideology of US imperialism are the religious messianic idea of "manifest destiny", the "balance of forces" theory, and militant anti-communism.

The idea of "manifest destiny" was formulated by US politicians and religious leaders in the late 19th century and turned into an ideological doctrine which directly affects the United States' policy and strategy, and sanctifies and promotes the expansion and aggression of US monopoly capital....

Present-day US political leaders do not often make direct references to "manifest destiny", which sounds much too affected and provocative. However, the "manifest destiny" spirit constantly makes itself felt in the words and deeds of US politicians. Characteristic of the policies of post-war presidents of the United States—Truman, Kennedy, Johnson, Nixon, Ford, Carter and particularly Reagan—is an attempt to transform the idea of the United States' "manifest destiny" into its mission of the world's policeman in regard to all national liberation movements, and primarily in regions which are particularly important for the implementation of US imperialism's global strategy. John Kennedy stated unequivocally: "We in this country, in this generation, are, by destiny rather than choice, the watchmen on the walls of world freedom."...

Rampant Anti-Communism

An important component of the ideology of US imperialism which permeates all aspects of its politics and strategy is anti-communism.

Anti-communism is rooted in a hatred for the ideology of Marxism-Leninism and the countries of the socialist community. In the United States ceaseless campaigns are waged in which the USSR is accused of "violations of human rights", of posing a "military threat", of "complicity in international terrorism", and so on. They create an abnormal attitude to everything that is in any way related to communism. Bourgeois ideologists see "the hand of Moscow" in all the social cataclysms inherent in capitalism and in the natural process of social, national, anti-imperialist and anti-monarchic revolutions, and blame communists for them. They are thus prevented from understanding the true meaning and the historical inevitability of the purifying thunderstorms sweeping over the planet and liberating it from out-dated despotic regimes of terror, be it the rule of the Shah in Iran or of Somoza in Nicaragua.

"The peoples of the emergent countries are seeing for themselves that the Soviet Union [is]...their true friend and guarantor of free and independent national and social development."

Soviet International Involvement Is Purely Humanitarian

Nikolai Sedov

Soviet economic and military aid is evident in many developing nations. This aid is a cause of alarm for many US government officials as they believe it is evidence of Soviet expansionism and must be stopped. Soviets defend this aid by saying it is purely humanitarian in nature: They are helping many Third World nations break from the insidious influence of the United States. In the following viewpoint, Nikolai Sedov argues that the Soviet Union helps emerging nations reach economic independence. Sedov is writing for *Soviet Military Review,* an official Soviet publication.

As you read, consider the following questions:

1. The author believes all revolutions stem from a particular ideology. What is it?
2. What are some of the improvements the Soviet Union has helped initiate in developing nations, according to the author?
3. Why does Sedov believe military aid is also important?

Nikolai Sedov, "The Irrepressible Process of Liberation," *Soviet Military Review,* August 1985.

The event-filled 20th century has witnessed more changes than any hundred-year span that preceded it. And no other country has made a weightier contribution to these changes than the Union of Soviet Socialist Republics—the homeland of the Great October Socialist Revolution and the first country of triumphant socialism.

A short historical period, literally the lifetime of a single generation, has seen the fall of age-old colonial empires, including the oldest, 500-year-old empire of Portugal. At present only remnants of them remain in the south of Africa, a few islands and other small territories. In place of yesterday's colonies and semi-colonies over 100 young sovereign states with an aggregate population of upwards of 2,000 million have been formed. On the whole, this is a huge world, which includes countries with highly different political, economic and social conditions, different levels of development, national specifics and cultural traditions. Extreme changeability and political instability are more particular to it than any other zone on the globe.

National Liberation Movements

The record has shown that national-liberation revolutions are intrinsically anti-imperialist, antifeudal and democratic. Virtually all the forces of society—the working class, peasantry, democratic intelligentsia, patriotic army circles, rural poor and the local bourgeoisie—take part in carrying out these revolutions.

The working class is the most consistent mainspring of national-democratic revolutions; however, its influence and role in the liberation struggle is dissimilar. In countries where the proletariat has taken shape as a class and set up its own working-class party, it has played the leading role in national-democratic revolutions.

In most developing countries as many as 90 per cent of the population are peasants, who live in extreme poverty and suffer from lack of land and ruthless exploitation by local landowners and foreign plantation owners; for this reason they, like other segments of the population, have a vested interest in the elimination of the colonial order and feudal oppression.

The national bourgeoisie of the developing countries is likewise interested in a victorious anti-imperialist, antifeudal revolution. However, in this struggle it is marching together with progressive forces only to a certain point. As class battles grow within a country, it, apprehensive of losing its privileges, colludes with international imperialism and puts the brakes on progressive development by embarking on a counterrevolutionary path.

Countries Fighting for Liberation

Today the struggle against imperialism, for the consolidation of political and the attainment of economic independence is simultaneously a struggle against reactionary internal forces from which the imperialists draw support. Among the young independent states,

33

at the forefront of this struggle are countries of socialist orientation, which after the triumph of anti-imperialist, antifeudal and democratic revolutions have embarked or are embarking upon the path of transition to socialism. The number of such countries has increased substantially over the past few years.

Represented on the political and social map of the world is a large group of Asian, African and Latin American countries which are restructuring society along socialist lines. They include Algeria, Angola, Afghanistan, Benin, Guinea-Bissau, the People's Democratic Republic of Yemen, the People's Republic of Congo, the Democratic Republic of Madagascar, Mozambique, Ethiopia, etc.

USSR Believes in Self-Determination

The Soviet Union believes that the policies of all countries and peoples, including the newly-free states, should further the realization of mankind's hopes for peace and progress. And therefore, it, placing its influence and its economic potential entirely in the service of peace and the freedom of nations, never remains indifferent to others' constructive initiatives, whoever they may come from.

Yuri Kuritsyn, *People's Daily World*, November 5, 1985.

Countries of socialist orientation are governed by progressive patriotic forces acting in the interests of the masses. Their struggle is headed by parties of the new type, such as the MPLA Party of Labour in Angola, the People's Democratic Party of Afghanistan, the Yemen Socialist Party in the PDRY, the Congolese Party of Labour, the Mozambique Liberation Front Party, etc. In their work these parties are drawing more and more on scientific socialism as the theoretical prerequisite for building socialist society.

Relations have already taken shape between the socialist-orientation countries and the socialist community countries which are based largely on a commonality of interests and goals and on principles of solidarity and mutual assistance, mutually beneficial cooperation and non-interference in each other's internal affairs.

Socialist Revolutionary Movements

The record of history has shown that in order to preserve and consolidate the progressive positions of the emergent countries it is highly important to have a revolutionary party which, acting on the basis of scientific socialism, guides society, constantly expands its ties with the masses, and involves the working people in the administration of state affairs. The overriding tasks under these circumstances are to consolidate bodies of democratic power, pursue balanced economic and social policies, enhance the defensive capability of the national armed forces, and also develop and solidify ties with the socialist countries—the most faithful and reliable friends of the independent peaceloving states. Only the successful implementation of these tasks will make it possible to surmount the numerous domestic and external difficulties which the developing countries are coming up against.

The struggle around the choice of which path of further development to take does not stop after a national-democratic revolution emerges victorious. The feudal elite and the bureaucratic bourgeoisie draw on imperialist support to effect fierce opposition to the revolutionary people and undertake attempts to undermine progressive regimes. The intrigues of imperialism and internal reaction cannot be underestimated. This is confirmed by the events which have taken place in Egypt and Somalia. Subterfuge, plots, economic blockade and even outright intervention, as is the case in Afghanistan, Angola and Mozambique, are but only a part of the dishonourable methods reaction uses to attain its selfish goals. . . .

Soviet Union Supports Freedom

Remaining true to the behests of Vladimir Lenin, the Soviet state and the socialist community countries have supported the peoples in their struggle and will continue to do so. Economic, technological and cultural cooperation is developing successfully. The Soviet Union has intergovernmental agreements on economic and technical cooperation with over 70 developing countries in Asia, Africa and Latin America. Over 1,800 industrial enterprises, electric power stations, hydrotechnical projects, transport and communications facilities, agricultural projects, hospitals, etc. have been built in the young emergent countries with Soviet assistance over the past 20 years.

The number of the USSR's trade partners from among the developing states is growing. Today the Soviet Union maintains trade relations with 110 emergent countries, while in 1960 the figure was only 44.

Also invaluable to the developing states is the assistance which the socialist community countries provide in enhancing their combat capability, creating national armed forces, training highly qualified military personnel, and equipping young armies with up-to-date hardware and weaponry.

The peoples of the emergent countries are seeing for themselves that the Soviet Union and other socialist countries are in deeds rather than words their true friends and guarantors of free and independent national and social development.

Solidarity with the peoples who have cast off the yoke of colonial dependence and have embarked upon the path of independent development has been and will continue to be one of the underpinnings of the foreign policy of the CPSU and the Soviet state.

"It isn't that the world is drawn to the Soviet
Communist vision of a better future, but rather
that people. . . find a willing source of assistance
in the Soviet Union."

Soviet International
Involvement Is Self-Serving

Richard N. Perle

Richard N. Perle is the assistant secretary of defense for international security policy under the Reagan administration. In the following interview by *American Legion Magazine*, Perle argues that the
USSR gives economic and military aid to other countries in order
to undermine burgeoning democracies in those areas. He believes
the Soviet Union is relentlessly expansionist and that by aiding terrorist groups and communist governments, it plans to eventually
dominate the world.

As you read, consider the following questions:

1. How can the US counter Soviet world influence, according to
   Perle?
2. Why does Perle believe that the Soviet model is losing its
   allure?
3. Does Perle think the differences between the US and the
   USSR can be solved? Why or why not?

Richard N. Perle, "Will the Russians Rule the World?" *American Legion Magazine*, October
1985. Reprinted by permission, **The American Legion Magazine**, Copyright 1985.

American Legion Magazine: Mr. Perle, what do you consider the most dangerous threat facing the United States today in terms of our international security?

Richard Perle: The single most significant threat is the Soviet Union and its growing military capability.

AL: Looking at the Soviet Union's rising support for communist movements around the world, what conclusions should be drawn as to that nation's ultimate goals?

Perle: It's important to be clear about the sources of support for movements aligned with or favorable to the Soviet Union, particularly in the Third World. I don't believe that such support arises from the effectiveness of the Soviet model as a magnet for leaders in other countries who are looking for a path to stability and prosperity for their people. It arises, rather, through an effective Soviet campaign to suborn potential leaders and leaders in power through a variety of devices. Military assistance, for example, which in some cases enables them to remain in power. The clearest example of that is Afghanistan where the Afghan government has been installed and is maintained in power by the Soviet Union and would, in my view, collapse at once without the active intervention of Soviet armed forces. Other devices include bribery, intervention in elections and the exploitation of social cleavages of an economic, ethnic and tribal nature.

Soviet Model Is Not Attractive

In short, it isn't that the world is drawn to the Soviet Communist vision of a better future, but rather that people who are prepared to achieve power with help from somewhere, find a willing source of assistance in the Soviet Union whose interest is not, in my view, in the long-term betterment of the people of those countries but, rather, in expanding Soviet influence.

AL: What are the most effective weapons being used by the communists in this world effort?

Perle: Their effort as a whole has to be seen against the background of their military power. The shadow of that military power is a significant element in their activities in a number of countries. That military power means they can supply weapons. It means they can join with countries that are weak relative to hostile neighbors. They may be the source of hostility, but, nevertheless, the Soviets have been prepared to sustain and support them with respect to their neighbors. Syria is a good example of that; Ethiopia is another. The Soviets also have been in a position to dispatch surrogates around the world: East Germans are engaged in subversive and intelligence activities; Czechoslovakia is supplying weapons; Bulgaria is supplying everything up to and including assistance in assassinations; and

Cuba, of course, is intervening massively in Africa and Central and Latin America with technical assistance, training, military equipment and troops.

A lot of places in the world are either lightly armed or not armed at all. Costa Rica comes to mind as a country that never saw the necessity to maintain a military force. The same thing is true in Angola. A small number of Cuban troops can make a very large difference in an area that has had relative peace and tranquility and, therefore, does not have a significant military establishment.

The Soviets know that and they have effectively used, worked with and supported their Cuban surrogates and other surrogates of Eastern Europe. One finds North Koreans flying aircraft in other countries. There is no technique for the extensions of Soviet power that one can not find examples of somewhere in the world.

A Resurgence of Expansionism

The [global] opportunities that have inadvertently and fortuitously been created may induce the Soviet Union to operate as if it is pursuing a grand design or stimulate it to formulate one to take systematic advantage of the situation. In this context, the threat and danger of Soviet envelopment of the Middle East and Persian Gulf region from the north are real. Since the Middle East is adjacent to Soviet borders, the natural resources of the region are close to the centers of Soviet power and lines of communication. Furthermore, no large bodies of water separate the USSR from these natural resources, and the countries lying between the USSR and the resources are small, internally unstable, and subject to both domestic turmoil and external penetration. . . .

In the recent past, Moscow has placed its ideological goals in cold storage, largely because it deemed too vocal an expression of them counterproductive and because the USSR did not have the capabilities to implement them in any case. But if Soviet global capabilities continue to grow while the capabilities of the United States wane, there could be a resurgence of ideology as a shaper of Soviet foreign policy.

Vernon V. Aspaturian in *Soviet Foreign Policy in a Changing World*, 1986.

AL: What should the United States be doing to effectively counter this drive?

Perle: The most effective thing we have going for us is the strength of our American model. The model of political democracy and a free and productive and growing economy is a very appealing model around the world. It doesn't take bribery and it doesn't take surrogates and it doesn't take intervention to persuade those who are given a choice, that the democratic model is the one they ought to pursue.

On the whole, the aftermath of the Russian Revolution which carried with it, in the minds of many around the world, the promise of a socialist utopia, has given way.

A Western Offensive

So, ideologically and philosophically, the West is on the offensive. Where stability can be achieved, we've had considerable success.

El Salvador is a good example. The turmoil of a couple of years ago in El Salvador has subsided. There clearly is still an insurgency in El Salvador, but there is now in that country a freely elected democratic government that's far stronger than many top-level observers would have predicted a couple of years ago.

AL: Does the very existence of this model explain why the Soviets are so virulent in their propaganda tirades against the United States and our system?

Perle: Yes. Propaganda is largely ineffective.

AL: People are beginning to see through it?

Perle: If people have access to alternative information, they see through it. This is why one of the first things the communists do after gaining a foothold anywhere is to seize control of mass communications, because the Soviet message does not stand up well in competition with information from the rest of the world. It is why the Soviets go to great lengths to jam Western radio broadcasts. They are comfortable with a situation only where the State controls utterly the flow of information. It is essential to the continuation in power of the Soviet elite. And *that* is a model they seek to impose elsewhere in the world, because they know from experience that the free flow of ideas and communications invariably leads to questioning of the Soviet model.

US Should Support Movements

AL: Should the United States be lending direct support to anti-communist revolutionary forces in such nations as Nicaragua, Afghanistan and Cambodia?

Perle: Absolutely. Indeed, I don't know how one would justify denying support to those groups and individuals in countries like Afghanistan and Nicaragua and elsewhere who subscribe in the main to our values or who wish to express some of our most important values.

There was a period in which the Soviets freely supported movements around the world aimed at destabilizing governments that were not to their liking, and there was little or no activity by the United States to support democratic forces. That has changed now, and the results are already evident. In some ways, reluctance to support the Contras in Nicaragua is an anachronism. The House

39

of Representatives already changed its mind on that issue once, and I think that is the beginning of a trend. Take the case of Grenada. Before Grenada it was standard practice for the Soviets to undermine countries, to install regimes friendly to themselves, to assist internal forces allied or prepared to ally themselves with the Soviet Union or with Soviet surrogates, as in the case of Cuba. And there was almost never a counter-strategy, almost never a counter-punch. . . .

Military Support of Third World

The Soviet Union continues to utilize military support to bolster its friends and clients in the Third World. For example, the Soviets doubled their arms shipments to Nicaragua. And Cuba remains a symbol of revolutionary internationalism, even though its faltering economy costs the Soviet Union a painful $10 million a day. Moscow has discovered that while concessional military assistance is still valued by many developing countries, its assets are less relevant to the immediate problems of famine and drought in Africa, debt in Latin America, or the desire for peace and reconciliation in the Middle East.

As the Soviet challenge is global, we require a global strategy that plays from our strengths and ideals and that blocks Soviet troublemaking. Such a strategy places a premium upon our ability to sustain the support of a large number of allies and friends, to foster the cohesion of new regional associations, to play the role of peacemaker in regional disputes, to supply moral and material assistance to those resisting tyranny, and to provide a steadfast and articulate defense of our ideas and values.

Michael H. Armacost, speech before the US Air Force Academy, May 1, 1985.

AL: What can be done to better alert the American people to the reality of Soviet arms and methods and the danger they pose?

Perle: The public needs access to information to inform itself. Its leaders have to be prepared to talk candidly to the American people in explaining the nature of the threat we face. There's no substitute for that. I think it's human nature to want to be relieved of the burdens that living in a difficult world imposes upon us. We have had historically the great benefit of being separated by large oceans from the wars of others. It's enticing to think that we can opt out and, protected by those great oceans and the distance from our shores of the Soviets and others who are allied with them, believe that we need not contend with them. I think in this shrunken world that would be a great mistake. But it's understandable that people would hope the danger isn't as great as it appears to be, that there are alternative explanations for Soviet behavior, and that improved communications will resolve our differences. I wish I thought we could resolve those differences by improved communications, but I rather suspect that the more we understand the Soviets, the less appealing we are likely to find their system and their objectives and their approach to achieving those objectives.

"The Soviet Union has achieved remarkable success in its utilization of Caribbean proxy forces to advance its strategic objectives not only in the Western Hemisphere but throughout the world."

Soviet Influence Is Expanding in Latin America

Timothy Ashby

Timothy Ashby is a policy analyst for Latin American Affairs at the Heritage Foundation and a fellow of the Foundation's Spitzer Institute for Hemispheric Development. Ashby has also worked with the US State Department conducting counterterrorism and crisis management exercises at US embassies in Latin America and the Caribbean. In the following viewpoint, he argues that the USSR's influence in Latin America and the Caribbean is increasing. Ashby believes the USSR is subtly taking over many of these countries in order to keep the US involved in as many small, expensive war efforts as possible.

As you read, consider the following questions:

1. What is the USSR's strategic objective in Latin America, according to Ashby?
2. What tactics does Ashby describe to make his case that the USSR is expanding its influence?
3. Based on US actions in Grenada, what does Ashby believe the US can do to counter this threat?

Reprinted by permission of the publisher from THE BEAR IN THE BACK YARD by Timothy Ashby. Lexington, Mass.: Lexington Books, D.C. Heath and Company. Copyright 1987, D.C. Heath and Company.

A new Soviet policy for the Third World developed during the Khrushchev era and was refined and expanded under Leonid Brezhnev. Recognizing the great opportunities for the projection of Soviet power in the postcolonial era, the USSR actively sought to penetrate the Third World in order to destabilize it and thus threaten and weaken the United States and its allies.

Moscow's grand strategy toward the Third World was an extrapolation of its foreign policy toward the "capitalist-imperialist" West. This policy was pursued on two levels. The first level sought penetration and influence via "peaceful" means such as diplomatic ties, trade and economic assistance, cultural links, and propaganda. The second level of policy was designed to achieve penetration and control through direct and indirect military means within the framework of "wars of national liberation," funding of Marxist revolutionaries, and KGB-sponsored "active measures" aimed at subversion of non-socialist governments. With the exception of the Soviet invasion of Afghanistan in 1979, the overt introduction of Soviet armed forces was avoided in order to support the fiction of indigenous "people's revolutions." . . .

Strategic Objectives

A strategy must, by definition, have an objective, and Soviet strategy for the Caribbean incorporates five major objectives:

1. Erosion of the United States' historical predominance in the region.
2. Expansion of Soviet influence and power.
3. Establishment and maintenance of Soviet proxies.
4. Proliferation of Soviet military and C^{3}I facilities.
5. Forced withdrawal of U.S. influence from other parts of the world due to an enhanced security threat along the U.S. southern flank, thereby leaving the "principal theaters" of Europe and Asia vulnerable to Soviet aggression. . . .

The USSR is fully aware of the United States' strategic dependence on what Boris Ponomarev has called "reliable rear lines of American imperialism." An article in the Soviet theoretical journal *Kommunist* noted that "U.S. industry draws a considerable share of its raw materials" from SLOCs [sea lines of communication] in this region, "including 40 to 100 percent of its imports of various strategic materials." Another Soviet geostrategist has commented that the Caribbean's importance "can hardly be exaggerated. In military strategic terms, it is a sort of hinterland on whose stability freedom of United States' action in other parts of the world depends."

The Caribbean is more than a U.S. hinterland. The region (covering a distance of more than four thousand linear miles from Bridgetown, Barbados, to Tijuana, Mexico) is in a very real sense the United States' fourth, and longest, border. History has demonstrated that a great power's ability to maintain its global balance of power can only be achieved by ensuring the security of its borders, including its littoral zones. The natural moat of the English Channel protected the borders of Britain from invasion attempts by its Continental enemies, allowing it to govern its vast empire even while engaged in numerous international conflicts. . . .

The Effect of a Communist Central America

The Soviet Union knows that a communist-dominated Central America would have a calamitous effect on U.S. allies and nonaligned nations in other parts of the world. Such an occurrence would be offered by Soviet propagandists as conclusive evidence that the "correlation of forces" had irrevocably shifted in favor of "socialism." This is a thesis that would probably be quickly accepted by vulnerable governments seeking to make an accommodation with the USSR. With the United States fully immersed in a region that Andrei Gromyko described as "boiling like a cauldron," Moscow would be free to impose its will on myriad countries that had heretofore felt protected not only by actual U.S. defense commitments, but by the relative balance of power that these commitments had provided.

Nicaragua and the Expansion of Soviet Interests

Nicaragua is now in the grip of utterly cynical and utterly ruthless men, exceeding even their sponsors in aggressive hostility to the United States. The Soviets may be the covert patrons of the world's terrorist plague, but not even they have had the temerity to embrace publicly the assassin Qaddafi as a "brother" the way the Sandinistas have. The aim of the Sandinista revolution is to crush its society from top to bottom, to institute totalitarian rule, and to use the country as a base to spread Communist terror and Communist regimes throughout the hemispheres.

The Sandinista anthem which proclaims the Yankee to be the "enemy of mankind" expresses precisely the revolutionaries' sentiment and goal. That goal is hardly to create a more just society—the sordid record would dissuade any reformer from choosing the Communist path—but to destroy the societies still outside the totalitarian perimeter, and their chief protector, the United States.

David Horowitz, *Commentary*, June 1986.

From the vantage point of the Kremlin, it must appear that this process is already well under way. Regardless of over $200 million in military aid given to the government of El Salvador between 1984 and 1986, Salvadoran guerrilla forces—trained, supplied, and coordinated by Managua—remain undefeated and continue their economic and political destabilization efforts. . . . Colombia, a country bordering the Caribbean that continues to support the flawed

Contadora proposal for a resolution of the Sandinista threat, has seen a significant increase in Soviet-sponsored guerrilla activity since the latter part of 1985. . . .

Diverting US Forces

As the Soviet Union knows, any serious threat developing close to the borders of the United States—such as a major revolutionary upheaval in Mexico—would probably lead to a retraction of U.S. forces from Europe, Asia, and the Middle East. These are the areas referred to by Soviet strategist Admiral Sergei Gorshkov as the "main sectors," as opposed to the "secondary sectors," of the Caribbean and Southern Africa. . . .

The weakening of the United States' historical, political and economic predominance in the region, with or without a concomitant increase in Soviet influence, serves to create the type of regional instability that fosters the growth of leftist insurgent movements. The economic crises besetting nearly all Caribbean and Latin American countries have led to anti-U.S. feeling and growing economic nationalism that the Cubans are actively exploiting to create even greater divisiveness between the United States and its southern neighbors. For example, the governments of Costa Rica, Guatemala, Colombia, and Venezuela have stated their opposition to the Reagan administration's policy of providing military assistance to the anti-Sandinista insurgent forces—positions that have received highly favorable publicity from Cuba, Nicaragua, and leftist opposition parties throughout the regions. To date, the U.S. government's much-vaunted Caribbean Basin Initiative (CBI) has largely failed to fulfill its promises of economic revitalization for the region, and will probably not have any significant impact on the area's problems even if fully implemented. As a result, Caribbean Marxists are regaining some of the political ground lost after the 1983 intervention in Grenada, where remnants of the New Jewel Movement have regrouped to enter the political arena again under the guise of the Maurice Bishop Patriotic Movement (MBPM). . . .

Moscow's Subversive Use of Cuba

Since Cuba's acceptance as the Soviet Union's most important proxy, subversive operations in Latin America and the Caribbean have generally been the responsibility of the DA and DGI [Cuban intelligence services] (notable exceptions include the work of Soviet agents among plantation workers in Costa Rica and unions in the Dominican Republic). The identification, cultivation, and training of potential revolutionaries, as in the cases of the New Jewel Movement and the Sandinistas, appear to be the favored form of initiating subversion in the region during the 1980s. This is usually accomplished by inviting young Caribbean leftists to conferences such as the First Consultative Meeting of Anti-Imperialist Organizations of the Caribbean and Central America, held in Havana in June 1984, which was attended by twenty-eight parties, fronts, and other organizations from twenty-one Caribbean regional countries. The attendance by several hundred young people from Central America and the Caribbean at the July-August 1985 Moscow Youth Festival may indicate a more overt trend on behalf of the Soviet Union to influence the next political generation throughout the Caribbean. Transportation and other expenses were paid for by the USSR, and festival participants included a significant number of representatives from moderate, traditionally anticommunist political parties.

Cuba's intelligence arms, as well as the Nicaraguan DGSE, are so closely connected with the KGB and GRU [another Soviet intelligence agency] that they effectively function as Latin American branches of the Soviet espionage services. The subversive activities of these proxies can and do draw on the resources of a comprehensive international subversive network, including terrorist advisers and operatives from the Soviet bloc, Vietnam, Libya, Ethiopia, the PLO, the Basque ETA, and various Latin American organizations.

Bill Garner, reprinted with permission.

The collaboration and joint action of these groups represent a powerful means of projecting a subtle Soviet influence over every nation in the Western Hemisphere, including the United States. Because of the Caribbean region's geostrategic importance and vulnerability, subversion has proven particularly effective in political coercion, economic destabilization through workers' strikes, assassinations, and clandestine support for coups d'etat. For example, ETA "internationalists" based in Managua were responsible for the 1984 assassination attempt on anti-Sandinista military commander Edén Pastora—a former FSLN hero who threatened the Managua regime by his enduring popularity throughout Nicaragua. Several Soviet client states, including Cuba, Nicaragua, Libya and Vietnam, have also been implicated in the Marxist M-19 guerrilla movement's continuing efforts to destabilize Colombia. . . .

Use of Proxies

The Soviet Union has achieved remarkable success in its utilization of Caribbean proxy forces to advance its strategic objectives not only in the Western Hemisphere but throughout the world. Today more than fifty-thousand uniformed Cuban military personnel are serving in sixteen known countries on four continents, and are engaged in combat against pro-Western forces in Nicaragua, Angola, and other countries. The permanent presence of Soviet surrogate naval, air, and ground forces in the Caribbean already represents a significant projection of Soviet power into this important geostrategic region; dealing with these forces in time of war would cause a serious diversion of U.S. military assets from other parts of the world.

The Soviet Union has enjoyed a high degree of success with its Caribbean surrogates because of their belief that they are *not* proxy forces controlled by an extrahemispheric superpower but *partners* with the USSR in a global crusade to replace "imperialism" with "socialism." Although some members of the Cuban, Grenadian, and Nicaraguan governments had undoubtedly given their primary allegiance to Moscow, the nationalistic leaders of these countries willingly accepted Soviet support and resources in pursuit of their personal revolutionary goals. The fact that the objectives of Fidel Castro, Maurice Bishop, and Daniel Ortega coincided with those of the Soviet Union was seen as completely natural within their shared ideological context. Although Fidel Castro has complained, probably correctly, that the Soviet Union has usurped many of his revolutionary initiatives, he nonetheless sees this as a form of self-vindication. As demonstrated by the Grenada documents, the Kremlin has grown adept at manipulating the egos and aspirations of those countries' leaders who are almost certainly regarded, albeit with great secrecy, as the USSR's proxies. . . .

In the Caribbean, Moscow's successful use of Cuba as a proxy had been extrapolated since 1979 by Havana's employment of its own surrogates—in effect, proxies of a proxy. Numerous examples of this primary and secondary system have been documented, especially in the areas of political subversion....

Soviet Opportunism

Whether or not the Soviets have a global strategy, they most certainly are determined to increase their political influence in the world. Since they find it difficult or impossible to exercise that influence through international economic, financial, or trading bodies or through regional groups, they seek instead to build military-political clients, the evolution of Soviet involvement in Africa, Southeast Asia, the Middle East, and the Caribbean Basin attest to this Soviet desire for influence through close alliances with willing or threatened nation states. The Soviets in this way seek to establish parity with the United States as a superpower, not only in the military but also in the political sphere....

The Soviets have no economic interests in the Caribbean Basin. Economic issues have played a decreasing role in Soviet policies toward the Third World. The Soviets believe that where their political and military influence expands is where regional strife is high. Central America seems now to be ripe for greatly expanded Soviet influence over the next few years as long as the Soviets can control and establish a military-security presence. The eventual financial cost of expanded influence and involvement in the region is not likely to be high even if it should eventually involve another client state. The current costs are low.

William H. Luers in *Soviet Foreign Policy in a Changing World*, 1986.

A Grenadian delegate to a conference of international radicals held in Libya admitted that "Cuba was using Grenada to influence the other Caribbean parties and organizations." Regardless of Cuba's command and control role and close cultural, racial, and geographic ties with its secondary Caribbean proxies, most regional Marxists maintained an ideological allegiance to Moscow. Grenada's NJM viewed its revolution as "a world-wide process with its original roots in the Great October Revolution," and were eager to enhance Grenada's "importance in the Soviet scheme of things." During a visit to Moscow in March 1980, Sandinista Defense Minister Humberto Ortega told his Soviet hosts that the FSLN was "willing to sacrifice the revolution in Nicaragua" in the interests of Soviet global strategy. In January 1977, Guyanese [guerrilla] leader Cheddi Jagan stated in Parliament that he was "not ashamed of being a Moscow puppet, if you want to put it that way, because Moscow stands for socialism, for democracy, for proletarian internationalism. It helps liberation movements."...

Confused U.S. responses to direct and indirect Soviet aggression in Africa, Asia, and Latin America during the 1970s served to encourage the USSR's expansionist tendencies, as Soviet theoreticians pointed to the seeming powerlessness of the Carter administration as evidence of the inevitable decline of the West. With the "correlation of forces" now perceived as visibly shifting in their favor, Soviet strategists appear increasingly determined to pursue Moscow's "mission" of hastening the spread of global communism. . . .

Eroding the West's Security

The USSR's strategic ventures in the Caribbean are part of one great strategic objective that has preoccupied Soviet strategists since the end of World War II: the destabilization and subordination of the Soviet Union's "main adversary," the United States. While the United States remains an international power, the Soviet Union will feel compelled to approach its goal of global hegemony cautiously. To gain the requisite freedom of action to defeat "imperialism," the USSR has decided to take the struggle to the United States' often overlooked, and therefore most vulnerable, southern flank.

The decisive U.S. and allied action to remove Grenada's pro-Soviet regime did not halt the proliferation of Soviet influence in the Caribbean. The incremental expansion of Moscow's power in "the traditional zone of U.S. dominance" continues to erode the security of the entire Western Hemisphere. Regardless of occasional, and perhaps expected, tactical setbacks, the Soviet Union's strategy toward the Caribbean continues to prove its effectiveness.

Soviet strategists have learned to exploit the United States' weaknesses—the "inherent contradictions" of a democratic society. Each display of weakness by the U.S. government has been met with an incremental expansion of Soviet power in the Caribbean region. Thus, it can be demonstrated that political decisions made in Washington may be as important to the Soviet Union's Caribbean, and other, strategies as military assistance to a communist guerrilla movement in Central America or the construction of a new Soviet military base in Grenada.

"Soviet attempts to expand their influence into Latin America have not been extensive, and their success has been limited."

Soviet Influence Is Not Expanding in Latin America

The Center for Defense Information

The Center for Defense Information (CDI) supports an effective defense. It opposes excessive expenditures for weapons and believes that strong social, economic, and political structures contribute equally to the national security and are essential to the strength and welfare of the country. In the following viewpoint, CDI argues that the fear of growing Soviet worldwide influence is a combination of myth and panic. Soviet influence is on the decline everywhere, the organization believes, including Latin America.

As you read, consider the following questions:

1. What event was a major setback to Soviet worldwide influence, according to CDI?
2. Why do the authors argue that the US should have more respect for Third World countries?
3. What does CDI think of the Soviet-Cuban alliance? Is it a threat to the US?

The Center for Defense Information, "Soviet Geopolitical Momentum: Myth or Menace?" *The Defense Monitor,* Vol. XV, Number 5, 1986.

For generations, the United States' activities around the world have been shaped by global competition with the Soviet Union. The U.S. has spent trillions of dollars on war preparations but has had no military combat with the Soviets. The struggle in other countries has largely been waged through diplomacy, military and economic aid, trade, and, occasionally, military intervention.

Many Americans fear that communist subversion and conquest are on the increase. In the 1970s, Soviet involvement in Angola, Ethiopia, Afghanistan, and elsewhere intensified fears of Soviet "geopolitical momentum." Ronald Reagan was elected President in 1980 in great part because of such fears.

While some Americans profess greater self-confidence today, the spectre of increasing Soviet influence continues to worry many in the United States. Central America is the latest focus of attention. We have expanded our military efforts there and elsewhere to combat the Soviet Union and its friends. The huge cost of this endeavor is increasingly burdensome. The combination of undiminished U.S.-Soviet rivalry and Third World instability creates constant dangers. . . .

Rising and Falling Influence

Trends of Soviet influence over the past 40 years have been analyzed by the Center for Defense Information by aggregating Soviet-influenced countries over this period according to their population and Gross National Product (GNP). Indices of power developed by former CIA official Ray Cline in his books on *World Power Assessment* were also examined. Because countries are not equally important, these methods may give a better picture of the trends of Soviet influence than simply counting the number of countries.

Population and GNP charts show the percentage of the world's total population and GNP for each year from 1945 through 1985 in countries under Soviet influence. With minor differences the population and GNP curves show similar patterns, rising and falling as Soviet influence in the world waxed and waned. Soviet influence rose sharply in the late 1940s with the addition of China and again less dramatically in the late 1950s with the addition of Indonesia and Iraq. Soviet influence plummeted through the first half of the 1960s with the loss of China and Indonesia but then rose in the late 1960s and early 1970s with the addition of Egypt and India. The loss of Egypt and India in the 1970s was only partially offset by successes in the former Portuguese colonies and elsewhere.

According to the population and GNP indicators, 1958 was the high point of Soviet influence in the world. At that time Soviet-influenced countries accounted for 31% of the world's population and 9% of the world's GNP, not including the Soviet Union. In 1985 the Soviets were influencing only 6% of the world's population and 6% of the world's GNP exclusive of the Soviet Union. . . .

51

Dan Wasserman. ©1987, The Boston Globe. Reprinted by permission of The Los Angeles Times Syndicate.

There is no evidence of inexorable Soviet geopolitical momentum and that both successes and failures have occurred on numerous occasions. These data describe a decline in Soviet world influence since the 1950s.

What emerges from the data is that, with the ups and downs over the years, the Soviet Union's bloc of friendly nations has less aggregate importance today than in the late 1950s, prior to the loss of China. Soviet efforts at influence-building since 1960 have not brought it back to the plateau it reached before China's defection.

Nothing that has happened since has really made up for the decline in the power of the Soviet bloc relative to the rest of the world that occurred when the Soviets "lost" China.

Another major conclusion that may be drawn from this analysis is that a handful of important countries account for nearly all of the significant fluctuation in Soviet world influence: China, India, Egypt, Indonesia, and, to a lesser extent, Iraq. It has been Soviet success or failure with these countries that has been the real story of the rise and fall of Soviet influence. *Soviet inability to hold the allegiance and support of important Third World countries over the long-term has been the major weakness of the Soviet Union in attempting to expand its influence.* While these more important countries have had more resources and options at their disposal to pursue their own road and acquire other patrons, even smaller countries such as Somalia and Guinea have been forceful in exerting their independence.

A final conclusion that may be drawn from this study of trends of Soviet influence is that a closer look at developments in the 1970s reveals no expansion of Soviet influence. During this period when there were so many headlines about the American debacle in Vietnam and alleged Soviet successes in Africa and the Middle East, the Soviet Union did not in fact expand its influence. Even in this alleged heyday of "Soviet geopolitical momentum" during the 1970s Soviet losses nearly equaled gains. . . .

Soviet Geographic Limitations

Despite the alarmist rhetoric of recent years, Soviet attempts to expand their influence into Latin America have not been extensive, and their success has been limited. The Soviets largely accept the geographic limitations on their reach. They are primarily interested in the big powers in Latin America, such as Argentina, Brazil and Mexico. Central America is an area of low priority. They do not want to commit their prestige in the region or justify further U.S. military involvement.

Cuba is probably the Soviet Union's most loyal and important ally outside of Eastern Europe. The 1970s were a decade of extremely close ties between the U.S.S.R. and Cuba, but the 1980s has seen a shift back in the direction of the friction-filled relations of the 1960s.

The overthrow of Somoza in Nicaragua by the Sandinistas in July 1979 was obviously a very positive development for the U.S.S.R. The anti-American/pro-Soviet orientation of the Sandinistas is clear, but Soviet influence in Nicaragua is still not significant, despite a large (by Central American standards) arms supply relationship. Cuban involvement and influence is extensive in Nicaragua.

Similarly, Grenada was never "in the Soviet camp." As in Nicaragua, Cuba exercised significant influence, but not the U.S.S.R. The New Jewel Movement was largely Marxist-Leninist in nature and Grenada did establish political, military, and economic ties with the Soviet Union, Cuba, and other Soviet friends, but Soviet involvement and influence was never extensive.

Over the past fifteen years, Cuba has emerged as the Soviet Union's key ally in the Third World. Cuba's near total dependence on the U.S.S.R. economically and militarily is indisputable. Cuba does not publicly oppose the Soviet Union on any major foreign policy issue. The Soviet military presence and use of military facilities in Cuba may be more important to Moscow than in any other Third World country.

Still, any notion that Cuba is a puppet of the Soviet Union which does not decide its own foreign and domestic policies is mistaken.

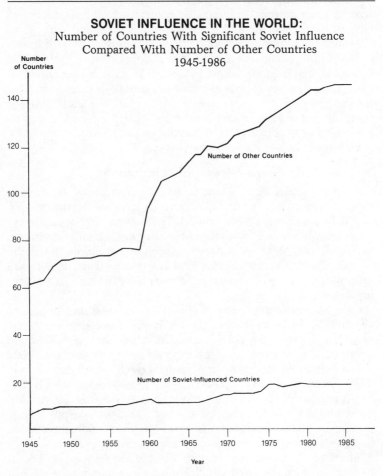

SOVIET INFLUENCE IN THE WORLD:
Number of Countries With Significant Soviet Influence
Compared With Number of Other Countries
1945-1986

Chart prepared by the Center for Defense Information

The Soviets exercise a great deal of leverage over Cuba, but Castro is a very strong, nationalistic leader. The two nations have found many areas for mutually beneficial collaboration, perhaps most visibly in Africa. But in many instances, the Soviets are less a cause of Cuban behavior than a facilitator, and even in some cases, a constraint.

Over the course of the 25 years since Castro's revolution, there have been ups and downs in Soviet-Cuban relations; serious tensions still exist today. While obviously beholden to the U.S.S.R. for political, economic and military support, Castro has tried to pursue his own aspirations and always puts the interests of Cuba ahead of those of the Soviet Union. On the other hand, the Soviets have never made as strong a commitment to Cuba's defense as Castro would probably like; no guarantee to defend Cuba against an American attack has ever been made, only vague commitments....

Breaking from the USSR

Castro has been increasingly outspoken in his public criticism of the Soviet inability or unwillingness to improve the economic lot of Third World nations. He has dropped his position of the "natural alliance" between the U.S.S.R. and the Third World. He has criticized the Soviets' lukewarm embrace of Nicaragua. Cuba was among the last nations to join the boycott of the Los Angeles Olympics, and did so only very reluctantly. Soviet actions in Afghanistan have embarrassed Cuba in the Non-Aligned Movement; Cuba has offered only perfunctory endorsement.

Cuba has also made efforts to improve ties with the West. U.S.-Cuban ties went through a warming phase in 1984 and 1985, before hitting a deep freeze. New immigration accords were signed in December 1984, Castro expressed interest in resuming diplomatic relations, a stream of U.S. politicians and businessmen visited Cuba, and Castro sought access to technology and increased trade and credit. The Reagan hard line—more precisely the establishment of the anti-Castro propaganda radio station Radio Marti—ended the tentative rapprochement, as Castro suspended the immigration accord and imposed new travel restrictions....

Cuba-Phobia

Former U.S. Ambassador to the Eastern Caribbean region Sally Shelton told Congress in 1982: "Our policy towards the Caribbean has traditionally been shaped to a substantial degree by our Cuba-phobia....Cuba is an integral part of the Caribbean; if we learned nothing else from years of attempting to isolate China, we learned that isolation is a policy tool that does not work."

The Reagan Administration maintains that Nicaragua has become a Soviet-Cuban surrogate, an "Eastern Bloc-style" nation which is doing the Soviets' bidding in the Western Hemisphere. This perception does not fit the facts.

Soviet influence in Nicaragua is limited. Cuban influence is extensive, and while the Soviets reap some benefits from Cuba's influence, the two are not the same. Clearly Nicaragua is favorably disposed to the Soviet Union—primarily as a result of Nicaragua's antipathy for the United States. But the Soviets have little, if any, input into Nicaraguan decision-making, especially on domestic issues.

The Soviet presence, especially the military presence, in Nicaragua is very small. According to the U.S. Department of Defense, there are only 50-70 Soviet military advisors in Nicaragua. There are perhaps 100-200 other Soviets in Nicaragua, mainly doctors, nurses and technicians at the one Soviet hospital. In contrast, Cubans are highly visible in Nicaragua. The U.S. government estimates 5,500-7,500 Cubans total, including 2,500-3,500 military advisors, as well as several hundred East European, Libyan and North Korean military advisors. The Nicaraguan government claims there are only a few hundred Cuban military....

According to U.S. government figures, Soviet bloc military deliveries to Nicaragua increased steadily each year, from $5 million in 1980, to $45 million in 1981, $90 million in 1982, $115 million in 1983, and $250 million in 1984, before falling sharply in 1985 to $75 million....

Nicaragua an Independent Nation

Nicaragua is not a member of the Soviet "bloc," and is by no means a full-fledged Marxist-Leninist state like East European nations, Cuba or Vietnam. That the Nicaraguan government is anti-American is of course not surprising in light of decades of U.S. support of the Somoza regime. The roots of Sandinista foreign policy have little if anything to do with the Soviet Union; indeed, until it became obvious that the Sandinistas would achieve a military victory, the Soviets instead supported the rival Nicaraguan Socialist and Communist Parties. Arturo Cruz, a former Sandinista official, has written that the Sandinistas were not close to the Soviet Union until mid-1982, when the Reagan Administration turned up the pressure as the contras grew and the economy deteriorated.

There have been signs of discontent and significant tensions in the Soviet-Nicaraguan relationship. Soviet economic aid has been meager, especially considering the severe difficulties Nicaragua has faced. For example, at a time when Nicaragua's economy was reaching a crisis point, Daniel Ortega returned from his June 1984 trip to Moscow empty-handed. The Soviets have turned down urgent Nicaraguan requests for foreign exchange and rejected Nicaragua's applications for full membership in COMECON.

Nicaragua is simply not a nation of great importance to the Soviet Union. While Nicaraguan leaders regularly visit Moscow, no important Soviet official has visited Managua. The Soviets have not offered a Treaty of Friendship and Cooperation. They have carefully avoided any public commitment to the preservation of the Sandinistas, stating that even in the event of a U.S. invasion assistance would be limited to political support. Peter Clement, a CIA analyst in the Office of Soviet Analysis, has written that authoritative Soviet statements have underscored their reluctance to openly tie their prestige to the Sandinistas: "In reviewing Soviet policy toward Nicaragua since 1979, one is struck by the general caution with which Moscow has proceeded."

No matter what the "truth" may be about the Sandinista government, about whether they are "better or worse" than the Somoza regime, it should be realized that there is no evidence of pervasive Soviet influence. In his testimony to Congress in February 1985, Dr. Carl Jacobsen concluded that, "Nicaragua may be Marxist-dominated and she may be inclined to authoritarianism, but she is not a Soviet satellite, either politically or economically—and a broader look at the evidence in fact suggests that she is not likely to become one. Moscow is resigned to minimal expectations."

Grenada

Both before and after the American invasion of Grenada in October 1983, the Reagan Administration attempted to portray that island's government as increasingly Marxist and increasingly part of the Soviet bloc. The New Jewel Movement was Marxist-Leninist in nature, and Grenada did establish political, military, and economic ties with the U.S.S.R., Cuba and other Soviet friends. However, Soviet involvement in Grenada was never very great and Soviet influence was never significant....

Many other countries in Latin America have established some political, economic, and cultural ties with the Soviet Union, but all remain closely tied to the West and most continue to be strongly anti-communist. Argentina, for example, now does over $1 billion per year in trade with the Soviet Union. Large grain sales at one time made the U.S.S.R. Argentina's number one trade partner.

Recognizing Ethnocentrism

Ethnocentrism is the attitude or tendency of people to view their own race, religion, culture, group, or nation as superior to others, and to judge others on that basis. An American, whose custom is to eat with a fork or spoon, would be making an ethnocentric statement when saying, "The Chinese custom of eating with chopsticks is stupid."

Ethnocentrism has promoted much misunderstanding and conflict. It emphasizes cultural and religious differences and the notion that one's national institutions or group customs are superior.

Ethnocentrism limits people's ability to be objective and to learn from others. Education in the truest sense stresses the similarities of the human condition throughout the world and the basic equality and dignity of all people.

Most of the following statements are derived from the viewpoints in this chapter. Consider each statement carefully. *Mark E for any statement you think is ethnocentric. Mark N for any statement you think is not ethnocentric. Mark U if you are undecided about any statement.*

If you are doing this activity as a member of a class or group, compare your answers with those of other class or group members. Be able to defend your answers. You may discover that others will come to different conclusions. Listening to the reasons others present for their answers may give you valuable insights in recognizing ethnocentric statements.

58

1. The Soviet Union is the most progressive and peaceful country in the world.
2. Socialism is the true progressive, patriotic system that will free the oppressed nations from their colonial chains.
3. Support for the Soviet Union arises not so much from the superiority of its model of development as it does from Soviet military power.
4. The more Americans understand the Soviets, the less appealing they are likely to find the Soviet system.
5. The continuing increase in the size of the Soviet armed forces, to the point where they enjoy superiority over the forces that can be easily brought against them, is preparation for war.
6. Capitalists are fundamentally opposed to the ideals of peace and progress.
7. The United States' greatest advantage is the strength of its American model of democracy.
8. The weakening of the United States' predominance in Central America serves to create instability, which fosters the growth of leftist insurgent movements.
9. It cannot be coincidence that the Soviet Union, having supported North Vietnam in its conquering of Indochina, should end up possessing air and naval bases there.
10. Socialist countries are governed by progressive patriotic forces that act in the interests of the masses.
11. The Soviet message does not stand up well when compared to the message the free democracies have to offer the world.
12. In the last few years the Soviet government has advanced a number of new initiatives for strengthening peace, preserving the existing military-strategic parity, and ensuring equal security.
13. The emergence of a pro-Soviet government in Mexico would cause the United States to pull back on its commitments in other parts of the world.
14. The Soviet Union is in the forefront of the peace-loving forces of the world.
15. Only Soviet-induced instability keeps pro-American nations from developing peacefully and democratically.

Periodical Bibliography

The following articles have been selected to supplement the diverse views expressed in this chapter.

Lev Alburt and
John F. McManus
"Interview: Lev Alburt's Defense," *The New American,* March 30, 1987.

Michael Binyon
"Still the 'Evil Empire?' " *World Press Review,* April 1987.

James J. Drummey
"Building the Evil Empire," *The New American,* July 20, 1987.

Matthew Evangelista
" 'New Thinking' in Foreign Policy," *The Nation,* June 13, 1987.

Nathan Gardels and
Regis Debray
"Interview: Beyond the Soviet Threat," *Harper's Magazine,* April 1986.

Philip Geyelin
"The World View of the Right," *The Atlantic Monthly,* March 1985.

Aleksandr Golts
"In a Frenzy of Anti-Sovietism," *Soviet Military Review,* June 1987.

Leon Gouré
"Developing Soviet Forces," *Society,* July/August 1987.

Mark N. Katz
"The Soviet Union and the Third World," *Current History,* October 1986.

Melvyn Krauss
"No More Rich Bully," *Reason,* November 1986.

Vladlen Kuznetsov
"Socialism: New Horizons," *New Times,* no. 18, May 11, 1987.

George Liska
"The US-Soviet Conflict: Concert Through Decompression," *Current,* January 1987.

Richard M. Nixon
"The Pillars of Peace," *Vital Speeches of the Day,* July 15, 1986.

Jean-François Revel
"Interview: How Democracies Perish," *American Legion Magazine,* July 1986.

I.F. Stone
"Wedded by Hate," *The Nation,* April 18, 1987.

George Urban and
Alexander Zinoviev
"The Myth of Imperial Russia," *Harper's Magazine,* September 1984.

Caspar W.
Weinberger
"Military Might of the Soviet Union," *Defense,* May/June 1987.

Vadim Zagladin
"War Is Anathema to Communists," *Political Affairs,* June 1987.

Does the Soviet Union Guarantee Human Rights?

the
SOVIET
UNION

Chapter Preface

If there is any issue that has become inextricably associated with the Soviet Union, it is that of abuse of human rights. The punishment of dissidents in inhumane gulags and in false psychiatric hospitals is vividly described in the work of renowned Soviet emigres like Andrei Sakharov and Aleksandr Solzhenitsyn. These accounts and others that report restrictions such as the censorship of newspapers, the banning of books, the lack of free elections, and stagnating economic conditions give those living in the West a bleak picture of the lives of Soviet citizens.

On the other side, officials in the Soviet Union and many people in the US claim the human rights issue is just another anti-Soviet campaign that does not reflect reality in the USSR. Most Soviet citizens, according to these advocates, are content and enjoy many benefits that Westerners should envy. These supporters point to the government's guarantees of full employment, housing, and child care. They argue that political dissidents are criminals who disguise their activities under the rubric of political and literary freedom. The authors in the following chapter include Soviet and American views on the debate over human rights.

VIEWPOINT

"Social justice is an inherent feature of life of the working people under socialism, that healthy moral and political atmosphere which has come to prevail in Soviet society."

The Soviet System Guarantees Basic Human Rights

Leonid Kazinov and Yaroslav Renkas

The following viewpoint consists of two articles, both taken from the Soviet publication *Soviet Military Review*. The two Soviet writers, Leonid Kazinov and Yaroslav Renkas, argue that the communist principles of the Soviet government guarantee social justice. The right to employment, a decent living wage, and full equality for men and women have made the Soviet Union one of the best places in the world to live.

As you read, consider the following questions:

1. Kazinov describes the Soviet insurance system. Does it sound better than that of the US?
2. What are some of the "guaranteed rights" that Renkas mentions?
3. According to Renkas, are the lives of Soviet citizens improving? Why or why not?

Leonid Kazinov, "The Country of Genuine Rights and Freedoms," *Soviet Military Review*, June 1987.
Yaroslav Renkas, "The Principles of Social Justice," *Soviet Military Review*, January 1986.

I

The basic principle of the USSR Constitution is that all Soviet citizens are equal before the law, without distinction as to sex or nationality, in every economic, political, social and cultural area.

Soviet citizens have the right to take part in the management and administration of state and public affairs. This constitutional right is being realised in many ways. One of them is the opportunity to vote and to be elected to Soviets of People's Deputies and other elective state bodies, to take part in nationwide discussions and referendums, in the work of public organisations, and in meetings of work collectives. Every Soviet citizen has the right to submit proposals to state bodies and public organisations on how they can improve their activity, and to criticise shortcomings.

At present 2,300,000 people's deputies and millions of volunteers for state bodies exercise state power. Workers and collective farmers represent nearly 70 per cent and women 50 per cent of all deputies. One in three deputies hasn't reached 30.

Soviet servicemen enjoy constitutional rights and freedoms in full measure and on an equal footing with all citizens of the USSR. Take, for instance, the right to vote and be elected to state bodies. Today 14,625 servicemen work fruitfully within the Supreme Soviet of the USSR, and Supreme Soviets of the Union and Autonomous Republics.

There are no national or social limitations for the USSR Armed Forces' personnel on the issues of promotion or education. "From soldier to general" is no mere phrase, but a reality. All Soviet military leaders and commanders come from the people. They were born into the families of workers, peasants and administrative staff. The majority of them came up through the lowest ranks. Chiefs and subordinates, privates and commanders have one and the same ideological and political views and interests. They are close-knit by a common aim, defence of socialist gains.

No Unemployment

As Soviet society blossoms and large-scale social and economic targets are reached, the working people's rights expand further.

For more than fifty years now the Soviet people haven't seen unemployment. Citizens of the USSR have a constitutional right to work, including the right to choose their trade or profession, type of job and work in accordance with their inclinations, abilities, training and education, with due account of the needs of society. The working people's rights are strictly secured by the state. There are established material, disciplinary and criminal liabilities for unlawfully sacking workers.

The right to rest and leisure is real and comprehensive for all Soviet people. A working week not exceeding 41 hours has been established for workers and other employees, by the provision of paid annual holidays of more than three weeks for workers and employees. The state promotes extension of the network of cultural, educational and health-building institutions and development of sport on a mass scale, physical culture and tourism.

The Soviet state was first in the world to establish free, qualified medical care. Allocations for the development of the medical system increase with every passing year, larger is the number of physicians, hospitals and polyclinics. There are 42 physicians per 10,000 people, the highest index of the world. Health protection and health-building is mostly vital for the state. Medical aid is comprehensive and fast and there is a highly-qualified prophylactic service.

State Insurance

The USSR has a state social insurance system based on the following principles. One, it is universal for industrial and administrative workers, employees, collective farmers and their families. Two, it is comprehensive, i.e., aid is rendered in illness, old age, disability, loss of the breadwinner, etc. Three, it is free, for one doesn't have to pay the bill for treatment, this coming from the state and social consumption funds.

Material Guarantees

The Soviet Union values the democratic acquisitions of the peoples of the Western countries, but it considers the rights and freedoms proclaimed by capitalist democracy as limited and often nominal. Socialist democracy treats with care the humanitarian heritage of the past, but goes farther and puts the main emphasis on the unity of humanity's political, individual, social and economic rights....

Material guarantees of fundamental human rights constitute a major asset of socialist democracy. A Soviet citizen knows that he or she will never be out of work and that, if he or she falls ill, it will not affect family income (all working people with a length of work of eight years are entitled to a disability allowance equivalent to their full monthly earnings) and this makes for confidence in the future.

Gennady Pisarevsky, *People's Daily World*, September 27, 1985.

The Soviet state takes particular care of the elder generation, of war and labour veterans. The material level of pensioners is constantly improving. Not just that retirement pensions are being increased. The idea is to create conditions for the elderly to live a fuller life, for them to be involved socially and even economically.

Soviet people enjoy a constitutional right to housing. This is guaranteed by state housing construction and maintenance. More than 2 million apartments are built annually. And rent takes just three to four per cent of a worker family's budget.

In the USSR all forms of education, including higher, are free. Illiteracy was done away with back in the mid-30s and today secondary education is universal. There are 892 higher educational institutions. A substantial part of students are provided with state scholarships and grants.

Soviet achievements in cultural life are widely known. The 27th CPSU [Communist Party of the Soviet Union] Congress stressed that the Party sees the main objective of its cultural policy in identifying people's abilities and making their lives intellectually rich and varied. The country has great opportunities to make the idea come true. There are 140,000 clubs, 134,000 public libraries, 628 theatres, etc. A great number of books, newspapers and magazines appear in all languages of the USSR nationalities.

The record-book shows the reality of the freedom of speech, of the press, and of assembly, meetings, street processions and demonstrations.

II

Socialism is a necessary and historically lengthy stage of the road towards complete social equality and, as a consequence, complete social justice. Having abolished private ownership of the means of production and essential differences between town and country and between blue- and white-collar work, in short, having secured social justice in the main, the new society, as V.I. Lenin pointed out, is not in a position yet to do away with what can be regarded as another form of injustice—distribution of goods "according to work" (and not according to want). To be able to do so, it has to develop its productive forces to a still higher level and every working person has to develop in himself a communist attitude towards work and public property and the culture of reasonable consumption.

The epoch-making significance of the Soviet Union's contribution to the social progress of mankind is determined by the content of the radical revolutionary changes that the Soviet people, led by the Communist Party, has made in all spheres of social life.

The concept of social justice has become richer in content since socialist construction began in this country. Today, with socialism having come into its own, social justice is not confined solely to rights and liberties, which people under capitalism have never enjoyed. Under real socialism, it embraces all aspects of human life and all relationships in society.

What are the present-day distinctive features of socialist community as one of social justice?

The guaranteed right to work and remuneration for work done, the community's concern for every person from birth to old age, broad access for everyone to objects of spiritual culture, respect for a person's dignity and human rights, ever growing participation of working people in the administration of state affairs—these are the permanent values of the Soviet way of life. Furthermore, such high ideals and values as humanism, democratism and collectivism are being increasingly fuller realised under developed socialism.

Soviet Optimism

Herein lies the source of Soviet citizens' social optimism. As yet further evidence of the indisputable advantage of socialism: for the first time in the history of mankind a multi-national state capable of solving the nationalities problem with fairness has been established and the inviolable brotherhood and friendship of dozens of peoples have evolved—things which are inconceivable under capitalism.

The Soviet state, which put an end to unemployment back in 1930, has in reality provided every citizen, for the first time in history, with the most important of human rights—the right to work. In the capitalist countries, mass-scale unemployment is still the number-one social problem.

A Wide Range of Rights

The [USSR's] Constitution has considerably enlarged the rights and freedoms of Soviet citizens in keeping with the new economic, political, social and cultural conditions of socialist society. Under the Constitution, the whole of Soviet legislation has been renewed and improved to ensure the fullest all-round satisfaction of the interests and requirements of Soviet citizens. This aim is also served by a system of economic, political, legal and organizational guarantees of the rights and freedoms of citizens.

All this is convincing proof of the indisputable fact that it is only real socialism that is capable of providing and guaranteeing citizens a wide range of rights and freedoms, ensuring the harmonious combination of the interests of the state, society, and the individual.

International Covenants on Human Rights and Soviet Legislation, 1986.

In the United States, the richest capitalist country, millions are living below the poverty line because of skyrocketing unemployment and burdensome taxation. To be more exact, there are 35.5 million people below the poverty line today, according to "Famine in America," a report by a team of Harvard University researchers. In New York alone nearly 80,000 are homeless and have to live a half-starved life in lodging-houses or in the streets.

In Britain, according to BBC [British Broadcasting Corporation] data, there are over 3 million unemployed. More than half the Englishmen who tried to commit suicide were unemployed.

In the Soviet Union and the fraternal socialist countries, free health service for all categories of the population, pensions for the elderly and the disabled, free education, the opportunity to choose an occupation, and open access to cultural and spiritual values have long become the order of the day. More than that, the practice of the socialist countries has made all these social benefits standards of life, without which no full-bodied human existence is conceivable.

Bourgeois propagandists in their attempts to diminish the importance of the social achievements of socialism assert that similar rights and privileges have been provided in the capitalist countries as well. Yet it is common knowledge that all such rights and privileges, if any, have been won by the working people of the West after a bitter class struggle which has forced the ruling circles to make concessions or perform social manoeuvring. Furthermore, in the Soviet Union and the other fraternal countries all spendings on health service, education and social security are almost entirely drawn from the public consumption funds, whereas in the capitalist countries every employee must contribute from his own wage to cover a great part of these spendings.

In the socialist countries the well-being of all working citizens is growing from year to year. In the Soviet Union, for instance, large-scale social programmes designed to increase the population's real incomes on a planned basis are well underway. The primary concern of the Communist Party and the Soviet state is to raise the standard of living. In 1985, some considerable measures to do so were implemented. The average wage of workers and office employees was raised substantially and the labour done by collective farmers was paid much better. Retail turnover was augmented and the amount of social amenities boosted. Housing conditions were improved for nearly 10 million Soviet citizens. All these measures, it will be noted, were implemented with no increase in retail prices of foodstuffs, everyday consumption goods and social amenities.

Improving Living Conditions

An impressive indication of the justice of the Soviet system is the ever-growing amount of benefits received by working people from the public consumption funds. In 1985, payments and benefits from the public consumption funds yielded a national per capita average of 530 roubles. They are spent on improvement of working people's living conditions.

It is important to stress that the public consumption funds are not the dole or some other charity handout. The steady growth of the funds is the outcome of the efforts made by working collectives and individuals. This means that if every individual works with ingenuity and initiative, his needs will be satisfied more fully via the public consumption funds.

The steady growth of the well-being of the masses in the Soviet Union is stable and dynamic. It is evident in all classes and sections of the socialist community.

The measures adopted by the Party of late to raise order and organisation, and strengthen production and state discipline are regarded by the working people of the country as a manifestation of their will and as an important guarantee of the principles of social justice.

In addition to satisfying the ever-growing material requirements of working people, socialism is expanding spiritual, socio-cultural and creative needs of the human personality. The achievements scored by socialism in augmenting man's spiritual wealth are great and indisputable. If the entire social environment created for the harmonious development of the individual is taken as the chief yardstick for measuring social progress, then there can be only one conclusion to be drawn: the socialist system embodies the main direction of the progress of mankind.

A Healthy Atmosphere

This conclusion affirms that social justice is an inherent feature of life of the working people under socialism, that healthy moral and political atmosphere which has come to prevail in Soviet society. The principles of social justice, as they are more and more fully realised in life, Mikhail Gorbachov, General Secretary of the CPSU Central Committee pointed out, will serve as a powerful factor in enhancing the working activity of the Soviet people and, as a consequence, in further strengthening the economic and defensive might of the USSR.

"The Soviet Union is infected from top to bottom with corruption."

Soviet Human Rights Are Undermined by Corruption

Konstantin Simis

Konstantin Simis is a native of the Soviet Union and was an attorney and member of the Moscow Bar Association. In the following viewpoint, excerpted from his book, *USSR: The Corrupt Society,* Simis argues that the structure of Soviet government is antithetical to human morality. He believes that Soviet society oppresses human ingenuity and decency. Basic human rights are subverted in every aspect of Soviets' daily lives.

As you read, consider the following questions:

1. Why does the author argue that Soviet "free health care" is a myth?
2. What does Simis believe is wrong with the Soviet educational system?
3. Does Simis believe Soviet people have adequate incomes? Why or why not?

Man's life begins with birth, and it is from the moment of birth that corruption enters his life.

Of course a woman about to go into labor will be taken to her local maternity home without any bribery, but if she wants to give birth in a hospital known for its high standards of service and its qualified staff, or if she wants specific midwives and anesthetists to perform the delivery, then a bribe will be required. In most segments of the state medical system, which is a part of the lives of all Soviet citizens without exception, corruption has become an everyday mass phenomenon over the past quarter of a century. . . .

Free Medical Service?

All medical services are provided completely without charge to all Soviet citizens. The patient gets everything free: hospitalization (including general medical care, operations, treatments, drugs, examinations, and food), visits to doctors in local clinics, and house calls.

The bulk of free medical services is provided through the network of district polyclinics that covers the entire country. Anyone in any district can visit his polyclinic and be seen by a doctor, or if his state of health does not permit this, can request to be visited in his home . . . .

Money or gifts can ensure more attentive care and more time being spent on one patient than on another. Almost all people—even the very poorest—seek to do this whenever they have to use the services of the local polyclinic doctors, and the desire for more and better attention has resulted in this kind of corruption really becoming nationwide in scope. . . .

In the summer of 1976 my wife was in Brest, Belorussia, where she was to appear in court. However, one morning on her way to the courthouse she fell down and suffered a very bad multiple fracture of the collarbone. She was taken, semiconscious, to the surgical department of the nearest polyclinic. When she arrived in the X-ray room, the surgeon, the radiologist, and the nurses (all women) were busily occupied in a lively discussion about the merits of a knitted cardigan from abroad which a patient had brought in to sell to one of them. They paid no attention to my wife, and only after they had exhausted their topic of conversation—about ten minutes later—did the radiologist tell her, without even asking how she felt, to climb up onto the high X-ray table. Then the surgeon put her arm and shoulder into a cast that was as heavy as medieval armor. (Back in Moscow our doctor could only shake his head as he removed the cast—together with the skin of her shoulder—and say, "Another week in that cast and you'd never have moved that arm again.") . . .

As soon as my wife returned home we called the doctor from the local polyclinic. She did not even look at the arm, which was still confined in its plaster armor, nor did she ask how my wife felt. The only thing she was interested in was when and in what circumstances the injury was sustained (facts determining how much insurance would be paid). After these questions were answered to her satisfaction she wrote out a doctor's certificate for three days' sick leave and told my wife to have the permission extended when the three days were up.

Avoiding "Free" Care

We realized immediately that free medical care was not going to get us anywhere, and so the very same day we arranged through friends who had the necessary entrée that my wife should be treated at one of the best hospitals in town by experienced surgeons, physiotherapists, specialists in therapeutic gymnastics, and masseuses, all experts in their fields and all thoughtful and considerate people. They saved my wife's arm, and we remember them to this day with feelings of profound gratitude. The total cost in cash and in gifts for all their work was probably not more than two hundred rubles.

Rampant Nepotism and Cronyism

Nepotism and cronyism are rampant in the Soviet Union and in many of the East bloc satellites. The offspring of party leaders are assured the best education and the best jobs. The result is not just what Yugoslavia's Communist-turned-critic, Milovan Djilas, denounced 24 years ago as a "new class"; it is a new aristocracy.

Strobe Talbott, *Time*, January 4, 1982.

Meanwhile, what did the free medical service do for us during this time? The treatment went on for more than three months, and throughout this time I would go every week to the polyclinic doctor who had originally called on us and every week she would extend the doctor's certificate. Throughout those months she never once asked me how the patient was or whether the cast had been removed.

The only way, then, to avoid free medical care is to go to the same free, state-run institutions—not, however, as a normal nonpaying patient but, rather, privately, by visiting a specific doctor by prior agreement and for a fee. . . .

Although there has been a massive spread of corruption in Soviet medicine, very few doctors have been taken to court on charges of receiving payment for hospitalizing or treating a patient. To some extent the paucity of court cases is due to the fact that under Soviet law bribery is an indictable crime only when money is taken by an "official person," not an ordinary doctor. So when an ordinary doctor receives money from a patient he is treating, he is not brought to trial. The main reason, however, lies elsewhere.

With rare exceptions, all Soviet doctors accept money, presents, or some kind of service from their patients. It is virtually impossible for doctors to keep their bribe-taking a secret, nor do they see any need to, since to their minds there is nothing immoral about it and it cannot impair their professional reputation or standards. Thus a "professional guarantee" has emerged making it highly improbable that cases of corruption will be exposed from inside the profession.

Free Education and Corruption

Like health care, education in the Soviet Union is free. The state provides all education from kindergarten to post-graduate studies, and most students in higher and special secondary colleges (that is, technical colleges) receive a small expense grant in addition.

Corruption enters the life of the Soviet citizen at a very early age, even before he or she is old enough to be aware of it. The five-year-old granddaughter of some friends of mine, who was a pupil in kindergarten, showed a full grasp of the situation when she told her parents that one girl's mother had given Antonina Ivanovna [teacher] some fabric to make a jacket for International Women's Day and that now Antonina Ivanovna was always praising the girl and had given her the leading role in the First of May show. Antonina Ivanovna had already informed all the mothers that her birthday fell in May, so now they were each giving five rubles to buy her a present. Then everything would be just great: Antonina Ivanovna would praise all the children in the kindergarten....

What a clear depiction of mass corruption, all-pervasive but somehow ordinary—for what is going on in the kindergartens is not real bribery. These are small-scale gifts, little sops to curry favor in a general way, to make sure the child gets more attention. The real corruption enters the child's life when he starts school. It is here, in the primary and secondary schools, that the line of demarcation between little gifts and bribery becomes more and more blurred....

Paying for Grades

There is corruption in Soviet schools that comes closer to real bribery: paying for high marks. This kind of corruption is gaining more and more ground in Russia and in other Soviet republics. Nowadays many teachers do not merely accept these bribes—they often extort them. I was told about this by many informants with firsthand knowledge of the facts or who had reliable sources of information. Details also came from articles on the subject appearing in Soviet newspapers from time to time. One such article was published on March 24, 1976, in *The Literary Gazette*; it related that one teacher had demanded a crystal vase from the parents of a pupil about to graduate from secondary school in exchange for putting a good grade on his diploma records. Another teacher demanded an imported umbrella for the same service.

As they climb higher and higher up the pyramid of the education system, boys and girls approach the threshold of higher education. By now they are psychologically prepared for this moment and they expect to encounter corruption at this stage as well.

BY PETT FOR THE LEXINGTON HERALD-LEADER

"YOU HAVE BEEN SET UP. YOU HAVE THE RIGHT TO REMAIN SET UP. YOU HAVE THE RIGHT TO HAVE AN INFORMANT PRESENT DURING INTERROGATION. ANYTHING WE SAY CAN AND WILL BE USED AGAINST YOU IN A SORT-OF LAW..."

©1986 Joel Pett for the Lexington Herald-Leader.

In the dock of Moscow City Court, there were nine defendants, all of them employees of one of the most prestigious institutes of Moscow. Sitting in the dock were the assistant dean of the institute, Professor B——, Assistant Professor L——, and a few teachers. All were accused of taking bribes from the parents of a number of candidates. In return they would arrange for candidates to be accepted at the school by giving them high marks on entrance examinations.

In the Soviet Union the system for entering higher educational institutions is by competitive examination; all candidates have to take written and oral examinations, each marked on a scale of one to five. The students with the highest total number of points on the various parts of the examination are accepted. . . .

Favoritism in Soviet Schools

Court evidence, given by teachers and school administrators appearing as defendants and witnesses, as well as private conversations with people who worked as executive secretaries on selection boards and with teachers who administered various entrance examinations in Moscow, Leningrad, and Tbilisi make it possible to assert that in the universities, institutes, and technical schools of the Soviet Union, a system of far-flung and imposed favoritism was practiced. The children of the ruling apparatus and those whom the apparat favor were accepted whether or not they did well on the entrance exams.

Ethnic discrimination is the lot of Soviet Jews. Quite a number of schools do not admit them at all: the institutions that train the upcoming ruling elite (the party schools, the Academy of Social Sciences, the Institute of International Relations) and also some institutes and university departments that train key nuclear scientists and electron physicists. Then there is another category that accepts Jews according to a strict quota system similar to that used in tsarist Russia. (This includes all humanities departments of the prestigious universities, the leading institutes of technology, medical schools, foreign-language institutes, and certain others.)...

That corruption in admissions to educational institutions is so integral a part of Soviet society is underscored by the fact that the average person with children about to apply to an institution of higher education has a firmly entrenched belief that you can get into any place you like for a bribe, and that everyone takes bribes. To try and convince such a person that by no means every staff member of every school takes bribes is not merely difficult, it is often impossible....

The commonly held conviction that bribery is an effective tool in the fight for admission to schools has created a psychological atmosphere in the country that makes it quite an easy matter to find clients willing to offer a bribe in order to get into an institute or university. What happens most of the time is that the clients—that is, the candidates' parents—use their own acquaintances to seek out contacts with likely go-betweens to pass along the bribes....

Everything Can Be Obtained Through Bribery

The corruption that has rotted the ruling apparat of the country has had the terrible effect of eating away the morals not only of the people who give or receive bribes but also of the innocent, those who have not been party to corruption but who have merely been living in an atmosphere of corruption and have been forced to breathe its tainted air.

The atmosphere of corruption has bred the conviction in the minds of the people that everything can be attained by bribery: a good job, a university diploma, or an undeserved judicial verdict. And although that conviction is far from justified in all cases, it has led to the climate of tolerance toward corruption that holds sway in Soviet society.

Apart from these moral preconditions for corruption, there is an absolutely fundamental material precondition as well: the need to find additional means to ensure a minimum living standard for one's family. The majority of Soviet people are faced by that need, since they are wage slaves, hired by the country's one monopoly employer, the state, which does not even provide them with the barest of living wages.

The average income of a wage earner in the Soviet Union may be stated with fair certainty. According to official Soviet statistics the average monthly wage for manual and office workers in the first half of 1979 was 163 rubles, or about $230 (my source for this is the issue of *Pravda* dated June 21, 1979). But it is impossible to obtain official statistics about the minimum subsistence requirements of an average Soviet family. Such information is simply not published; it is a state secret.

A Privileged Class

Certain groups in Soviet society (the party, the military officer corps, the diplomatic corps, the scientific-technical intelligentsia, the cultural and sports establishments) have deliberately shielded themselves from the social and economic hardships faced by the rest of the population. A privileged 5% of the Soviet population, known as the *Nomenklatura*, has access to special "closed" stores that are specially stocked with foreign goods not available in regular stores, as well as bountiful supplies of Soviet goods that are in short supply elsewhere. . . . Housing space is allocated by state authorities on the basis of social status. Many leading Soviet organizations have their own housing facilities, which are of good standard and centrally located.

The Fourth Directorate of the Ministry of Health runs a closed system of hospitals, clinics, and dispensaries for the *Nomenklatura*, providing far better services than those available to the general population. . . . To quote from George Orwell's *Animal Farm*: "All animals are equal, but some are more equal than others."

Richard Schifter, address to Conference on Security and Cooperation in Europe, Ottawa, Canada, May 22, 1985.

We do, however, have one official indicator, which was published in the Soviet press: the decree passed by the Central Committee of the Communist Party of the Soviet Union and the Council of Ministers regarding allowances for families with many children. In this decision the poverty line was set at 50 rubles per month per person, or 150 rubles for a family of three.

That is the poverty line as officially recognized by the state; but official statistics have to be disregarded when calculating the true minimum needs of an average Soviet family, which most typically consists of three people—mother, father, and child. I am able to calculate these figures because I lived in the USSR for almost sixty years, thirty-five of them in a large apartment building full of factory workers and engineers, and I have my own experience and my observations of my neighbors to go by. . . .

Supplementing the Family Income

The average wage of a manual or office worker in the Soviet Union is below even the poverty line fixed by the state itself at 150 rubles. The average wage of 147 rubles covers less than 60 percent of the 250 rubles needed by a family of three as a more realistic subsistence minimum; the remainder—more than 40 percent—of 103 rubles has to be met from other sources.

One should bear in mind here that these are the calculations for a Moscow family that is able to buy produce in state shops and at state prices (although with difficulty and only by waiting in long lines). What, then, about a family living in any city or town in the country apart from the few, like Moscow, that enjoy special supply privileges? In these other places practically no basic staples are to be found in the stores, so people have to buy them at the markets for prices three to five times the state prices. In such cases the subsistence minimum must be increased by 150 rubles even by the most conservative estimates; it thus climbs to 400 rubles. Accordingly, the deficit that must somehow be made up rises to 253 rubles.

Does the average Soviet family really live on 147 rubles a month, by half starving and denying itself the very basic necessities, or does such a family make up the shortage of funds from other sources? It does indeed supplement its basic income, and it not only covers the deficit in the family budget—it does much more than that. According to official data the people of the Soviet Union keep more than 140 billion rubles in savings accounts. This is money that is clearly not being spent on current expenses. Where do these billions come from?

To begin with, they come from legal sources: from the wages of the second working member in a family. For, according to sociological samplings, both husband and wife work in one family out of two. This is how the problem of the subsistence minimum is solved in families in which that wife is able to leave her child with someone and go out to work. There are, however, other sources of additional income—moonlighting, pilfering from employers, private trade, and many other semilegal or totally illegal activities. . . .

The need to be assured of a subsistence minimum income and the desire for not just this minimum but also the things that more privileged people may clearly be seen to possess have led to a pervasive determination to get hold of money by any means, whether legal and moral (such as moonlighting) or illegal and immoral (such as theft and prostitution) . . . .

Thus the Soviet Union is infected from top to bottom with corruption—from the worker, who gives the foreman a bottle of vodka to get the best job, to Politburo candidate Mzhavanadze, who takes hundreds of thousands of rubles for protecting underground millionaires; from the street prostitute, who pays the policeman ten rubles so that he won't prevent her from soliciting clients, to the former member of the Politburo, Minister of Culture Ekaterina Furtseva, who built a luxurious suburban villa at the government's expense—each and every one is afflicted with corruption.

Working for Nothing

Comrade Lenin set the heroic example by relieving the workers of any need to worry about free speech, voting for the party of their choice, the right to assemble or to strike. He called this setup the dictatorship of the proletariat and everyone was happy. He also freed the workers from the tyranny of capitalist exploitation so they could work all the time for the glorious Soviet state for practically nothing. Things would get better, Comrade Lenin assured the proletariat. He was right. Things did get better—for the few proletarians running the system.

Arnold Irvine, *Washington Inquirer*, May 2, 1986.

I was born in that country and lived there for almost sixty years. Year after year since childhood and throughout my whole conscious life I watched as corruption ate more deeply into society until it turned the Soviet regime in the sixties and seventies into a land of corrupt rulers, ruling over a corrupted people. . . .

But even if the ruling elite undertook a decisive battle against corruption, such an attempt would be doomed to failure, since at the root of the general corruption of the Soviet Union lies the totalitarian rule of the Communist party, single-handedly ruling the country. This power is checked neither by law nor by a free press. And the nature of any unrestricted power is such that it inevitably corrupts those who wield it and constantly generates the phenomenon of corruption. So it is that corruption has become the organic and unchangeable essence of the Soviet regime.

"In the name of human survival, peacemakers. . . must tolerate, in patience and compassion, a large volume of inhumanities in order to prevent even worse inhumanities."

Soviet Human Rights Violations Must Be Tolerated

Theodore H. Von Laue

Should the US and Western Europe restrict relations with the Soviet Union on the basis of human rights violations? In the following viewpoint, Theodore H. Von Laue argues no. He believes the Western world should attempt to understand the historical and social causes for the lack of human rights in the USSR. By asking the Soviet Union to comply with American standards, he argues, the Western world is applying a kind of human rights imperialism. Von Laue is Frances and Jacob Hiatt professor emeritus of European history at Clark University in Massachusetts.

As you read, consider the following questions:

1. What does the author believe causes the Soviet disregard for human life?
2. Why does the author believe the West should tolerate Soviet human rights violations?

Theodore H. Von Laue, "Human Rights Imperialism," *Bulletin of the Atomic Scientists,* August/September 1983. Reprinted by permission of the BULLETIN OF THE ATOMIC SCIENTISTS, a magazine of science and world affairs. Copyright © 1983 by the Educational Foundation for Nuclear Science, Chicago, IL 60637.

The central force escalating the arms race is not the frightfulness of the weapons. Rather, it is the instinctive hostility of most Americans—as of most Westerners—toward the Soviet system and its inhumanities. Put bluntly, it is the American unwillingness to recognize the legitimacy of the Soviet system.

Implicitly or explicitly, Americans insist that Soviet policy and Soviet institutions conform to American standards, especially in regard to human rights. This moral imperialism prevails not only among hawks but even among doves. Admittedly, there are corollaries on the Soviet side—mostly in response to and in direct imitation of Western initiatives. But as the American government has persistently taken the initiative in escalating the arms race, so Americans as a people, long before nuclear weapons, have been forever on the offensive in prescribing political morality to the rest of the world, and most of all to the Soviet Union.

These abrasive assertions, bound to arouse instant resentment, need to be made, considering what is at stake. As long as the arguments focus on weaponry alone, the peace movement and public agitation over arms limitation will never prevail. Before arms limitation can be negotiated, there has to be a process of psychological disarmament which allows us, individually and collectively, to accept the Soviet system, with all its inhumanities, as a tragic but legitimate system, deserving our compassion, even our admiration, but most of all our unbiased rational comprehension.

Soviet Inhumanities

All arguments in favor of nuclear arms limitation run up against not only the reality of Soviet military strength (which is debatable) but also the undeniable record of Soviet inhumanities, beginning with the Revolution, reaching a climax under Stalin, and ever-present under Khrushchev and Brezhnev. We are all aware of Soviet violations of the Helsinki agreement, of the treatment of dissenters (among whom Andrei Sakharov deservedly has a large following among scientists in the West), and of the measures of repression reaching into Eastern Europe and Afghanistan. In the face of Soviet violations of human rights, even ardent leaders of the peace movement are apt to turn militantly anti-Soviet. How can we defuse the moral revulsion against the Soviet system which is the trump card of the hawks?

The point here is that, in the name of human survival, peacemakers in America and in Western Europe must tolerate, in patience and compassion, a large volume of inhumanities in order to prevent even worse inhumanities. In the face of a nuclear holocaust, we cannot afford to compound the hostility and tension that arise out of our own indignation. Our foremost moral obligation is to understand, rationally and dispassionately, what prompts those violations before we condemn their instigators. Maybe the inhumanities are symptoms of a deeper malaise to which we, as Americans, conceivably contribute. Do we really know why the Soviet regime acts as it does? As we side with the Sakharovs and other heroic dissenters, are we sure that *they* know? Or do they, like us, apply Western liberal-democratic values and expectations to a political culture deficient in the pre-conditions that make freedom work? Do we apply our Western standards to countries and people that have never shared our values? Do we practice an aggressive moral imperialism that contributes to the arms race? The answer, for the sake of psychological disarmament, is: yes, indeed we do.

Can't Negotiate Internal Reforms

The [arms control] agreements that failed had in common efforts in some way to change the behavior of the Soviet state. Whether the goal was to encourage religious freedom, to bring about free elections, to induce Soviet restraint in the Third World, or to promote human rights, the initiatives proceeded from the assumption that diplomacy could be used to bring about fundamental changes in the way great nations conduct their internal affairs. Negotiations, it was assumed, could provide not only a means of managing conflicts, but could also serve as instruments of reform.

Again, history offers little encouragement that this strategy works. Changes do occur within the Soviet Union. . . . But, as is the case in our system, these changes proceed chiefly from internal causes and are not susceptible to management or manipulation from the outside. To insist that diplomacy serve the interests of reform as well as those of global stability is to impose on it a task considerably beyond its capabilities. It is quite enough, for the moment, to concentrate on keeping the peace.

John Lewis Gaddis, *Shared Destiny*, 1985.

We do it unconsciously, subliminally. Our moral imperialism is embedded in our thinking and collective experience; it lies at the core of the American national character. Our gut reaction is that the Soviet system is starkly incompatible with the American way of life, a constant provocation. But the reverse is also true: the American presence in the world is an intolerable provocation to the Soviet system, or to any effective government ruling the vast Russian empire. The symbolic essence of the American way of life is freedom; the same freedom is a state-busting force in the Soviet setting. Are we then to let this mutual provocation promote an unending moral, political and military escalation toward conflict? Can we allow the defense of our way of life to push us inescapably toward a nuclear holocaust? The steady escalation of American hostility to the Soviet system since 1917 and the redefinition of American identity as being in direct contrast to that of the Soviet Union (and to communism) since 1947 suggest an irresistible historical dialectic, dooming, in the upshot, everything Americans stand for. . . .

A Long Tradition

Disregard for human life and dignity has a long tradition on the ground floor of Russian life, as it does in other parts of the world. Open boundaries, a harsh climate and pervasive bitter poverty combined with the ruthlessness of government in shaping a brutal popular culture, especially on the open frontiers as in Siberia. Russians did not lack kindliness but such traits remained regressive; they did not enter into the country's political culture.

Consider the origins of the Soviet regime in the battles of World War I and in the revolution and civil war that followed; brutality and terror escalated into a fine art. How was it possible to build a new and better state, capable of preventing a repetition of the disasters of World War I, with the human raw material so totally unsuited for the peaceful give-and-take that underlies government by consensus? The evidence reflected in the histories and novels of the time shows an embittered people, militantly anarchist and anti-modern, fractious, hostile to all government authority, united only by command and terror. Terror-enforced command came wrapped in the exalted vision of communism as a secular paradise, taking the place of earlier illusions of Russian superiority derived from the Orthodox Church. But neither orthodoxy nor Marxism could uphold individual rights while the polity was on the brink of disaster.

Among the multiple disasters facing any Russian government trying to fashion law, order and power out of highly fissionable human raw material, invidious comparison with the West took top rank. Military defeat was intermittent; but defeat resulting from such comparison was a daily threat. Those humiliations had begun in earnest after the French Revolution; they increased as contact with the West became more frequent and intense. And they are a stark reality today. Americans visiting the Soviet Union are a subversive force merely by their presence.

Responding to Daily Emergencies

Confronted with daily emergencies of this nature, Russian governments have long since evolved countermeasures: censorship; control of contact between Russia and the outside; promotion of an aggressive creed of indigenous superiority, always enforced by terror. The satisfactions of superiority that cemented American consensus and thereby safeguarded human rights never had a chance in the Russian setting. While the legitimacy of Russian autocrats and Soviet leaders has thus been fiercely challenged by comparisons, Western governments—above all the United States—were not only immune to subversion from without but also totally unaware that cultural subversion constituted a potent form of political power.

Put more bluntly, the West has engaged in the power game of cultural aggression, not by a formal or deliberate policy but unwittingly, by its very existence and its role as a universal model of wealth and power. In response, Russia's rulers adopted a deliberate policy of self-defense, including counter-offensives like supporting subversive revolutionary movements wherever possible. In recent decades, of course, U.S. policy has enthusiastically adopted Soviet Cold War tactics. In the dirty business of intelligence work with its disregard for human rights the two camps have become surprisingly alike.

Human Rights Delusions

With respect to political subversion by example, however, the differences are great: the United States is reasonably secure in the loyalty of its citizens and the goodwill of its largest neighbors; the Soviet Union lacks the support of a dedicated, skilled and loyal population, and faces the outright hostility of satellite nations, ready to break into open revolt whenever the Soviet regime shows signs of weakness. The openness of cultural relations with the outside, promised under the Helsinki agreements, was a delusion based on unrealistic hopes on both sides. The "worst-case" syndrome—fear of a combined external attack and an internal rebellion—continues to hang over Soviet policy-making. It determines Soviet planning for conventional and nuclear war. . . .

Reduce Pressure on Moscow

No nation responds well to pressure, certainly not the Soviets. Increased economic and military pressure will only help convince them their vital security is being threatened, and if they respond by increasing domestic repression and aggression abroad, who can blame them? Under such circumstances, we would no doubt do the same. A much more reasonable course of action would be to reduce the pressure on Moscow as best we can, while at the same time seeking to work out just and reasonable agreements on a wide range of issues, including arms reduction and trade. This strategy would not only benefit us economically, but would greatly lessen international tensions which are growing to alarming proportions.

Jay Higginbotham, speech at Auburn University, April 12, 1983.

What moral right does the Soviet regime have to proliferate its influence? Does the world want still more repression, slave labor and dictatorship than already exists? Why cannot some sensible Soviet leaders reduce their over-extended territorial sway and concentrate on solving the pressing internal problems of their country? Dissenters like Solzhenitsyn have long urged a contraction of Russian ambition, letting the satellite peoples go for the sake of promoting the interest of the Russians and reducing tension throughout Eurasia.

How little these critics know of the dynamics of power! It is safe to say that a significant reduction of Soviet ambition would bring into the open all the national and ethnic conflicts of Eurasia that have been simmering under the surface: How could the tensions be contained? Where should the new boundaries be drawn? What would become of the distribution of raw materials like oil, coal, iron or food? How soon after settling old scores would there arise sufficient goodwill to restore the former network of economic interdependence and cooperation? And what, meanwhile, of the starving human multitudes in the industrial cities, or the settlements in the far north that depend on long lines of supply? The standard of living would sink drastically and, considering the intensity of conflict and suffering, concern for human rights would vanish, as it did in the civil war after 1917. . . .

Soviet Justice and Morality

What then should we do? First, we should expand our sense of reality by taking into account the insights and perspectives of the other side. There is justice and morality even in the policies of the Politburo. Second, we should tolerate Soviet inhumanities in order not to add to them out of ignorance and incomprehension. The patent inhumanities of the Soviet system are not inherent in that system, but in the conditions that gave rise to it and preserve it.

Such tolerance, alas, is an infinitely saddening, disorienting and even repulsive endeavor for a liberal conscience. Are we then—to take the sharpest provocation—to ignore the Polish bid for freedom and betray Solidarity? The question dramatizes the challenges we face, but the answers here suggested do not imply a lack of compassion or a betrayal. Above all, we have to make certain that in attitude or policy we do not escalate hostility between the Superpowers. Rising hostility inevitably worsens life in Poland; a nuclear holocaust wipes it out. As the future of their country is tied by geography and history to the temper of relations between the Superpowers, the Poles too will benefit by what I have called psychological disarmament. By geopolitical necessity they must be one of its chief practitioners. Encouraging the Polish people in a rash bid for self-determination contributes to the arms race; helping them to promote a cooperative relationship between the Superpowers, in which all participants scale down their political ambitions and moral righteousness, is a move toward peace and humanity.

The initiative for such reversal of natural impulses, however, can hardly be expected to come from Poland. Rather, it must come from the United States, the prime mover in the game of global preeminence. We must learn to turn our human rights imperialism inward upon ourselves, demanding that we withhold moral judgment until we understand fully what we judge; that we re-evaluate our expectations about the American role in the world and project a more humble image of ourselves and our global responsibility; that we become more capable of comprehending the needs of other peoples and other countries and of adjusting our own priorities accordingly. There is a desperate urgency for managing the Earth's resources in the common interest; it calls for a raised awareness of ourselves and our interests as inhabitants of the Global City.

Nuclear Midnight

These may be fine words, but they lack the power to alter the trends of the times and the moral temper of society. Thus the arms race escalates. How close must we approach the nuclear midnight flash before we undertake the big changes in ourselves and our society which global interdependence and nuclear weapons demand?

Stopping the arms race is a far bigger challenge than even people of goodwill are ready to admit. It means, in questions of political power and morality, putting ourselves occasionally inside the minds of leaders on the other side and seeing ourselves as they see us. By thus doubling our vision we greatly enhance our grasp of the realities that push us toward the midnight flash. Maybe with such understanding we can even reverse that deadly course.

"To maintain U.S. and Western pressure on Moscow to improve its human rights practices, the U.S. should keep the issues of human rights high on the Soviet-American negotiating agenda."

Soviet Human Rights Violations Should Remain a Concern

Mikhail Tsypkin

Mikhail Tsypkin is a Salvatori Fellow in Soviet Studies at the Heritage Foundation, a conservative think tank. An émigré from the Soviet Union, Tsypkin holds a Ph.D. in political science from Harvard University and also has served as a research consultant at the US Naval War College. In the following viewpoint, he argues that the Soviet Union under Premier Gorbachev continues to show a blatant disregard for human rights. Tsypkin asserts that the US must continue to make human rights a priority in all discussions with the Soviet Union. Allowing the Soviet government to avoid improving human rights is a moral injustice.

As you read, consider the following questions:

1. Does the author believe Reagan's "tough stance" on human rights helped or hindered Soviet dissidents? Why?
2. What "tactics" are the Soviets using to project an image of improved human rights, according to Tsypkin?

Mikhail Tsypkin, "Soviet Human Rights Under Gorbachev," The Heritage Foundation *Backgrounder*, February 10, 1987. Reprinted with permission.

Soviet Communist Party General Secretary Mikhail Gorbachev has been seeking to project an image of "openness" and flexibility on human rights issues. He has taken some dramatic steps to demonstrate that the Soviet regime's policies on these matters are changing. He has released Dr. Andrei Sakharov and his wife Elena Bonner from their nearly seven years of internal exile. He has released the dissidents Anatoly Shcharansky and Yuri Orlov from prison and internal exile and sent them to the West in exchange for Soviet spies held here. He has released the poet Irina Ratushinskaya from prison and allowed her to leave the Soviet Union.

Freeing a couple of internationally known Soviet human rights activists guarantees worldwide headlines. It also masks the fact that for most Soviet citizens, there has been no general improvement in Soviet human rights practices under Gorbachev.

Consistent and widespread violations of human rights by the Kremlin have been a major reason for Western mistrust of the Soviets. Moscow has ignored its commitment, under the 1975 Helsinki Final Act on security and cooperation in Europe, to respect human rights and fundamental freedoms, including freedom of thought, conscience, and religion, as well as the free flow of ideas and people across state borders.

While Gorbachev's policy of *glasnost*, the Russian word for "openness," has allowed the Soviet mass media to write about social ills in the Soviet Union, the Kremlin continues to harass, imprison, and even torture human rights activists, independent peace activists, religious believers, would-be emigrants, and free thinkers. Indeed, shortly before Sakharov's release, Anatoly Marchenko, a prominent human rights activist, died in prison after a long hunger strike. And the flow of emigres from the Soviet Union practically has been stopped.

New Tactics

At the same time, Gorbachev's regime is using new public relations tactics to shield itself from international censure. In the past, high-ranking Soviet officials shunned any discussion of human rights abuses. Now these officials, including Gorbachev, distort and lie about these issues to Western audiences. Example: In an interview with the French communist daily *L'Humanite* in February 1986, Gorbachev stated that Andrei Sakharov was exiled to Gorky "in accordance with Soviet law" and that Sakharov was "living in normal conditions" and "was conducting scientific work." This was untrue: Sakharov was never tried, and there is no law in the Soviet criminal code permitting internal exile of indefinite duration and isolation from practically all human contacts. Sakharov could not really engage in scientific work because he was largely isolated from his colleagues, and his life under the KGB cameras was anything but normal.

After his release from exile, Sakharov said that Ronald Reagan's tough stance toward the Soviet Union has helped Soviet dissidents. The Reagan Administration thus should continue its policy on human rights: openly criticize Soviet human rights abuses; demand that the Soviets fulfill the human rights provisions contained in the 1975 Helsinki Final Act; deny the Soviets the most favored nation treatment (MFN) in trade relations until they permit free emigration; insist on including human rights issues in the agenda of high-level Soviet-American meetings; and retain the issue of human rights as the centerpiece of the Helsinki process. It is only continuing and unremitting pressure by the U.S. and the West on human rights that may lead to improvements in individual situations and the possibility of long-term systemic change.

We Must Not Desist

It is the responsibility of the Free World to clarify the relationship between security and human rights. Western insistence on freedom in the Soviet Union is *not* an artificial demand that can be balanced with a counterdemand by the Soviet negotiators. The Helsinki accords officially recognized the obligation of the Soviet Union to respect civil liberties, and linked the future of the East-West relationship to the honoring of those liberties. Is our continuous pressure for human rights and for freedom of emigration raising the price the Soviets demand? Should we desist?

The answer is an emphatic *no*. We are not in a marketplace. We must not use the Jews as currency for or against SDI. We cannot accept the Soviet concept that accepts trade in human lives. We must intensify the struggle for the release of every prisoner of conscience. We must stress the need to allow free emigration for all Soviet Jews who desire it. Real success in any future arms-reduction talks is intrinsically linked to their release.

Natan (Anatoly) Shcharansky, *The Wall Street Journal*, November 4, 1986.

Observance of human rights is not only a moral issue, but a crucial indicator of a nation's intentions. According to Reagan: "a government that will break faith with its own people cannot be trusted to keep faith with foreign powers." This has been underscored for years by such Soviet human rights activists as Sakharov, who said that "as long as a country has no civil liberty, no freedom of information, and no independent press, then there exists no effective body of public opinion to control the conduct of the government . . . . Such a situation . . . is a menace to international security.". . .

Soviet Prisoners of Conscience

There has been no reduction in the number of political prisoners incarcerated for their political or religious beliefs or attempts to leave the Soviet Union. Natan (Anatoly) Shcharansky, using the data he collected while in Soviet prisons and forced labor camps, has estimated the number of these prisoners to be between 10,000 and 20,000. No international organization, such as the Red Cross or Amnesty International, is permitted to collect data on the condition of Soviet prisoners of conscience. The KGB has cut off many possible channels for passing information on human rights violations from the Soviet Union to the West and has virtually destroyed the network for gathering such information within the USSR.

Persecution of Human Rights Advocates

Gorbachev's regime has continued persecuting human rights advocates. After the signing of the Helsinki Final Act in 1975, nongovernmental "Helsinki groups" were established in Moscow (the Russian Federation), the Ukraine, Lithuania, Georgia, and Armenia to monitor Soviet adherence to the principles of human rights. These Helsinki groups no longer function because of state persecution....

While the reality of the Soviet's systematic violations of human rights remains unchanged, Gorbachev has launched a public relations drive to improve the Soviet image.

An important element of the public relations campaign is the highly publicized release of some prisoners. In the past, the Soviets occasionally released prisoners of conscience from prison and granted exit visas to Jewish refuseniks (Soviet Jews whose visa applications previously had been turned down) in response to requests from American politicians, but Moscow never acknowledged doing this. Soviet Foreign Minister Eduard Shevardnadze told a New York audience last September 30, [1986] however, that the Soviet Union "sometimes takes into consideration requests of the U.S. Administration, some appeals by members of Congress" on behalf of dissidents and refuseniks. This statement signals that Moscow seeks to score public relations points with American policy makers and mass media by resolving selected cases of human rights violations. The Soviets also apparently hope to reap political dividends by exchanging some of their political prisoners for Soviet spies imprisoned in the West. These actions then are trumpeted as goodwill gestures. This was the case with the exchanges of Natan (Anatoly) Shcharansky and Yuri Orlov for Soviet and East European spies.

Feigning "Openness" on Human Rights

Until very recently, any attempt to raise human rights concerns publicly with Soviet officials triggered shrill warnings against "interfering" in Soviet domestic affairs. Now Soviet officials confront the issue calmly—with falsehoods and half-truths.

Example: In his interview to the French communist daily *L'Humanite* in February 1986, Gorbachev stated that those imprisoned for political offenses in the Soviet Union had called for "subversion or destruction" of the Soviet state. This is true only if criticizing human rights abuses, exercising religious freedom, or attempting to leave the Soviet Union—the rights guaranteed in the Helsinki Final Act—are acts of subversion....

At the same time, Moscow has taken a tough stand on changing the definition of fundamental human rights. Instead of addressing such traditional rights as freedoms of speech, religion, and movement, Moscow stresses that what is truly important are "humanitarian issues." This Moscow defines narrowly as problems affecting divided families and cultural exchanges. Gorbachev here apparently is attempting to lure the West into protracted haggling over family reunification....

Soviet Goals

1) *Diverting the Helsinki Process from Human Rights*

The Soviets' only interest in the 1975 Helsinki Final Act was that document's recognition of the post-World War II division of Europe. According to former Soviet Ambassador Arkady Shevchenko, who defected to the U.S. in 1978, Western resolve to hold the Soviets accountable for violating the human rights provision of the Helsinki Final Act came as an unpleasant and embarrassing surprise to the Kremlin.

Dick Wright, reprinted with permission.

Now the Soviets are trying to make the Helsinki process more to their liking. First, the Soviets are striving to downgrade fundamental human rights to the "humanitarian" issues. Speaking at the Vienna conference opening, Soviet Foreign Minister Shevardnadze proposed convening a special conference on humanitarian affairs in Moscow. The Kremlin obviously hopes to win Western recognition of the Soviets' extremely limited interpretation of human rights and to keep Western nongovernmental human rights organizations away from the review process, since their activity would be impossible or severely restricted in Moscow.

Second, the Soviets hope to decouple the linkage, enunciated by the Helsinki Final Act, between human rights and European security. With review of human rights performance effectively delayed until the proposed humanitarian conference in Moscow, the Soviets would find it easier to tilt the Vienna conference toward exclusive preoccupation with Soviet plans for new arms control schemes in Europe.

2) *"Quiet Diplomacy"*

The Soviets strive to create an impression of a "dialogue" with the United States on human rights and thus foster a climate for "quiet diplomacy." This would make human rights exclusively the issue of private discussions between Soviet and Western diplomats and would spare the Kremlin from public criticism for human rights abuses.

3) *Blaming the U.S. for Soviet Abuses*

The Soviets would like to shift the blame for their abuses of human rights onto the Reagan Administration by linking the lack of progress in this area to the American refusal to give up the Strategic Defense Initiative. For instance, after no arms control agreement was reached at Reykjavik, the Soviets hinted to Western reporters that no progress on human rights could be reached without an arms control deal eliminating the SDI.

4) *Emphasis on Arms Control at U.S.-Soviet Summits*

The Soviets want to allow Gorbachev to concentrate on arms control in his meetings with the U.S. by relegating "humanitarian" discussions to routine mid-level working groups of professional diplomats. In such discussions the pressure to reach any progress would be lower than at top-level talks.

Policy Recommendations

To maintain U.S. and Western pressure on Moscow to improve its human rights practices, the U.S. should:

• Keep the issues of human rights high on the Soviet-American negotiating agenda. Raising individual cases with the Soviet leaders is necessary and can bring positive results. More important, the Soviets should be reminded constantly that they must fulfill the human rights provisions of the Helsinki Final Act.

• Protect the integrity of the Helsinki process, which realistically

91

links relaxation of international tensions to strict observance of human rights.

- Emphasize human rights in their entirety as a key subject of U.S.-Soviet discussions, since the Soviet definition of "humanitarian affairs" is limited to family reunification problems.
- Reject the Soviet invitation to hold a Moscow conference on humanitarian affairs within the Helsinki framework until all Soviet prisoners of conscience are released; large-scale emigration from the Soviet Union is renewed; and guarantees are received for freedom of activities for nongovernmental organizations in Moscow, freedom of contacts between Western delegations and nongovernment organizations, and full uncensored coverage of the conference in the Soviet mass media.
- Avoid the trap of quiet diplomacy on human rights. While quiet diplomacy might be appropriate to gain the release of specific prisoners of conscience or to increase emigration, Washington should continue to insist that the Soviets fulfill completely the human rights provisions of the Helsinki Final Act and publicly criticize Soviet violations of human rights. Otherwise, it would appear that the pressure on the Soviets to correct their human rights abuses had been turned off.

Conclusion

Human rights are systematically violated in the Soviet Union under Gorbachev. There has been almost no improvement since the KGB campaign to eradicate all dissent was begun in 1979. At the same time, Gorbachev and his advisors are using new public relations tactics to reduce the damage to the Soviet world image over their poor human rights record. This new strategy includes releasing select prisoners of conscience and refuseniks; narrowing the issue of human rights to such "humanitarian issues" as family reunification; removing human rights from the agenda of top-level Soviet-American discussions by creating mid-level working groups on humanitarian affairs; having high-ranking Soviet officials, even including Gorbachev, present a false picture of Soviet human rights abuses, rather than shunning questions about them as before; and diverting the Helsinki process away from human rights issues.

The U.S. should respond to the new Soviet tactics with its own strict agenda: conducting all human rights discussions at top-level U.S.-Soviet meetings; linking security issues with human rights within the Helsinki process; criticizing Soviet human rights violations publicly; and insisting that strict implementation of human rights provisions of the Helsinki Final Act is central to East-West relations.

"Soviet women enjoy equal possibilities with men in participation in all spheres of life of our society, including social activities and politics."

Soviet Women Have Full Equality

Galina Sukhoruchenkova, interviewed by Lyudmila Zabavskaya

Women are officially guaranteed equal rights with men in the Soviet Union. But whether or not this official stance reflects reality for Soviet women is debated. In the following viewpoint, Galina Sukhoruchenkova, secretary of the All-Union Central Council of Trade Unions, is interviewed by Soviet journalist Lyudmila Zabavskaya. Sukhoruchenkova asserts that women in the Soviet Union fully and equally participate in politics, education, and employment.

As you read, consider the following questions:

1. According to the author, what are the "special privileges" women are granted in the Soviet Union?
2. In what kind of daily activities do Soviet women participate, according to the author?
3. After reading this article and its opposing viewpoint, do you think the role of women in Soviet society is easier or harder than that of women in the US?

Galina Sukhoruchenkova, interviewed by Lyudmila Zabavskaya, "Genuine Equality," *Soviet Military Review,* March 1987.

The Constitution of the USSR guarantees equal rights to man and woman. Could you, please, explain to our readers how these rights are actually guaranteed?

Soviet women enjoy equal possibilities with men in participation in all spheres of life of our society, including social activities and politics. They exercise equal powers with men in the administration of state affairs. Women account for 30 odd per cent of the members of the USSR Supreme Soviet (Parliament), for 40 per cent of the members of the Supreme Soviets of the Union Republics (Regional Parliaments) and for 50 per cent of the members of local Soviets (or Councils). More than one third of the people's judges and more than half of judges' assessors are women.

Soviet women enjoy equal rights with men in all other spheres: education, work, pay and promotion. Today the educational level of women and men employed in social production is the same. Out of every thousand working women, 862 have either a higher or secondary education.

Active Women

You will find women in all jobs at factories, plants, in the fields, on the farms. There are women who are managers of big industrial enterprises or hold executive posts in ministries. One thousand three hundred and fifty-two women were elected delegates to the 27th CPSU [Communist Party of the Soviet Union] Congress. These are the best female workers of the nation. Among them are Zinaida Kondrashova, Hero of Socialist Labour, a lathe operator at the Lenin Novokramatorsk Engineering Works; Valentina Polikarpova, leader of an interior decorating team; Mariya Belyayeva, manager of a department store in Kemerovo; Galina Soldatova, deputy chief physician of a hospital in Saransk; and Tatyana Trofimova, an operator at the Novo-Ufimsk Oil Refinery. During the Eleventh Five-Year-Plan period (1981-1985) she submitted 20 rationalisation proposals on process control. Tatyana Trofimova is also an active social worker. Her comrades have elected her their Party group organiser. She has a good family. Tatyana is a loving mother of three daughters. Soviet society has created for our women conditions that would enable them to cope with their duties at work and their tasks at home. The USSR has endowed women with special privileges.

What are those privileges?

They include special female health and work safety measures. Female labour is not employed in arduous physical jobs, underground or in other conditions hazardous for the health. With every passing year the Soviet Union is allocating more and more funds for pre-natal and childbirth allowances, benefits to working mothers off work caring for children and to mothers of large families and single mothers, and payments for children born into low income families.

The 27th CPSU Congress resolved to improve the working and domestic conditions of women. In the Twelfth Five-Year-Plan period (1986-1990), working women will have opportunities to work shorter hours, a shorter week or work at home. The part-paid post-natal leave will extend to when the child reaches 18 months. Paid leave to care for a sick child will also be extended. In the next few years the demand for accommodation at pre-school establishments—nurseries and kindergartens—will be met in full.

The state is doing a lot to help the family bring up the rising generation. It has built for the children Young Pioneer Palaces and Houses, young technicians' and young naturalists' stations, and schools of art and choreography. These establishments help develop the children's abilities, kindle their social activity, and interest in work, science, technology, art and sports. There are over 10,000 such palaces, houses and schools and they are attended by several million children. They are maintained by the state, and participation in their activities does not involve payment by the families.

Genuine Equality

Soviet women have received genuine equality, the opportunity to partake of all benefits ensuing from social progress....

Women's growing confidence in their strength, in the forces of peace and progress enables them to look with optimism and hope to the future and to work with increasing energies and persistence for the implementation of the great ideals of humanism, democracy and social progress.

Socialism, March 1987.

The decisions of the 27th CPSU Congress have activated the work of women's councils in the work collectives and in residential neighborhoods. What are their main tasks?

Women's councils help resolve a wide range of social issues. Their main purpose is to help improve the working and domestic conditions of women in order to enable them to combine work and social activity with motherhood. Women's councils are becoming important centres of ideological education and other work among women.

Important Work of Women's Councils

In Lithuania, in Panevezhis District for instance, the women's council organises events to which female representatives of all collective farms and state farms are invited. They study the documents of the Party and government bearing on working women's working and living conditions, and child training and education. Some are open door events. This means that the event is held on a collective farm or state farm which has properly organised work and provides excellent working conditions for the women with proper facilities for leisure and rest. The guests attending such an event can also learn from the experience of the host farm.

Here is another aspect of their work. The women's council of the Kirov Kondopoga Pulp and Paper Mill appealed to the workers to help collect gifts for the children of Nicaragua. In a few days the room in which the activists were collecting the presents was tightly packed with boxes and packages with books, toys and children's clothing. The Soviet Women's Committee awarded the women's council of the mill an Honorary Diploma for rendering material assistance to the women and children of developing countries.

Soviet women are active on social and political issues in more than the USSR. They are a powerful force in the international women's movement too. How is this done?

Above all in cooperation with the women's organisations of other countries in the fight for peace and security. The Soviet Women's Committee plays an active role in this. It is affiliated to the International Democratic Women's Federation.

On the Committee's initiative, an International Peace School was opened in a suburb of Leningrad in May 1986—International Peace Year. It was attended by female representatives of 56 national and international women's and anti-war movements. Women's conferences were held in many Soviet towns and cities.

Participation in Peace

A mass anti-war rally was held in Moscow. Anxiety for the fate of the world caused Soviet women and their friends from other countries active in the International Democratic Women's Federation to attend the event. The participants forwarded an Appeal to Mikhail Gorbachev, General Secretary of the CPSU Central Committee, in which they approved of the Soviet Government's peaceful policies. They also adopted an Appeal to Ronald Reagan, President of the USA, urging him to discontinue nuclear explosions, and to heed the voice of the peoples all over the world and put an end to the nuclear arms race.

Along with women in capitalist countries, Soviet women are fighting against acts of imperialist aggression, and against direct and indirect intervention in the affairs of the peoples of Asia, Africa, Latin America and the Middle East. . . .

The solution of the women's question in the USSR is a major contribution to the campaign for women's social, economic and political rights all over the world.

"Soviet women have failed to win social equality in a land where traditional Russian sexism is still overwhelming."

Soviet Women Do Not Have Full Equality

David K. Willis

David K. Willis spent over four years in the Soviet Union with his wife and three children. As Moscow bureau chief for *The Christian Science Monitor,* he traveled all over Russia. In the following viewpoint, Willis argues that the role of Soviet women leaves much to be desired. While most women work in the USSR, they are also completely responsible for child care, shopping, and household chores.

As you read, consider the following questions:

1. According to Willis, do women hold much political power in the USSR?
2. In what kinds of jobs do women participate, according to the author?
3. The author believes Soviet women have made legal progress, but not social progress. What does he mean?

David K. Willis, *Klass: How Russians Really Live.* New York: St. Martin's Press, ©David K. Willis, 1985. Reprinted with permission.

The Soviet Union has long held itself up as a model for women's liberation movements. With more than 90 percent of women holding full-time jobs, it is certainly a country where women have won a considerable measure of economic freedom. Yet for all but a few, Lenin's creation is only a partial female liberation. Soviet women have failed to win social equality in a land where traditional Russian sexism is still overwhelming. There are exceptions, of course, and attitudes are beginning to change among young people and the intelligentsia. But Soviet society is still behind the United States and Western Europe in the emancipation of females at home. . . .

Many women dislike the system, but with Slavic fatalism they make the best of it. The Party reserves for itself the sole right to determine the conditions under which Soviet men and women may live and it moves quickly against any dissenting movement, including female power. Women's liberation as a cause has no place in the Soviet Union, except in the dreams of a few. In the Soviet Union today, women are more useful than equal. Of the status and privilege dispersed by the Party, women receive considerably less than men.

As in so many other fields, Soviet society is a mixture of Western and Eastern attitudes. The Western side shows in a woman being able to rise to a full professorship; the Eastern side comes into play when she returns to her apartment to drudgery, toil, and dirt.

If you question the average Urban and Rural Class male about his attitude toward women, he is often incredulous. Just as his grandfather did, he considers it his right to spend his free time drinking with the other men, and to use his apartment mainly as a place to eat, sleep, and watch television. Men do no cleaning, no cooking, and little shopping. Sons learn from their fathers' indifference. In another socially conservative society, Britain, a recent survey of 1,082 people over the age of eighteen revealed that only 2 percent of husbands performed housework. Only 6 percent claimed to help with the cooking. Such a survey would show less than one percent in both categories in the Soviet Union.

Surface Achievements

On the surface, Soviet achievements for women look good. The state has brought legal equality to women along with the principle of equal pay for equal labor. A woman's working life can be personally and financially rewarding. Almost three quarters of all doctors and teachers, as well as one third of the engineers, half of all students in universities and institutes, and 60 percent of vocational and technical students in and beyond high school are women. Soviet hotels, museums, theaters, apartment houses, and construction and repair enterprises would close without the women who manage, supervise, and clean them. The chief of Moscow's Metro construction team and one third of the chief engineers on the gigantic Bratsk Dam were women. The wife of one of our émigré friends in London is a mechanical engineer and designer specializing in industrial refrigeration. (She was unable to find a job in the United Kingdom, partly because her English is not perfect, but partly, she believes, because of a British bias against women in her profession.)

It all seems to be a picture of enlightened recognition of the part that 140 million Soviet women—53.4 percent of the population—can play in a modern society. It might not satisfy the feminist firebrand of the early Bolshevik days, Alexandra Kollontai, who campaigned against any inequality between the sexes and considered the family to be an outmoded, bourgeois institution. But to feminists in the United States and Europe there seems much in the Soviet record to study and admire.

Yet the official Soviet picture is far from complete....

Working for Men

Almost all Soviet women work full time, but they often work for men, just as they do in the West. Even women teachers and doctors, who make up about three quarters of both professions, find themselves reporting to male hospital and school directors. The occasional woman does become head of an Academy of Sciences research institute, and in the 1960s, a woman headed the prestigious Moscow Institute of Physical Engineering. But women scientists and engineers often work under men, just as women bureaucrats work for male Party bosses.

"ONE THING WE BEAT U.S. ON, WE GOT EQUAL RIGHTS!"

Jim Dobbins, reprinted with permission.

Women hold little political power in the USSR. Only one woman has sat on the ruling Party Politburo in recent decades: Ekaterina Furtseva, a former Moscow Party worker who was a Politburo member from 1957 to 1961 and minister of cultural affairs. She was appointed and later ejected by Nikita Khrushchev, and no woman has since risen to a similar height. Women do not sit on the powerful secretariat of the Central Committee of the Party; none ranks high in Party committees in the republic capitals around the country.

Twenty-five percent of the Party membership at large is female, and 33 percent of the 1,500 deputies of the Supreme Soviet, or "legislature," are women, but the deputies hold no real power. They are selected by the Party amid stage-managed hoopla and transported to Moscow twice a year to ratify decisions already made by the Politburo and Central Committee Secretariat. Only 3 to 4 percent of the Central Committee are women. The idea of a Soviet Margaret Thatcher or Golda Meir is remote.

Less than one percent of the members of the Academy of Sciences are women, and there are no women among Soviet admirals or generals. One American military attaché in Moscow said he had spotted only one significant female officer, a lieutenant-colonel in the ground forces, in several months. Women do much better in the trade unions, but Soviet labor unions have little power. They are merely conveyor belts on which Party discipline and rewards reach the work force, and which carry back reports on workers' mood and complaints. Typically, when a woman's name becomes a household word, she is either in a traditional role—ballerina, singer, actress— or she is a token in a male-dominated field. . . .

Accepting Propaganda

Many women, ignorant about conditions in other countries, accept that at least part of the Party's propaganda about the West must be true: that America and Europe are plagued by drugs, crime, unemployment, and moral degeneracy. Women can still be fervent patriots even as they blame the Party for food shortages.

Despite their stoic patriotism, however, the majority of Soviet women, compared to men, remain the statusless sex. "I am a quiet person," observes émigré Marina Voikhanskaya, "but the only time I cannot remain quiet in England is when someone tells me how wonderful women's liberation must be in Russia. Then I become agitated. I cannot push the words back down my throat." Women were largely statusless under the tsars; since then they have made much legal but only limited social progress toward the equality with men that the Party would have us believe Lenin created overnight in 1917.

"Arrests of Hebrew teachers and Jewish cultural activists on trumped-up criminal charges are common, as are beatings and other mistreatment."

Soviet Jews Are Repressed

Roger Pilon

The tenets of communism and the tenets of religion are in direct conflict. Communist political philosophy refutes the existence of God and argues that religion distracts and deludes the masses. In spite of this official stance, whether or not freedom of religion is tolerated in the Soviet Union remains a debatable issue. In the following viewpoint, Roger Pilon, director of policy for the Bureau of Human Rights and Humanitarian Affairs for the US government, documents Soviet repression of its Jewish citizens and argues that this repression is getting worse under Premier Gorbachev.

As you read, consider the following questions:

1. What particular types of repression do Soviet Jews experience, according to the author?
2. Why, according to Pilon, must the Soviets repress the Jews?
3. What does Pilon believe the US must do to counter this repression?

Roger Pilon, a speech before the Metrowest Conference on Soviet Jewry in East Orange, New Jersey on September 28, 1986. From the Bureau of Public Affairs, Current Policy No. 878.

By design, citizens of the Soviet Union are subjugated, at virtually every turn in their lives, to the interests of the state, as determined by the Party. With a centrally planned economy, the daily decisions of life, from production to distribution, from education to employment, to income, housing, and on and on, are all out of the hands of the individual to a degree vastly greater than anything we know in a free society. Over this public control of the daily affairs of life, the individual has very little influence. There is no effective franchise, of course, nor any effective way to object to the decisions that determine one's daily life. Indeed, the attempt to protest is itself a sign that you don't understand your own best interests, that you may, in fact, be a candidate for psychiatric incarceration. At the very least, protest is a threat to the authority and integrity of the all-encompassing system and thus marks the protester for repression.

The result, of course, is a drab and mean existence and a constant daily struggle just to survive. Far from a life of meaning, a life that inspires, it is a life that suffocates. Surrounded by scarcity, by bureaucracy, by the constant din of slogans, propaganda, and lies, is it any wonder that people turn inward, to themselves, or to their religious and cultural heritage? Even among those formerly committed to the system, there is broadening realization that, after seven decades of struggle and sacrifice, the building of communism is going nowhere, except for more of the same. The rebirth of interest in religion across the Soviet Union should not surprise, therefore, despite relentless efforts to stamp it out.

The Repression of Soviet Jews

But Jews have come in for particular repression—insults, deprivation of cultural rights, quotas at institutions of higher learning, denial of professional opportunities, not to mention outright arrest and incarceration for practicing their traditions—all based simply upon their being Jewish, all of which urges us to reflect upon why this is so. There are the usual explanations from anti-Semitism, of course, couched in the Soviet Union as anti-Zionism, which have a long history in Russia. But there are other, systemic reasons at work as well, which in many ways are more interesting.

There is first the belief that Jews, as a class, cannot be trusted, a thesis developed recently by Professor Matatyahu Minc of the Diaspora Institute at the University of Tel Aviv, a student of the history of the Jews in the Soviet Union. Observing that the ruling *Nomenklatura* selects its members primarily on the basis of evidence of total loyalty to the system—loyalty, above all, to one's fellow *Nomenklatura* members and complete subservience to one's superiors—Professor Minc argues that Stalin's successors concluded, just as Stalin had, that Jews, as a group, came from a cultural pattern that made them unfit for a system of this kind. Drawing upon this thesis, Ambassador Richard Schifter, presently Assistant

Secretary of State for Human Rights and Humanitarian Affairs, observes that "gradually, almost imperceptibly, the job level beyond which Jews may not rise in the Soviet Union was lowered. Increasingly, prestigious institutions of higher learning closed their doors to them entirely or permitted only a tiny number of applicants to enter. As the years passed, Jews thus began to be moved to the margins of Soviet society."

Yet another, closely related explanation for the particular repression of Soviet Jews returns us to the character of the Soviet political system. Although Jews were repressed under the czars, the character of that repression was not totalitarian: the czars allowed Jewish cultural and religious institutions to flourish, for example. Soviet rulers, by contrast, distrust any institutions they do not control; in fact, they will not, indeed cannot, allow independent institutions to coexist with the state since these are a threat not only to their total control but, more importantly, to the rationale for that control. The "new Soviet man," after all, does not need independent institutions. The return of Soviet Jews to their religious and cultural heritage is thus a slap in the face of the system itself. It must be repressed, especially when it takes the form of group or institutional activity.

In recent years, however, that repression has increased substantially, to the point of a crackdown, over the past 2 years, even upon teachers of Hebrew. Arrests of Hebrew teachers and Jewish cultural activists on trumped-up criminal charges are common, as are

Jeff MacNelly. Reprinted by permission: Tribune Media Services.

beatings and other mistreatment. Is it any wonder then that Jews are asking to leave?

But there, of course, is the rub, for the Soviet Union does not recognize any right of free emigration, notwithstanding that it is a signatory of the Helsinki accords wherein it promised recognition of such a right. In practice, as we know, emigration is possible, for reasons, primarily, of family reunification. Yet the regulations governing emigration are unavailable to applicants; and procedures are lengthy, usually arbitrary, and invariably surrounded by persecution. Those denied permission, the *refuseniks,* frequently endure years of suffering. Fired from their jobs, or at least demoted, they are shunned by their friends out of fear of guilt by association. Often their apartments are searched, their mail seized, and their telephones disconnected. Moreover, the more vocal they become about their right to emigrate, the more they expose themselves to official harassment and possible repeated refusals of permission. When this suspended animation goes on for years, life can become all but unbearable.

Regrettably, these conditions describe the Soviet Union even, indeed especially today. In fact, emigration of Soviet Jews is at its lowest level in 20 years. During the first 9 months of 1986, only 631 were allowed to leave. At its present rate, emigration [during 1986] will be down by about 99% from the rate in 1979. Yet we know the names of at least 11,000 Soviet Jews who have been refused permission to emigrate; and approximately 380,000 others have requested invitations from relatives abroad as required by Soviet law. Clearly, the situation under Mr. Gorbachev is not improving, notwithstanding a few high-visibility gestures such as the release of Anatoliy Shcharanskiy and the visit of Yelena Bonner. In fact, the situation is as bad as it has been at any time in the post-Stalin era. The loose associations of dissenters have been destroyed. The arrest and punishment of dissenters has discouraged others from following the same path. We are back to the days of total repression.

The Administration's Response

Well, what are we in the Administration doing about this? Perhaps a better question would be what *can* we do about this? One thing that comes readily to mind, of course, is conditioning trade agreements upon an improvement in the human rights area. But here the possibilities are limited by the fact that it is a world economy we need to coordinate if we are to be effective; and that economy is by no means ours to coordinate. Nevertheless, where we can be effective in this area, we try to do so.

In general, however, we have followed a dual policy of private and public diplomacy by way of trying to improve the situation. In particular cases where we believe we can be effective, that is, we try quietly to obtain relief. Clearly, however, we have had only limited success in these efforts at quiet diplomacy. Accordingly, we have had increasingly to go public in our criticism, in the belief that Soviet leaders have at least some concern for their standing in the international community. Rightly or wrongly, that is, we have assumed that if we speak often and loudly enough, the public relations price Soviet leaders will have to pay will influence them to improve the situation.

No Sign of Improvement

The Kremlin, long a master at manipulating public opinion, has clearly entered a more sophisticated stage in its ongoing international public-relations offensive to divert attention from its anti-Jewish policies.

It is true that 470 Jews were permitted to emigrate in March [1987].

It is true that this number compares favorably with the average of less than 80 per month who emigrated in 1986.

But this hardly constitutes a trend, especially since there are an estimated 11,000 "refuseniks" still waiting—some for a decade and more—for exit visas. And this is to say nothing of the hundreds of thousands who have indicated a desire to leave but, fearing intimidation, have not pursued this goal.

Alan D. Pesky, *The New York Times*, May 2, 1987.

There is considerable evidence, of course, that Soviet leaders do care about Western public opinion—else why the intense media efforts of Mr. Gorbachev since he came to power. They care because, notwithstanding all their military might, they can effect favorable deals with the West most efficiently by manipulating constraints on Western decisionmakers. It is democratic public opinion, therefore, and Western democratic opinion in particular, that is up for grabs here—the only public opinion that matters because the only opinion that can be translated into public policy. And let us be clear, more precisely and more fundamentally, it is *moral* opinion that is ultimately at issue.

Soviet Reaction

Which brings me to my final considerations: the Soviet response to our human rights public diplomacy is presently going through an interesting change, which presents a fundamental challenge to us. No longer do we hear what we used to hear so often when we complained, namely, that we were interfering in the internal affairs of the Soviet Union. Rather, we are met today with a two-pronged counterattack. The first is to charge, in reply, that the United States, too, has massive human rights problems, from hunger, to homelessness, to unemployment. The second is to try to shift the name of the game from "human rights" to "humanitarianism." These two threads, let me note, are closely connected. Moreover, they play to patterns of thought that have evolved in the West, and especially in Europe, for nearly a century now, from at least the Progressive Era—patterns that have come under serious intellectual scrutiny only in the last decade or two and serious political challenge only in this decade.

Let me briefly address these two lines of response in order. The first points to what we in the West loosely call "social problems," which the Soviets then convert into "human rights" abuses. But, in doing so, they point as well, by implication, to the great international debate over two very different conceptions of "rights": our own conception of "civil and political rights," derived from the classical liberal trinity of life, liberty, and property; and the socialist conception of "social and economic rights," so-called rights to the goods produced by the society organized along socialist lines. In this country, for the most part, we have steadfastly resisted recognizing these social and economic "rights," not least because attempts to enforce them involve both the planned economy, with all its massive inefficiencies, and repeated violations of our traditional rights.

An Unfree System

In this last connection, recent scholarly work has shown clearly that you cannot have it both ways: every attempt to compel the production and distribution of these social and economic goods and services, that is, ineluctably amounts to a violation of individual rights to be free. Here again, it is no accident that the Soviet system, which attempts to secure these "rights," is as unfree as it is. The better approach to these admitted social problems, we have said, is to encourage private, voluntary solutions and to turn to forced solutions only when and to the extent necessary. Only thus do we conform to the principles that define us as a free society.

The second tactic we have increasingly seen from the Soviets by way of response to our charges is to attempt to shift the terms of the debate from "human rights" to "humanitarianism." Witness, for example, their recent creation of a Humanitarian and Cultural Affairs Office in the Ministry of Foreign Affairs. This move plays, again, to confusions that have set in in our own understanding of our moral foundations, which is why the remarks of the President on the subject before the UN General Assembly were so critically important. Indeed, they state the point so well as to bear repeating here:

> I note that Mr. Gorbachev has used in recent speeches the same categories I have used here today: the military, the political, and the economic; except that he titled his fourth category: humanitarian.

> Well, the difference is revealing. The United States believes that respect for the individual, for the dignity of the human person—

those rights outlined in the UN Universal Declaration of Human Rights—does not belong in the realm of charity or "humanitarian" causes. Respect for human rights is not social work; it is not merely an act of compassion. It is the first obligation of government and the source of its legitimacy.

How clear and to the point those remarks are. It is up to us now to bear them in mind as we press on with our important work, as we cry out against the suffering that is going on in the Soviet Union today.

Persecution Increasing

Despite the much-publicized release of dissident Anatoly Shcharansky, Sakharov and his wife, Yelena Bonner, we know that the number of Jewish prisoners of conscience in Soviet camps and jails has doubled since Mikhail S. Gorbachev came to power. Harassment and intimidation by the KGB are increasing. As the level of emigration falls to its lowest figure in 15 years, the pressures on Jews rise. They cannot live as Jews, and they cannot leave—and all the Soviet efforts at deceiving the West into believing that a new era has begun cannot change that fact.

Morris B. Abram, *Los Angeles Times,* January 6, 1987.

This is not a pretty picture I have drawn for you. I wish I could be more sanguine, but as the legal latinate has it, *res ipsa loquitur*—the case speaks for itself. I am here, in part to tell you about it, in part to assure you we are listening, but mostly to try to make it clear just what the nature of the problem is and what we must do about it. We must be resolute, but we must also realize that we are in this for the long haul. It is, after all, our children and our children's children who will inherit this world from us.

"Of all Anti-Soviet fabrications, none is more blatantly false and pernicious than the allegations of 'anti-Semitism in the Soviet Union.' "

Soviet Jews Are Not Repressed

Florence Fox

Whether or not religious persecution exists in the Soviet Union is continually debated. Soviet officials argue that religion is tolerated, and many Americans who visit the Soviet Union have verified this. On the other hand, Jewish émigrés to the US tell of rampant anti-Semitism. In the following viewpoint, Florence Fox, author of *Poland Answers*, argues that Soviet repression of the Jews is a malicious myth, fabricated by the US in order to inspire hatred of the USSR.

As you read, consider the following questions:

1. What historical events does Fox relate to prove her point that Soviet Jews are not persecuted?
2. According to the author, why do most Jews emigrate?
3. Why does Fox believe Soviet Jews' lives are better in the USSR than they are after they have emigrated to the US?

Florence Fox, "Saving Soviet Jews, Parts I and II," *The Churchman*, April/May and June/July 1986. Reprinted with permission.

Of all Anti-Soviet fabrications, none is more blatantly false and pernicious than the allegations of "anti-Semitism in the Soviet Union."

Soviet socialism delivered the Jews from the ghettoes and pogroms of tsarist Russia.

Jakov Sverdlov, a Jew, was the first president of Soviet Russia, and the Soviet Union was the first nation to recognize the state of Israel.

On U.N. Day (12/10/45), Albert Einstein, a Jew, expressed his gratitude to the Soviet Union, the only state to open its borders to tens of thousands of German, Polish and other Jews fleeing the Nazis in 1938-39.

When Hitler launched World War II, only the Soviet Union protected its Jews by evacuating them to safety beyond the Urals. Israel's former leader, Menachem Begin, one of the Jews rescued, wrote in his autobiography: "I cannot forget, and no Jew should forget that . . . thanks to the Soviet Union, hundreds of thousands of Jews were saved from Nazi hands."

If the Red Army had not checked fascism, Jewry today would be reduced to a mere handful of hunted survivors. Soviet Jews now share the freedom, democracy, economic security and human rights guaranteed to all citizens by the Soviet Constitution.

In 1985, Boris Gramm, leader of the Jewish community in Moscow, ordered 20,000 copies of a Jewish pocket calendar in Hebrew and Russian to be produced by the state printing house in time to celebrate Rosh Hashanah at the recently renovated Moscow Choral Synagogue. It had previously published prayer books and the "Five Books of Moses."

Evidence of Tolerance

As an example of the good relations between the Jewish community and the municipality, Gramm cited the closing of Arkhipov Street, the site of the synagogue, during certain holidays to permit traditional dancing in the street by Jewish youth. He noted [that] . . . Jews enjoy absolutely the same rights as all other Soviet people. . . . We'll never forget it was the Soviet Army that saved us from extinction. Our duty today is to devote all our energy to efforts for peace against the threat of nuclear war.

The population of the USSR is 270 million, of which 1.8 million— only 0.7%—are Jews. However, Jews comprise 15% of Soviet doctors; more than 8% of all writers; over 10% of all judges and lawyers; 5.7% scientists—half of them top specialists (8 times more than other Soviet nationalities); and 8% of all artists, musicians, actors and actresses.

Two Cabinet members are Jews. Eight Jews are members of the Supreme Soviet. Jews are heavily represented in the USSR Council of Ministers, Republics and Party bodies. There were more than 100 Jewish Soviet Army generals in World War II, 160,000 Jews received military honors, and 117 were awarded the nation's highest honor—

Hero of the Soviet Union.

Jewish members of the Soviet Academy of Science, Yiddish writers, and other valued Jewish citizens are recorded in the Great Soviet Encyclopedia.

The American Jewish Year Book (1985) acknowledged Soviet encouragement of Jewish culture in literature, research, music, drama, religion and art, and notes awards of state prizes to Jews for distinguished achievement.

Don't Worry About Us

In a Kiev synagogue, the guests talked with Mikhail Katz, leader of the religious community, a war veteran and retired medical corps captain.

Katz spoke at length about the life of believers in the Soviet Union. He asked the guests to convey shalom and wishes of peace and happiness to American Jews. Let them not worry about us, Mikhail Katz added. We are free to profess our religion and exercise our rights. And, above all, we are free forever from anti-Semitism, which was rampant under tsarism, its terrible pogroms, and the horrors nazism brought to our country.

A. Gurevich and A. Nikolenko, *New Times*, no. 20, May 1986.

There are more Soviet Jews with advanced education in proportion to their numbers than in all western countries and Israel combined. The proportion of educated Jews (25%) is higher than that of any other nationality in the USSR—329 per 100 as against 196 per 1000 other inhabitants, and 65,000 Jews have PhDs.

The Leningrad Institute for Eastern Studies, and the Judaica collection of rare books and manuscripts in Moscow's Lenin Library are world famous—unparalleled sources for Judaica research by Jewish scholars worldwide.

Soviet Scholars

Soviet scholars study ancient Hebrew history, culture and philology in institutes attached to the USSR Academy of Sciences. At the Gorky Institute of World Literature in Moscow, advanced literary courses are conducted for aspiring authors, including those writing in Yiddish. A rabbinical college (yeshiva) is attached to the synagogue in Moscow to serve the 10% of Jews who are religious. Jews train their rabbis, observe religious holidays, perform traditional rites, bake matzohs, prepare kosher foods, publish their literature, and maintain ties with Jews in Israel and other countries.

More Jewish literature is published in the USSR than any other country in the world. "Sovietish Heimland" publishes both Soviet and foreign Jewish authors and has a special section for the self-teaching of Yiddish. It is read throughout the USSR and thirty countries abroad, and has the widest circulation of any Yiddish magazine worldwide.

A new Jewish-Russian dictionary published in 1984 includes 40,000 entries and a grammar text.

The books of over 100 Jewish writers have been translated into fifteen other Soviet languages in the last decade. Lev Kvitko's books alone sold 9,300,000 copies. Hebrew literature is also reproduced, e.g., the revered 11th-century Hebrew poet, Jehuda Hallewi.

Central Television recently presented a TV mini-series, "Tevye the Milkman" by the celebrated Jewish writer, Sholem Aleichem, in whose honor a Kiev street was named. Hundreds of other respected Jews have Soviet streets named for them. Jewish theatrical and musical companies tour the country, playing to packed houses. The United States, with over three times as many Jews as the USSR, hasn't a single permanent Yiddish theatre.

In 1928, twenty years before Israel became a state, the Soviet Union gave Jews their own autonomous region on 36,000 sq. kilometers of arable land—twice the size of Israel, and as big as Belgium and Holland combined, with Birobidjan its capital. Their newspaper, "Birobidjaner Shtern," is published in Yiddish, and books in both Yiddish and Hebrew fill their libraries.

"An Open Letter to Jewish Americans from Jews in the Soviet Union" (1983) was signed by prominent Jewish leaders in the Soviet government, sciences, industry and arts: ". . .We Soviet Jews do not need self-appointed 'protectors' from across the ocean. We have no need to be protected from anyone or anything in our own country. . . .The reality fully refutes the slanders of western propaganda to the effect that 'official anti-Semitism' exists in the USSR. Only people who know nothing at all about the situation in our country can believe that invention. . . ."

Reasons for Emigration

Despite the favorable egalitarian, economic and political environment, some Jews emigrate for reasons which have nothing to do with the way they are treated in the Soviet Union.

1. Some leave for reasons of religious orthodoxy which mandates return to the land of their biblical ancestors, expressed in the centuries-old prayer: "Next year in Jerusalem."

2. The late Golda Meir stressed to members of the Knesset that it cost Israel 30,000 pounds to educate a doctor, which is could ill afford. Her solution was simple—lure to Israel the Soviet Jews whose education and training had already been paid for by the Soviets. This massive brain drain was to be justified by a propaganda campaign to "Save the Russian Jews."

The Soviet law which permits emigration for reunification of families dispersed throughout the world during World War II precipitated a flood of invitations from Israel to Soviet Jews to "reunite" with real as well as bogus relatives in Israel. Israeli officials note with alarm that most Jews who leave the Soviet Union, presumably to rejoin relatives in Israel, do not truly intend to settle in Israel. The campaign to recruit Soviet Jews grows increasingly urgent as Israel faces an exodus—not only of immigrants but native Sabras as well. Since the mid-70s, disenchanted emigre Jews began returning to the USSR in droves.

The Truth About Jewish Emigration

In the arsenal of anti-Sovietism, after the Goebbels-invented big lie of the Soviet military threat, the next biggest lie is that the Soviet Union violates the human rights of its citizens, particularly those who are Jews. And among the many lies that support this lie of "official Soviet anti-Semitism," the biggest one, which is designed to lend credence to the others, is that the Soviet Union does not allow Jews to emigrate.

The truth is that in a country that lost 20 million people in World War II and has a permanent labor shortage, one of every nine or ten Soviet Jews, over 275,000 of a post-World War II Jewish population of about 2,250,000, have emigrated in the last four decades. According to Soviet authorities, this amounts to about 99 percent of all Jews who have applied to leave the country. . . .

Jewish emigration from the Soviet Union peaked in the 1970s, with 51,000 leaving in 1979, and has since decreased to a few hundred a year. Soviet authorities attribute this to the fact that most Jews who wanted to leave have done so.

Alfred Kutzik, *People's Daily World*, November 13, 1986.

Phillip Bonofsky *(Political Affairs)* has stated: ". . . It is Zionism and America's Middle-East policy and not the Soviets who need anti-Semitism in the Soviet Union! And where it doesn't exist, it must be made to exist, one way or the other. . . . A campaign of letter-writing to Jews in the USSR organized by Jews in the U.S.A. and Israel, describes life in America (less so, now, in Israel where the dream has faded) as still the gleaming paradise of opportunities where rewards are instant. Although emigres tell themselves that they are going to America to better themselves, they know in their hearts that they are selling anti-Sovietism. And America is buying it." The truth is that most emigres come to the U.S.A. to get rich under capitalism.

Emigration is instigated by Jewish "tourists," Zionist activists promoting emigration to Israel (aliyah), and by CIA-sponsored anti-Soviet propaganda beamed by Voice of America, Voice of Israel and Radio Free Europe—which incite defection. It is ironic that some of the most strident voices protesting alleged mistreatment of Jews in the Soviet Union have been those of rabid anti-Semitic Nazi war criminals who were given sanctuary after World War II by the U.S. Some, like Nazi-collaborator Anton Adamovich, were assigned to lucrative posts on Radio Free Europe/Radio Liberty. (Washington's disgraceful protection of Nazi perpetrators of the holocaust was later compounded by President Reagan's gravesite tribute to Hitler's S.S. at Bitburg.)

Jewish Criminals

Although anti-Sovieteers claim that Jews emigrate to escape "oppression," some flee to escape prosecution for criminal acts. A *New York Daily News* report (4/1/84) cited a "nationwide network of lawless Russian immigrants...involved in murder, drug trafficking and counterfeiting...the country's newest crime syndicate...hardened criminals from Soviet jails with bogus documents saying they were imprisoned as political dissidents.... Information gleaned by the FBI and police departments across the country reveal that the mob's power base is in the Russian enclave in Brighton Beach, Brooklyn, where they terrorize other members of the Soviet emigre community. At least 150 ring-leaders and top associates nationwide...are involved in systematic crimes."

Detective Charles Damiano of the 60th police precinct in Brooklyn stated (*Jewish Times,* Feb. 1984) that the criminals are referred to simply as "Soviet emigres," but a listing of their names reveals that they are Jewish, something that is not widely publicized. The crime network extends to Atlanta, Chicago, Cleveland, Dallas, Miami, Philadelphia, Portland, Montreal, Toronto and Winnipeg—with international connections.

Jews who request exit visas from the USSR for *any* reason are termed "dissidents" by the West. However, the West, which exploits them as "champions of human rights," fails to publicize their crimes. Shcharansky, for instance, was convicted for espionage—arranging to deliver intelligence data on Soviet defenses to the West, and collaborating with foreign centers of anti-Soviet subversion.

Emigre Lies

Soviet emigres learn that the more tales of "oppression" they relate, the more acceptance, sympathy and favors they receive from Jewish communities in the U.S.—which they milk to the limit. Most of those who claim the need for "religious freedom" by-pass the religious state of Israel, and surveys show that most Soviet Jewish emigres do not practice their religion or participate in Jewish affairs in the U.S....

Only 1.2% of Soviet Jews emigrating to the U.S. have found employment in occupations related to their professional training. Most must settle for low-paying menial jobs and substandard working conditions. After a few months in the U.S., their sponsoring agen-

cies leave them to shift for themselves. They are further American-
ized in unemployment and welfare offices.

The majority of emigres experience culture shock when they
discover that in this free country, nothing is free, and they are confronted with problems of survival they did not have back home. And
they are shocked to learn that anti-Semitism exists in the United
States. The Anti-Defamation League of B'nai B'rith records hundreds
of anti-Jewish incidents—unknown in the USSR where such deeds
are officially outlawed.

Nazi-type movements in the U.S. are free to publish anti-Semitic
literature for distribution in the U.S. and to fascists in West Germany.

Whereas Jewish doctors practice their profession freely in the
Soviet Union, they encounter unaccustomed discrimination when
they "defect" to the United States. Arkady Fishman, spokesman for
34 Jewish emigre doctors, lodged a complaint with the U.S. government when, after passing all qualification exams in medicine and
English, their applications were turned down by 800 hospitals, including some in Alaska. U.S. medical establishments do not welcome
foreign-born doctors practicing medicine in the land of the free.

Some Emigres Commit Suicide

Some emigres, their illusions shattered, and unable to return to
their homeland, have committed suicide. Their stories have not been
publicized. An official of HIAS [Hebrew Immigrant Aid Society] told
me sadly: "How I wish someone would tell the Jews in the Soviet
Union how much better off they would be to stay where they are."

Disillusioned emigres succumb to feelings of guilt for having
betrayed their country, their family and friends. Their letters to Soviet
officials pleading for readmission to the USSR have reached flood
proportions. They find life in the capitalist jungle alien after growing up in the spirit of socialism in a country which provides lifetime
security for all. They belatedly appreciate all the benefits guaranteed
by the Soviet Constitution which they had taken for granted.

Jewish Colonel-General David Dragunsky, twice honored Hero of
the Soviet Union, denounced the "Save Soviet Jews" propaganda:
"Save us from what? From the full equality we enjoy? From the
peaceful and steady progress we have made under socialism? The
enemies of peace base their insane nuclear arms race, their mad
Star Wars, on lies about the Soviet Union. Jewish people should
remember who saved millions of Jews from the gas chambers, who
shed so much blood to defeat fascism."

As a Soviet Jew who remains loyal to his country, Dragunsky was
not welcome in the U.S. which denied him a visa to attend a dinner
in his honor in New York City in 1985.

Shalom.

Recognizing Deceptive Arguments

People who feel strongly about an issue use many techniques to persuade others to agree with them. Some of these techniques appeal to the intellect, some to the emotions. Many of them distract the reader or listener from the real issues.

When evaluating an argument, it is important to recognize the deceptive, or distracting, appeal being used. Here are a few common ones:

a. *bandwagon*—the idea that "everybody" does this or believes this

b. *scare tactics*—the threat that if you don't do this or don't believe this, something terrible will happen

c. *strawperson*—distorting or exaggerating an opponent's ideas to make one's own seem stronger

d. *personal attack*—putting down an opponent *personally* instead of rationally debating his or her ideas

e. *hyperbole*—extravagantly exaggerating one's own claims or the weaknesses of opponents

f. *testimonial*—quoting or paraphrasing an authority or celebrity to support one's own viewpoint

g. *generalizations*—making unfounded blanket statements about a population, place, or thing

115

Below are listed several statements, many of them taken from the viewpoints in this chapter. *Beside each one, mark the letter of the type of deceptive appeal being used. If a statement is not any of the listed appeals, write N.*

1. As Soviet society blossoms and moves closer to social and economic perfection, the rights of working people will also develop toward perfection.

2. Americans are forever prescribing political morality for the rest of the world.

3. Soviet officials calmly address the subject of human rights with lies and half-truths.

4. Soviet society is recognized as the world leader in bringing equality and social justice to women.

5. The current persecution of Jews in the Soviet Union is simply a contemporary expression of the ageless Russian hatred of the Jews.

6. Because they are tools of the US government, Soviet émigrés cannot be trusted to give an objective account of conditions in the USSR.

7. The most strident voices protesting alleged mistreatment of Soviet Jews are in fact rabidly anti-Semitic Nazi war criminals who have been given sanctuary by the US.

8. With the development of the Soviet Union, for the first time in history a multinational state that insures the inviolable brotherhood and friendship of dozens of peoples is a reality.

9. We must learn to sacrifice our moral indignation toward the Soviet Union if we are to avert a fiery global holocaust.

10. Most Soviet émigrés come to the US not to escape so-called human rights abuses but to become rich under capitalism.

11. An official with the Hebrew Immigration Aid Society told me: "How I wish someone would tell Soviet Jews how much better off they would be if they stayed where they are."

12. The Soviet government attacks the US on its inability to provide so-called "economic human rights" to divert attention from their own brutal and oppressive police state.

13. Because Soviet society is so rigid, free-thinking Americans visiting the Soviet Union are a subversive force merely by their presence.

Periodical Bibliography

The following articles have been selected to supplement the diverse views expressed in this chapter.

Robert L. Bernstein
"A Ray of Light for Soviet Rights?" *The New York Times*, December 28, 1986.

Boris Bolotin
"Socialist Society's Priorities," *New Times*, no. 51, December 1985.

Anita and Peter Deyneka Jr.
"The Church Under Gorbachev," *Christianity Today*, December 12, 1986.

Marshall I. Goldman
"Can Anybody Fix the Soviet System?" *U.S. News & World Report*, February 9, 1987.

Irving Kristol
" 'Human Rights': The Hidden Agenda," *The National Interest*, Winter 1986/87.

Ye. Krylova
"Women in the USSR," *Soviet Military Review*, August 1984.

Susanna McBee and Miriam Horn
"From Russia With Love," *U.S. News & World Report*, April 21, 1986.

Mikhail Makarenko
"Testament to Torment," *American Legion Magazine*, May 1986.

Stephen Miller
"God and Man in the Soviet Union," *Catholicism in Crisis*, January 1985.

The New Republic
"Not Only Jews," April 8, 1985.

Yuri Orlov
"My Life in Exile," *The New York Times Magazine*, March 15, 1987.

Yuri Orlov and Nicholas Bethell
"Out of the Gulag & into Exile," *Encounter*, May 1987.

Roger Pilon
"Human Rights: Marxist-Leninist Theory," *Vital Speeches of the Day*, November 15, 1986.

Vladimir Posner and Yuri Kudimov
"Americans' Ghost Images," *World Press Review*, February 1986.

Natan (Anatoly) Shcharansky
"Human Rights, Arms Talks Must Be Linked," *The Wall Street Journal*, November 4, 1986.

David K. Shipler
"After They Defect . . ." *The New York Times Magazine*, December 7, 1986.

George Shultz
"Human Rights and Soviet-American Relations," *Department of State Bulletin*, December 1986.

William E. Smith   "Sounds of Freedom," *Time,* February 23, 1987.

Vsevolod Sofinsky   "Human Rights: Advocates Real and Apparent," *Soviet Military Review,* October 1986.

Soviet Military Review   "Tried and Tested Leader of Soviet People," January 1985.

Galina Vishnevskaya   "Galina," *Encounter,* December 1986.
and George Urban

Vladimir Vladimirov   "In the Name of Human Rights," *Soviet Military Review,* December 1985.

Elie Wiesel   "What Shcharansky Means to the World," *The New York Times,* February 19, 1986.

How Strong Is the Soviet Economy?

the
SOVIET
UNION

Chapter Preface

The accompanying chart, prepared by Radio Free Europe/Radio Liberty, shows that Soviet consumers must work longer to pay for goods and services than American consumers. This consumer price chart represents the viewpoint that despite ambitious "five-year-plans" and other measures, the Soviet economy lags behind that of the United States, not only in affordability of goods, but also in trade and general economic productivity.

Comparing costs

How many minutes (unless otherwise noted) of work time it takes an average industrial worker in Washington and Moscow to purchase various goods and services.

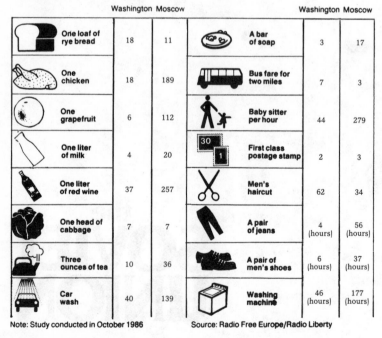

	Washington	Moscow		Washington	Moscow
One loaf of rye bread	18	11	A bar of soap	3	17
One chicken	18	189	Bus fare for two miles	7	3
One grapefruit	6	112	Baby sitter per hour	44	279
One liter of milk	4	20	First class postage stamp	2	3
One liter of red wine	37	257	Men's haircut	62	34
One head of cabbage	7	7	A pair of jeans	4 (hours)	56 (hours)
Three ounces of tea	10	36	A pair of men's shoes	6 (hours)	37 (hours)
Car wash	40	139	Washing machine	46 (hours)	177 (hours)

Note: Study conducted in October 1986   Source: Radio Free Europe/Radio Liberty

However, many people argue that this bleak economic picture is changing. Mikhail Gorbachev has begun a program of reform designed to overcome problems inherent in the Soviet system. Gorbachev's proposals include an emphasis on free enterprise, more trade with the West, and worker incentives such as merit pay and worker-elected managers. These reforms, which place more power in the hands of the individual, suggest to many that the Soviet bureaucracy that has traditionally hindered economic reform is being changed.

This chapter deals with questions about whether these reforms will effectively improve the economy.

---

*"In the sum total of economic indicators, [the
Soviet Union] has surpassed the United States in
a number of most important areas."*

The Soviet Economy
Is Healthy

Gennady Kobyakov

Gennady Kobyakov is a Soviet journalist who writes for Novosti Press
Agency, a Soviet publishing house. In the following viewpoint, he
gives statistics that refute Western claims that the Soviet Union is
in an economic crisis. He goes on to state that the Soviet economy
continues to grow and will overtake that of the United States.

As you read, consider the following questions:

1. In what economic areas does the Soviet Union lead the
   United States?
2. What evidence does the author cite to refute the claim of a
   Soviet economic crisis?
3. According to the author, what is the USSR doing to further
   improve its economy?

Gennady Kobyakov, "Is There an Economic Crisis in the USSR?" in *Socialism: Theory and
Practice.* Moscow: Novosti Press Agency Publishing House, January 1987.

National income is known to be a source of the ever growing development of social production, of strengthening the economic might of any country and improving people's welfare. It is also an indicator which most fully reflects the economic development of a state. Today, in our country the average material wealth per capita is almost 12 thousand roubles, twice the 1970 figure. The USSR's average annual national income increase between 1951 and 1981 was 7.3 per cent; in the USA it amounted to 3.4 per cent.

As for the volume of Soviet industrial output, from 1971 to 1980 it almost doubled. It took Great Britain, the FRG [Federal Republic of Germany], France and the USA, 26, 18, 18 and 17 years respectively, to double theirs. During this period US industrial production suffered a recession three times. In the USSR, industrial growth rates at that particular time averaged out at 5.9 per cent a year, in Britain 1 per cent, Italy 3.5, Canada 3.4, the USA 3.1, France 2.9, Japan 4.5 per cent.

What kind of a crisis has hit the Soviet economy if in the last 25 years the USSR has left the US behind in the production of many major industrial items? In 1960, Soviet production of oil (gas condensate included) was 42 and of natural gas 12 per cent of the corresponding levels in the USA. In 1985 the figures were 136 and 116 per cent, respectively. If we take steel, mineral fertilizer and cement, their production in those years jumped and the corresponding percentage ratios were 71 and 191, 43 and 158, 81 and 170.

Other, less important indicators over different years also witness the fact that economically the USSR is catching up with the USA. And now, although the Soviet Union ranks second in the world (after the US) in the sum total of economic indicators, it has surpassed the United States in a number of most important areas.

Our agriculture is steadily progressing. Its gross output rose 2.4 times between 1940 and 1981. In the 1951-1981 period the average annual increase in farm produce was 2.9 per cent in the Soviet Union and 1.8 per cent in the United States. Labour productivity grew at an average of 6.2 per cent a year in this country and 2 per cent in the USA.

Soviet people's welfare is also improving. Large-scale social programmes have been started which are regularly raising the population's real incomes, expanding the production of consumer goods, increasing the scale of housing construction, etc. Each five-year plan period saw imposing investments in the social sphere, and these have borne fruit. To illustrate.

In twenty-five years per capita real incomes increased 2.6 times. In 1965, only four per cent of the population earned more than 100 roubles a month, in 1970 this stratum made up 18 per cent, and in 1985 over 60 per cent. Average monthly wages and salaries in 1985 were double the 1965 figures, and payments to collective farmers were 2.5 times higher. In 1985, a decision was passed on raising the earnings of some categories of medical personnel, workers in science and technology, and on bettering the living standards of a significant proportion of pensioners. In the last ten years consumer goods production has almost doubled and the new houses built in the USSR over the last twenty years constitute 70 per cent of the total built in the country under Soviet power.

Scientific Progress

All-round development of Soviet science moved it to the forefront in the fields of mathematics, mechanics, quantum electronics, solid state physics, nuclear power engineering, and so on. The achievements made in space exploration are a concentrated expression of scientific progress in the USSR.

Perfecting Socialism

Soviet society is entering a crucial stage in the perfecting of socialism and in its advance towards communism on the basis of the acceleration of the country's social and economic development. Within a historically brief space of time a multitude of complex problems of unprecedented magnitude are to be resolved. The economic potential of the country is to be doubled and all areas of life—from working and living conditions, health care, and recreation facilities to class and national relations—are to be carried to a new and higher plane by the year 2000.

Gennady Pisarevsky, *New Times*, no. 48, November 1985.

Well, the reader may ask quite a logical question: if Soviet society and its economy has progressed so successfully, why then all this talk about the fundamental restructuring mapped out by the 27th Congress of Soviet Communists. During his talk with the Chief Editor of the Algerian magazine *Révolution Africaine*, M.S. Gorbachev, General Secretary of the CPSU [Communist Party of the Soviet Union] Central Committee, answered that question thus: "The point is that while giving credit to what has been accomplished we want to move forward faster, on a new qualitative basis. The creative potentialities of socialism are such that we can now tackle much more complicated and ambitious tasks than we could before. Complacency contradicts the very nature of the Communist Party, the nature of socialist society and our morals. That is why our mistakes and oversights, as well as our accomplishments, were openly and honestly discussed at the 27th Congress."

In the late 70s-early 80s some negative tendencies were discerned in the Soviet economy's development. These were due to several factors, mainly, an unfavourable demographic situation (resulting in labour shortages) and enormous material spending on arms forced upon the Soviet Union. However, there are other factors. Namely, we did not properly assess the new economic situation which had taken shape after the extensive growth lived its day; we were not persistent enough in introducing the achievements of science and technology, in restructuring the economy and managerial system in line with the new situation. Other negative tendencies, too, had their effect. As a result, economic growth rates reduced somewhat.

Acceleration Strategy

Having critically analysed the state of affairs in our country the CPSU adopted measures that would accelerate socio-economic development. What does this mean? It means, above all, raising the economic growth rates. But there is more to it than just that. As noted in the Political Report of the CPSU Central Committee to the 27th Party Congress, the acceleration means a new quality of growth; all-round intensification of production on the basis of the achievements of science and technology; restructuring of the economy; more effective forms of management, better organization and stimulation of labour. Steps are being made to do this, to strengthen labour and state discipline and introduce strict economy. In other words, great, intensive efforts are being made in every sphere of social life, and they are bearing fruit. This is proved by the results achieved in our national economy in the first ten months of 1986.

As N.V. Talyzin, First Deputy-Chairman of the USSR Council of Ministers, Chairman of the State Planning Committee, noted in his report at the November 1986 session of the USSR Supreme Soviet, high growth rates have been attained in almost all branches of the economy. The increase in the national income and industrial output has been the highest in the current decade. The produced national income is 4.3 per cent more than that in the first ten months of 1985; the total volume of industrial production has grown 5.2 per cent. These are the results of the first year of the twelfth five-year plan period (1986-1990), and they show that in its major areas the Soviet economy is approaching the average annual targets set in the five-year plan.

The development of engineering, the chemical and petrochemical industries has been accorded priority. It is precisely these branches that ensure the national economy's progress. The output of the latest production equipment is expanding, and the key industries—metallurgy, the coal and oil industries—are making steady headway.

The output and state purchases of grain, potatoes, vegetables, fruits and animal produce have expanded. The growth rates of agricultural production are almost double the average annual plan targets. The gross yield of grain was about 210 million tons in 1986, almost 30 million tons more than the average annual amount of grain produced between 1981 and 1985.

Judge and jury

Ollie Harrington for the *Daily World*.

Large-scale technological reconstruction and retooling of enterprises are gaining momentum. Some 25 per cent more funds than in 1985 have been earmarked for the purpose.

Labour productivity in industry has grown 4.8 per cent which is above the annual target (4.1 per cent). This was equivalent to a 95 per cent increase in industrial growth.

Measures are being taken to raise people's living standards. Average monthly wages and salaries amounted to 194 roubles in 1986 as against 189 roubles in 1985. Over the same period farmers' wages increased 4 per cent. Housing, social and cultural construction has grown in scale significantly. In the country as a whole 14 per cent more houses were built in the first ten months of 1986 than in the same period in 1985, the number of schools, pre-school institutions, hospitals and out-patient clinics also rose, 13, 27 and 60 per cent, respectively.

What else will be achieved in the twelfth five-year plan period? What economic results can we expect? National income, which reflects the end results and efficiency of the economic activity, will swell to 124 billion roubles (79 billion in the eleventh five-year period). The planned increase in industrial production will amount to 200 billion roubles (133 billion in the previous period). The average annual output of farm produce will be 29 billion roubles worth (10 billion in the previous period).

A characteristic feature of the plan is to raise the incomes of almost all strata of the population, and solve social problems. About four-fifths of the national income will go to improve people's welfare. Some 90 million white- and blue-collar workers (as against 20 million in the eleventh five-year period) will get higher pay. Better living conditions will be provided for war and labour veterans, and more funds will be allocated to help families having children. These measures will improve the living standards of more than 55 million pensioners and mothers.

Wage and Salary Increases

In the 1986-1990 plan period the average wages and salaries will jump almost 15 per cent to reach 218 roubles a month in 1990. As for the collective farmers, the respective figures will be 18 per cent and 180 roubles. And if one takes into account the money rural dwellers derive from their personal holdings, then it will be clear that their real incomes will actually equal those of blue- and white-collar workers. . . .

The Real State of Affairs

There is no denying that existing socialism has not yet solved all of its problems, and these are being discussed in the socialist countries openly and honestly. Difficulties arise in any society. However, reports about an "economic crisis in the USSR" made in the West are a gross misrepresentation of the real state of affairs. The point to be made here is that bourgeois ideologists view Soviet realities through the prism of the interests of the ruling class which they serve. Because of this they cannot be objective in their evaluations. Socialist economy will never know the crises inherent in capitalist society. Soviet society faces difficulties but only those that arise as its economy develops.

"Official speeches, newspapers, and the radio have trumpeted the successes of Soviet industry; in fact it is an ailing organism."

The Soviet Economy Is in Crisis

Aleksandr Solzhenitsyn

Aleksandr Solzhenitsyn is one of the most visible and controversial Soviet expatriates. Solzhenitsyn served during World War II as commander of an artillery battery, receiving two medals for bravery. He was imprisoned immediately after the war for a letter highly critical of Stalin and sent to Siberia. "Rehabilitated" by the Soviet government, Solzhenitsyn began to attack its policies and its bureaucrats. During the 1970s, the Soviet government sent him into exile in the West. He has written poetry, dramatic literature, as well as books criticizing the Soviet Union. In the following viewpoint, he argues that the whole Soviet economy is in such a degenerate state that only radically transforming the system will ensure economic recovery.

As you read, consider the following questions:

1. According to the author, what are the fundamental problems with the Soviet economic system?
2. What evidence does Solzhenitsyn give of an economic crisis?
3. The author states that "Absurdity besets the economy." What aspects of the economy does the author think are absurd and why?

Aleksandr Solzhenitsyn, "Communism at the End of the Brezhnev Era," *National Review,* January 21, 1983. World ©1983 by Aleksandr Solzhenitsyn. Reprinted with permission.

The agricultural economy in a Communist country is not designed according to calculations for achieving an optimum harvest, but is determined "ideologically." It is controlled by a grotesquely bureaucratic central plan incapable of anticipating real-life circumstances or of giving thought to the future, striving only to plunder the earth, as if this same earth will not have to sustain us tomorrow. For decades on end, the regime has handed down absurd and ruinous prescripts that the people have had no choice but to follow. The peasant is no longer devoted to the land and to his work as he was for centuries. What an achievement! Peasants have been numbed into indifference, obediently carrying out stupid orders, sowing and harvesting at the wrong times, irreparably turning the best meadowlands into unproductive plowed fields, cutting down forests until the rivers dry up, or draining good lakes to satisfy the formal requirements of "land reclamation." (But as they reclaim land in one spot, the same amount of acreage is abandoned elsewhere for lack of manpower.) Harvested grain and vegetables rot because of poor storage and inadequate transportation. Farm machinery rusts in the open air in winter and is soon out of commission. When there is too little time to spread all the fertilizer required by "the plan," the unused portion is burned so as to leave no trace of the infraction. Or consider this picture: a combine driver sells seed grain on the side at cut rates instead of sowing it. No one will check to see how much he has sown, and he doesn't care what comes up. For two months every year, teenagers from city high schools and other city dwellers inexperienced in agriculture are shipped in to "help" on the dying fields: their time, quite uselessly spent, is paid for by the regular salary they continue to receive at the various institutions from which they are absent. During the past ten years imports of foodstuffs to the USSR have increased forty-fold, and there have been four poor harvests in a row—such is the worth of this system of agriculture. For decades, the state has paid artificially low, indeed contemptible, prices for the produce of collective farms, so that the labor of the farmer has in effect been appropriated without any recompense whatever. For the person weeding a field all day long, the rewards have been only the tough weeds themselves—food for his cow or goat. Having arrogated the collective farmer's full working day at no cost to itself, the state permitted him to earn a livelihood by working his tiny private plot—about three-fifths of an acre—during what was left of the day and evening. These plots consume the remaining strength of old men and women (retired collective farmers until recently drew no old-age pension; they now receive a miserly sum), of invalids, and of children. (Fifteen million rural children don't know what it means to play; rural teenagers are smaller and more disease-prone than their urban counterparts.) In terms of area, the private plots make up only 2 per cent of the land under cultivation in the country, yet they generate one-third of the total production of vegetables, eggs, milk, and meat. But since up to a third of the collective farms' production of these same items is lost because of spoilage, the peasants—doubly exploited, deprived of fertilizers and modern technology, and working only with their hands, as they did long ago—produce on their private plots almost *half* of the USSR's supplies of those foodstuffs. But they cannot even sell all of this freely on the market. They have to give up a part to the state—formerly as a "tax," today in the form of "voluntary" sales at cut prices.

Economic Crises

The USSR has for more than ten years been in a *structural crisis*, whose effects are superimposed upon those of cyclical crises. The incapacity of the Soviet leaders to overcome this crisis cannnot be attributed to their "stupidity." It is the product of objective contradictions. In order to eliminate them or to reduce their effects, it would be necessary, in the absence of spontaneous changes in economic practices and relations, for the leaders to take appropriate action. The fact that the crisis is deepening confirms that the leaders do not act "freely." They are paralyzed by the contradictions of the system, which render them incapable of taking the steps necessary to overcome the structural crisis in their country. The half-measures they are taking are not enough to overcome this structural crisis: their effects are limited.

Charles Bettelheim, *Monthly Review*, December 1986.

The disproportions of the Communist agricultural system speak for themselves: the entire adult rural population spends its days working on 98 per cent of the cultivated area, while the remaining 2 per cent is worked by invalids and children, and by adults in the evenings. But even this last refuge is being eliminated by the regime in its ideological madness: more and more collective farms *(kolkhozy)* have in recent years been reorganized into state farms *(sovkhozy)*, a process that transforms the farmer into an industrial worker deprived of his private plot; these plots will therefore soon disappear altogether. Entire villages are being razed, the remnants of the peasant way of life eradicated, and the people resettled into multi-storied structures where cattle and fowl can no longer be kept. Once again the Soviet regime is demolishing its own base of production while "triumphing" ideologically.

The same type of absurdity besets the entire economy. By assuming complete control of production, the state has wrecked it. For sixty years official speeches, newspapers, and the radio have trumpeted the successes of Soviet industry; in fact it is an ailing organism,

130

plagued by numerous afflictions that are temporarily relieved only by illegal "microcapitalistic" means (administered in circumvention of socialist remedies). The essential goal of the Soviet economy is not economic growth, not a general increase in production, not even a rise in productivity or profit, but the functioning of a mighty military machine and the abundant provisioning of the ruling caste. The party bureaucracy is unable to organize either production or commercial distribution; it knows only how to confiscate goods that have already been produced. It is a system that cannot tolerate independence. Incapable of effective economic management, the regime substitutes coercion for leadership. The economy is fettered and hemmed in by a multitude of administrative restrictions, the aim of which is to prevent the emergence of any free social force. An obtuse extension of these rules has a deadening impact on many fruitful scientific undertakings; to offset this, key technology is either purchased or stolen in the West, and productivity rises only as a result of technical advances that have come into common use the world over. The result is foreign debts in the fantastic billions and depletion of the mineral and fuel resources that are used as payment. During their years in power, the Soviet leaders have sold or squandered reserves sufficient for their own generation and the two following generations. A great power, yet one that must import everything from electronics to grain, and that exports only its natural riches and arms, the Soviet Union has a standard of living below that of more than thirty other nations. Meanwhile, 12 per cent of the state's income is derived from the sale of exorbitantly priced vodka (which brings the populace to the point of induced idiocy) and of inferior wines prepared in unsanitary conditions: the government is literally driving the people to drink in order to finance its global designs.

Rigid Detail

The central plan controlling the economy does not take into account local circumstances or concrete events, yet it must be followed in rigid detail. The result is absurdity and chaos. Local officials work full-time devising ways of resisting or circumventing the plan, risking criminal charges at every step. Construction, for example, could not proceed if the laws were adhered to strictly: neither materials nor manpower would be available. Only illicit methods work. Everyone trembles at the threat of prosecution, yet nothing whatever would get built in any other way. The restrictions hinder action to the point that industrial managers are afraid to introduce obviously advantageous new technology: that would affect the plan and disrupt the schedule; it is far less trouble to announce that it will be instituted during the next five-year plan. Bold men with initiative have here and there attempted to set up the finances at their factories so as to get around petty state regulations and to be able to pay accord-

131

ing to the quality and quantity of work performed. The results have always been spectacular, but such managers are immediately reined in from above with new restrictions, cuts in budget allocations, and sometimes even with criminal proceedings. The emergence of free economic forces is seen as a threat to the bureaucracy's control of events.

The plan is not based on the quality of goods, nor on their variety, but on their gross value; thus whoever produces the greatest number of expensive, unnecessary, and unsalable items is "ahead" and is awarded a prize. To satisfy the plan, more timber is cut and floated downstream yearly than can later be hauled away; the rest rots. The plan means that Siberia, the richest part of the country in energy resources, has a shortage of electric power. An outstanding black-earth region is pointlessly chosen as the site of the huge Kama industrial complex. The Baikal-Amur railway line is a high-priority "national construction project"; no resources, materials, or manpower are spared. Yet the line is exceedingly poor in quality, with settling of the roadbed and derailments, even though the cost of five million rubles per kilometer surpasses the cost of an equivalent unit of railway construction in pre-revolutionary Siberia by a factor of twenty (taking into account the changed value of the ruble). . . .

It goes without saying that this lunatic conduct of economic policy, which anticipates nothing but military needs and exhibits a contemp-

Bill DeOre, reprinted with permission.

tuous disregard for the everyday requirements of the populace, leads to irreparable abuse of the environment. It is the plan at any cost, no matter what may be ruined in the process, particularly if this is merely some historical site or an unsullied natural region. Numerous hydroelectric stations are being constructed across rivers in flat country, flooding cultivated fields, grasslands, and populated districts; the hastily constructed dams ruin fishing. The price of all this is far greater than the benefits in increased electric energy. Beneath the waters of such new "seas," about which, incredibly, the Communists like to boast, there now lie a dozen towns, many hundreds of villages, and valuable forests. In contrast, the highly prized Sea of Azov, which used to provide more fish than the Black, Caspian, and Baltic Seas put together, has had its water level lowered by the Volga-Don Canal and has been turned into a dump for industrial wastes. The fish population has decreased ninety- to a hundred-fold compared to pre-World War II levels. . . .

Communism Cannot Be Corrected

There has been a great deal of excitement in the West in connection with the change of leadership in the Soviet Union, and, naturally, there are great hopes. And just as naturally, a few small but seemingly meaningful steps taken by the new leadership, particularly in the area of intellectual freedom and emigration, would be enough to "signal" that everything is improving. A survey of Soviet reality shows, however, that neither a change of leadership nor dozens of symbolic gestures could improve the situation. This can only be achieved if the life of the nation is restored to health in a fundamental way.

To improve or to correct Communism is not feasible. Communism can only be done away with—by the joint efforts of the many peoples oppressed by it.

"The Soviet Union has increased its national income fourfold and its industrial output fivefold. No advanced capitalist country, except Japan, has such high growth rates."

The Soviet Economy Is Improving

Abel Aganbegian

In the following viewpoint, Anatoli Lepikhov, a correspondent from a Soviet publishing house, interviews Abel Aganbegian, deputy academic secretary of the economics department of the USSR Academy of Sciences. Aganbegian is also the founder and editor-in-chief of the magazine *EKO* (Economics and Organization of Industrial Production), the largest publication of its kind in the USSR. Aganbegian discusses the current state of the Soviet economy and he argues that new economic reforms will augment an already successful economy.

As you read, consider the following questions:

1. What evidence does the author present to indicate that economic reforms only supplement an already healthy, growing economy?
2. According to the author, how does the Soviet Union's economic system compare with Western systems in terms of growth?
3. Specifically, how will Gorbachev's reforms affect the economy, according to Aganbegian?

Abel Aganbegian, interviewed by Anatoli Lepikhov, "Bigger, Better, Faster," in *Make the Economy Responsive to Innovation*. Moscow: Novosti Press Agency Publishing House, 1986.

In twenty-five years the Soviet Union has increased its national income fourfold and its industrial output fivefold. No advanced capitalist country, except Japan, has such high growth rates. Nevertheless, in the Soviet Union it is considered that the potentialities of the socialist economic system can be used more efficiently, that more can be produced much better and faster, and with less expenditure of labour, energy and materials.

At the 27th Congress of Soviet Communists a new strategy for the country's economic and social development was worked out. This strategy involves the overall intensification of production on the basis of scientific and technological progress, the restructuring of the economy and the improvement of the forms of economic management and labour organization and stimulation. It is a radical, carefully considered and comprehensive programme aimed at making development more dynamic, finding optimal methods of solving problems, and at eradicating all that is outdated and obsolete. The programme is based on a balanced combination of innovation and realism.

Soviet Progress

The Soviet Union had scored impressive achievements in the 25 years after the Third CPSU [Communist Party of the Soviet Union] Programme was adopted in 1961. The fixed production assets of the national economy had grown sevenfold. Thousands of enterprises had been built and new industries appeared. National income had increased almost fourfold, industrial output fivefold and agricultural output by 70 per cent.

Whereas the economic level of the United States seemed difficult to reach in the 1950s, by the 1970s the Soviet economy had already made substantial progress in approaching this level in terms of scientific, technological and economic potential, and had exceeded it in the output of several highly significant products. Below are listed a few of the features of scientific and technological progress in the Soviet Union before the 27th Party Congress. In 1985 alone, 23,000 inventions were put into practical use in the national economy. The implementation of important programmes for the development and application of highly efficient equipment and technologies continued. Joint studies had been conducted with CMEA [Council for Mutual Economic Assistance] member states, and the Comprehensive Programme for Scientific and Technological Progress of CMEA Member Countries up to the Year 2000 had been drafted and approved by the heads of government.

The technical level of production and output in the Soviet Union had risen and the scale of retooling and modernizing existing enterprises grown. In industry, 3,600 models of new machines, equipment, instruments and automation facilities had been developed. Over 11,000 mechanized, automatic and rotary transfer lines and over 13,000 robots had been installed and 775 automated process control systems built. . . .

The economic situation in the USSR has radically changed in the past 10-15 years. Certain difficulties, including objective ones, have affected the country's economic development. First, there are external difficulties: I have in mind the arms race that has been forced on us. And, second, there are internal difficulties, such as a considerable growth of expenditure on the extraction and transportation of oil, gas, ores, and virtually all other raw materials. Let us consider just one figure—5,000 million tons—which is the annual output of all fuels in our country. With this output we are able not only to meet our own demand but also to supply large quantities to those socialist countries that have insufficient sources of fuel or raw materials. But the extraction of natural resources at such a rate leads to the quick depletion of easily accessible deposits, so our main fuel and energy production centres are constantly being relocated to the east and to the unsettled northern areas.

Dynamic Development

In the course of many years the USSR's economy has been developing dynamically, with full employment of the entire able-bodied population. In the 1961-1985 period alone the national income of the Soviet Union had increased almost four times and industrial production five times. No developed capitalist country, except Japan, has such rates. In 25 years real per capita incomes had grown 2.6 times and social consumption funds more than five times. There had been built 54 million flats and most of the families had had their living conditions improved. There had been a transition to universal secondary education, and the number of persons who had graduated from higher educational institutions had increased four-fold.

Gennady Pisarevsky, *Soviet Economy: The Strategy of Intensification*, 1987.

The demographic situation is also a problem for us, as Soviet society is suffering today from the "second echo" of the demographic damage caused by the war. The children of those born when the birth rate dropped sharply are now joining the able-bodied work force. At the same time those who did not fight in the war have started to retire and receive pensions, and their number is 2-3 times greater than that of pensioners who fought in the war. As a result, the work force is shorthanded by about eight million workers in each five-year period as compared to the previous one. Thus we can no longer depend on the enlistment of additional natural and manpower resources in order to maintain high growth rates.

But these difficulties are only a partial explanation for a considerable reduction in the rate of socio-economic development in the past three five-year periods. National income that was used increased by 41 per cent in the 8th five-year period (1966-1970), by 28 per cent in the 9th, by 21 per cent in the 10th, and by 16.5 per cent in the previous, 11th five-year period (1981-1985). But the primary causes for these negative trends stem from mistakes and shortcomings in economic management....

The concept of acceleration, underlying the targets of the new five-year plan for 1986-1990, is realized not only in growth rates but also in a substantial rise in the absolute increment of key economic indicators. For example, national income, which reflects the end results and efficiency of economic activity, is planned to grow by 124,000 million roubles in the 12th five-year plan period as compared to an increase of 79,000 million roubles in the previous five-year period (in 1983 prices). The resulting growth rate is 4.1 per cent. In the 13th and 14th five-year periods, the growth rate is projected to reach five per cent or higher, and thus the country's national income should nearly double in the course of 15 years. I emphasize the fact that these targets are not only feasible, but also scientifically substantiated. However, due to the continually diminishing growth of resources for objective reasons, these targets can be reached only through a sharp increase in economic efficiency.

All-Around Intensification

The country has launched a course of all-round intensification of the entire national economic complex, the further development and efficient use of the scientific and technological potential, and a more exact correspondence between the forms of socialist economic management and the conditions and requirements of modern society. As Mikhail Gorbachev stressed in his report to the congress, only with this approach will it be possible to raise labour productivity by 130-150 per cent by the end of the century and at the same time reduce power consumption per rouble of national income by 29 per cent and metal consumption by nearly 50 per cent. It is intended to reverse radically the tendency of diminishing capital productivity by the stabilization of this ratio followed by the acceleration of its growth.

Soviet science holds a strong position and is advancing pioneering projects. An increasing number of new technologies are developed from the achievements of basic research. These technologies include laser and radiation machining of materials, powder metallurgy, and genetic and cellular engineering.

Integral technological systems are being gradually developed to transform whole production cycles and not only individual parts of these cycles. Examples of such systems are many: the converter process of steelmaking with continuous casting and controlled rolling, rotary and rotary-conveyor transfer lines, flexible production systems in engineering, and various biotechnological processes....

In my opinion, the assertions that scientific and technological progress in the Soviet Union may result in unemployment testify to the insufficient or simply erroneous knowledge of the real conditions in our country. This is a peculiar interpretation of our plans to release about 30 million manual workers by the year 2000. But the overwhelming majority of these workers are of relatively advanced age, and replacing them has already become a problem since young people tend to be unwilling to work on these jobs. We have difficulties, for instance, with manning assembly lines. Of course, some of the relieved manual workers will have to be retrained, and the appropriate measures are being taken. Some jobs will simply cease to exist. But the reduction of monotonous and arduous manual labour is a natural and progressive development. In socialist society the scientific and technological revolution is aimed at lightening the work load and enhancing the creative character of work.

The Main Achievement

The Land of Soviets has risen from age-old backwardness to the heights of social progress, registered signal accomplishments in all spheres of life, become a great power exerting a decisive influence on all areas of international life. The main achievement, as the draft of the new text of the CPSU Programme states, is the "final and complete victory of socialism in our country."

Mikhail Kobrin and Victor Tsoppi, *New Times*, no. 8, September 1986.

Workers replaced by machines will be moved in a regulated manner to other sectors of production where the appropriate opportunities for employment and retraining are being provided. This process will last several years in the course of which those unwilling to quit their jobs will go to work at other enterprises where their specialties will still be in demand. Those inclined to change their occupation will have time to retrain. Suitable jobs can be found in sectors where the work force is growing. In production these include, above all, high-tech industries. There are also vast opportunities in the fields of service, housing and utilities, public health, education and culture. The development of this social infrastructure is one of the basic conditions required for increasing economic efficiency of production as a whole. To sum up, the centralized planning of economic development under socialism provides every opportunity for total employment....

We have to achieve a breakthrough in economic, scientific, technological and social development. The human factor is certainly decisive here. We will be able to resolve the complex problems of our development if we achieve a breakthrough in human minds and attitudes, learn effectively to stimulate work at all levels and concentrate on accelerating scientific and technological progress.

The Party's Principal Goal

The principal objective of the Communist Party's policy has always been and remains the concern for man and his needs and for the steady rise of the material and cultural level of the people. The Party associates the attainment of this goal with the renovation of the productive forces on the basis of the highest achievements in science and engineering, the improvement of production relations and of the system of management and administration, and with the carrying out of profound changes in the sphere of labour. These are the most vital conditions for social progress today.

In conclusion, I would like to emphasize that the policy of the 27th Party Congress with regard to scientific and technological progress will enable the Soviet Union's economy to become responsive to constant innovations and will help in solving the complex problems of accelerating our social and economic development.

"Even according to the more optimistic scenarios... the Soviet Union will face an economic crunch far more severe than anything it encountered in the 1960s and 1970s."

The Soviet Economy Is Not Improving

Paul Kennedy

Paul Kennedy is the J. Richardson Dilworth Professor of History at Yale University. Kennedy has written a number of books, including *The Rise and Fall of British Naval Mastery,* and *Strategy and Diplomacy, 1870-1945.* This viewpoint is part of his book, *The Rise and Fall of the Great Powers: Economic Change and Military Conflict from 1500-2000.* In his viewpoint, Kennedy argues that Gorbachev's program of reform will make no substantial and lasting impact on the Soviet economy. The author concludes that Gorbachev can hope only to slow the rate of inevitable economic decline.

As you read, consider the following questions:

1. What inherent features in the Soviet system will keep new reforms from having any impact on the Soviet economy, according to the author?
2. What causes for concern does the author discuss in his viewpoint? How do these concerns affect the economy?
3. What relationship does the bureaucracy have with Soviet industry? According to the author, how does this relationship prevent the economy from improving?

Paul Kennedy, "What Gorbachev Is Up Against." Condensed from *The Atlantic Monthly,* June 1987. To be published in *The Rise and Fall of the Great Powers* in January 1988 by Random House. Copyright © 1987 by Paul Kennedy.

Whether Gorbachev can effectively reform the system *without* abandoning the fundamentals of the Communist ideology is extremely doubtful. The evidence of the past seventy years of Party rule suggests that the real problem is the Leninist system of government and the economy itself. If they remain, fundamental reform is impossible; if they go, the USSR will no longer be a "Soviet" and "Socialist" republic. No amount of partial or cosmetic change will allow Gorbachev and his Party to escape this basic contradiction.

Economic Irony

In Marxist terminology the word *contradiction* is a very specific one, referring to the tensions that (it is argued) inherently exist within the capitalist system of production and will inevitably cause its demise. It may therefore seem deliberately ironic to employ the same expression to describe the position in which the Soviet Union, the world's first Communist state, now finds itself. Nevertheless, in a number of absolutely critical areas there seems to be an ever-widening gap between the *aims* of the Soviet state and the *methods* employed to reach them. The state proclaims the need for greater agricultural and industrial output, yet hobbles that possibility by collectivization and heavy-handed planning. It asserts the overriding importance of world peace, yet its enormous arms buildup and its links with "revolutionary" states (together with its revolutionary heritage) serve to increase international tensions. It claims to require absolute security along its extensive borders, yet its unyielding policy toward its neighbors' security concerns worsens Moscow's relations with Western and Eastern Europe, with the Middle East, with China and Japan, and in turn makes the Soviet Union feel "encircled" and *less* secure. Its philosophy asserts that the ongoing, dialectical process of change in world affairs is driven by technology and new means of production, and inevitably causes all sorts of political and social transformations, yet its own autocratic and bureaucratic habits, the privileges that cushion the party elites, the restrictions upon the free interchange of knowledge, and the lack of personal incentive make it horribly ill equipped to handle the explosive but subtle "high-tech" future that is already emerging in Japan and the United States. Above all, while Party leaders frequently insist that the USSR will never again accept a position of military inferiority, and even more frequently urge the nation to increase production, the state has clearly found it difficult to reconcile those two aims and, in particular, to check a Russian tradition of devoting too large a share of national resources to the armed forces—with deleterious consequences for the ability of the USSR to compete commercially with other societies. Perhaps there are other ways of labeling all these problems, but it does not seem inappropriate to term them "contradictions.". . .

Whatever the noises about reform from the highest levels, however, the indications are that the Soviet Union is not contemplating large-scale agricultural changes to anything like the extent of Deng Xiaoping's recent "liberalization" measures in China, even though it is clear that Soviet grain output is falling far behind that of its adventurous neighbor.

Why the System Is Inflexible

Although the Kremlin is unlikely to explain openly why it will make only marginal improvements in the present system of collectivized agriculture, despite the system's manifest inefficiencies, two reasons for this inflexibility stand out. The first is that an enormous extension of private plots, the creation of many more private markets, and increases in the prices paid for agricultural produce would mean significant rises in the peasantry's share of national income—to the detriment of the resentful urban population and, perhaps, of industrial investment.

Economic Deficiencies

It should be emphasized that these Marxist deficiencies—industrial accidents, Chernobyl, housing shortages, high infant mortality, poverty—are admitted, although cautiously, in the name of Mr. Gorbachev's *glasnost* ("frankness") policy.

But no one, not even Mr. Gorbachev, would dare ask the deeper question—of what further use is Marxism-Leninism except to bring greater and greater misery to the victims forced to live under that antihuman system of exploitation of the many and privileges for the few? Nor do the Soviet hierarchs tolerate those who raise such questions.

Arnold Beichman, *The Washington Times*, October 24, 1986.

Second, fundamental reform would mean a decline in the power of the bureaucrats and managers who run Soviet agriculture, and would have implications for all other spheres of decision-making. If it is obvious that "individual farmers making day-to-day decisions in response to market signals, changing weather, and the conditions of their crops" can manage agriculture far better than any "centralized bureaucracy, however competently staffed," what might that imply for the future of the centralized bureaucracy? In its impressive wide-ranging survey of global trends in agriculture, the Worldwatch Institute's publication *State of the World 1986*, came to the conclusion that there appeared to be a consistent, embarrassing relationship between socialism and national food deficits, and that fact can hardly have escaped the Politburo's attention. But from its own perspective, it may seem better—safer, certainly—to maintain "socialist" (collectivized) farming, even if that implies rising food imports, than to admit the failure of the Communist system and to

142

remove the existing controls on so large a segment of society.

By the same token, it is difficult for the USSR to amend its industrial sector. To some observers, it may hardly seem necessary for it to do so, given the remarkable achievements of the Soviet economy since 1945 and the fact that it outproduces the United States in, for example, machine tools, steel, cement, fertilizers, and oil. Yet there are many signs that Soviet industry, too, is stagnating, and that the period of relatively easy expansion—made possible by fixing ambitious output targets and then devoting masses of money and manpower to meeting those figures—is coming to a close. This is owing in part to increasing labor and energy shortages. . . . Equally important, however, are the signs that manufacturing suffers from an excess of bureaucratic planning, from being too much concentrated upon heavy industry, and from being unable to respond either to consumer choice or to the need to alter products to meet new demands or markets. Being among the world's leading producers of cement is not necessarily a good thing if excessive investment in that industry takes resources from a more needy sector, if the cement-production process is very wasteful of energy, if the final product has to be transported long distances across the country, further straining the overworked railway system, and if the cement itself has to be distributed among the thousands of building projects that Soviet planners have authorized but the nation has never been able to complete. The same holds true for the enormous Soviet steel industry, much of whose output seems to be wasted—causing Robert V. Daniels, among other scholars, to marvel at the "paradox of industrial plenty in the midst of consumer poverty." There are, to be sure, some efficient sectors in Soviet industry (usually related to defense, which can command large resources and must seek to be competitive with the West), but the overall system suffers from concentrating on production regardless of market prices and consumer demand. Since Soviet factories cannot go out of business, they also lack the ultimate stimulus to produce efficiently. However many tinkerings there are to speed industrial growth, it is difficult to believe that they will produce a sustained breakthrough if the existing system of a planned economy remains more or less intact. . . .

Hordes of Uzbekis

[Another] major cause for concern about the Soviet Union's future economic growth lies in demographics. The prognosis here is so gloomy that one Western expert, Murray Feshbach, of Georgetown University's Center for Population Research, began his recent survey of the Soviet population and labor force with the following blunt statements:

> On any basis, short-term or long-term, the prospects for the development of Soviet population and manpower resources until the end of the century are quite dismal. From the reduc-

tion in the country's birth rate to the incredible increase in the death rates beyond all reasonable past projections; from the decrease in the supply of new entrants to the labor force, compounded by its unequal regional distribution, to the relative aging of the population, not much glimmer of hope lies before the Soviet Government in these trends.

All of these trends are serious, and they interact, but the most shocking has been the steady worsening in life expectancy and infant-mortality rates since the 1970s and perhaps earlier. Because of a slow erosion in hospital services and general health care, poor standards of sanitation and public hygiene, and fantastic levels of alcoholism, death rates in the Soviet Union have increased, especially among working males. According to some calculations, the average Soviet man can now expect to live for only about sixty years—some six years less than he could in the mid-1960s. Nearly as shocking has been the rise in infant mortality (the USSR is the only industrialized country where such a rise has occurred), to a rate three times that in the United States—despite the enormous number of Soviet doctors. Yet as the population is dying off faster, the birthrate is slowing down sharply—presumably because of urbanization, greater female participation in the work force, poor housing conditions, and other disincentives to have a family. The birthrate has dropped most among the Russian population of the country, with the consequence that the male Russian population of the country is barely increasing at all. . . .

No Economic Boom

The Soviet Union is experiencing an economic boom, or so the CIA and the Defense Intelligence Agency say in a [1987] report. They conclude that the Soviet economy grew more than 4 percent [in 1986] compared with about 2 percent for the U.S. How accurate is the estimate? Not very, in all likelihood.

Let us assume, for sake of assuming, that Mikhail Gorbachev's ballyhooed "restructuring" has indeed stimulated the rattletrap Soviet economy. All that means is a few more drops squeezed from the turnip. Force people to work harder, and output can be boosted slightly. But in the long run only an economy based on individual initiative can sustain high-level output.

The Washington Times, April 7, 1987.

Two main political obstacles stand in the way of taking a "leap forward" on the Chinese model. The first, already referred to, is the entrenched positions of Party officials, bureaucrats, and other members of the elite, who enjoy an array of privileges that cushion them from the hardships of everyday life in the Soviet Union, and who monopolize power and influence. To decentralize the planning and pricing system, to free the peasants from communal controls, to allow managers of factories greater freedom of action, to offer incentives for individual enterprise rather than Party loyalty, to close outdated plants, to refuse to accept shoddy products, and to allow a freer circulation of information would be seen by those in power as a dire threat to their positions. Exhortations, more-flexible planning, new investments in this or that sector, and disciplinary drives against alcoholism and "decadent" youth styles are one thing; but all proposed changes, Soviet Party officials have stressed, must take place "within the framework of scientific socialism" and without "any shifts toward a market economy or private enterprise." In the opinion of Leonard Silk, a business columnist for *The New York Times*, "the Soviet economy needs its inefficiencies to remain Soviet"; that is to say, far from "stagnation" being "alien to socialism," as the Soviet leader claimed in his January [1987] speech, the reverse might be true. If that is so, Gorbachev's speeches about the need for a "profound transformation" of the system are unlikely to make much impact upon long-term growth rates. . . .

Gorbachev's Problem

Economics matters to the leaders of the Soviet military, not only because they are Marxist and not only because it pays for their weapons and pays their wages, but also because they understand its importance to the outcome of a lengthy coalition war. It *might* be true, the *Soviet Military Encyclopaedia* conceded in 1979, that a global coalition war would be short, especially if nuclear weapons were used. "However," it added, "taking into account the great military and economic potentials of possible coalitions of belligerent states, it is not excluded that it might be protracted also." If such a war were "protracted," the emphasis would again be on economic staying power, as it has been in the great coalition wars of the past. With that assumption in mind, it cannot be comforting to the Soviet leadership to reflect that the USSR is responsible for only 12 or 13 percent of the world's GNP (or about 17 percent, if one dares to include the Warsaw Pact satellites as plus factors), and that it not only is far behind the United States and Western Europe in total GNP but also is being overtaken by Japan and may—if current growth rates continue over the long term—even find itself being approached by China in the next thirty years. As *The Economist* coldly observed, in 1913 "Imperial Russia had a real product per manhour 3½ times greater than Japan's [but the USSR] has spent its nigh 70 socialist years slipping relatively backwards, to maybe a quarter of Japan's rate now." However one assesses the military strength of the USSR at the moment, therefore, the prospect of its being only the fourth or fifth among the great productive centers of the world by the early twenty-first century cannot but worry the Soviet leadership, simply because of the implications for long-term Soviet power.

This does not mean that the USSR is close to collapse. It does mean that it is facing awkward choices. One Soviet expert, Professor Seweryn Bialer, of Columbia University, has said, "The policy of guns, butter, and growth—the political cornerstone of the Brezhnev era—is no longer possible," and "Even according to the more optimistic scenarios. . . the Soviet Union will face an economic crunch far more severe than anything it encountered in the 1960s and 1970s." It is therefore to be expected that Gorbachev's efforts and exhortations to improve the Soviet economy will intensify. But it is highly unlikely that even an energetic regime in Moscow would either abandon "scientific socialism" in order to boost the economy or drastically cut the burden of defense expenditures and thereby affect the military core of the Soviet state.

A Continual Decline

It is a grim dilemma, made no less grim by the fact that whatever Gorbachev's freshness of style, he shows no intention of either abandoning control from the top or disregarding Russia's preference for military security over anything else. Obviously, his shake-up of the system could make the pace of the Soviet Union's relative decline much slower than it was during the Brezhnev years; but the evidence suggests that its decline will continue nonetheless.

"Getting our economy out of the pre-crisis situation. . .calls for in-depth, truly revolutionary transformations."

The Soviet Economy Is Undergoing Economic Reform

Mikhail Gorbachev

Mikhail Gorbachev as general secretary of the Central Committee of the Communist Party is the highest ranking official in the Soviet government. Since taking office, Gorbachev has become a highly visible and controversial world leader. Many observers believe that his new policies of perestroika (restructuring) and glasnost (openness) have made him more accessible and made obsolete the stereotype of the staid, unapproachable Soviet leader. In the following viewpoint, taken from a speech given at the Plenary meeting of the Central Committee, Gorbachev discusses how perestroika and glasnost will reform the Soviet economy.

As you read, consider the following questions:

1. What specific steps does Gorbachev outline for reforming the Soviet economy?
2. What specific effect, according to the author, will these steps have on the economy?
3. What conditions does Gorbachev cite as necessary for economic reform?

Mikhail Gorbachev, "On the Party's Tasks in Fundamentally Restructuring the Management of the Economy," a speech presented to the Plenary Committee of the CPSU Central Committee, June 29, 1987.

Guided by Leninist teaching and creatively developing it, the Soviet people and the party continue the cause of the revolution through their drive toward restructuring.

I refer to a radical reform of the management of the economy, to qualitative changes in the system of the economic mechanism—changes that will open up new possibilities for using the advantages of the socialist system. . . .

We understand more clearly all the time that the restructuring was necessitated by the mounting contradictions in the development of society. These contradictions, gradually accumulating and not being solved in time, were actually taking on pre-crisis forms.

The process of democratization of all aspects of life is expanding and deepening. Public organizations are displaying more initiative. Democratic principles are gaining momentum in the management of production. Public opinion is having a clear and important voice. The mass media have begun working more actively in the interests of the renewal drive.

Increased Labor Productivity

The new situation has affected economic results to a certain extent as well. The growth rates of labor productivity have increased. On the average over the past two years they have exceeded the growth rate during the Eleventh Five-Year Plan period in industry and construction by 30 per cent, in agriculture by 100 per cent and in rail transport by 200 per cent.

Industrial production increased by 4.4 per cent and agricultural production by 3 per cent on the average in 1985-1986.

The January 1987 Plenary Meeting gave a powerful impetus to labor and social activity. It became obvious that no one can stand on the sidelines of the restructuring drive—every person must take his or her position.

The revolutionary transformations in society have brought to the fore the contradiction between the demands for renewal, creativity and constructive initiative on the one hand, and conservatism, inertia and selfish interests on the other hand.

The imbalance between the growing vigor of the masses and bureaucratism, which survives in the most diverse fields, and attempts to freeze the renewal drive are manifestations of this real contradiction.

Overcoming this contradiction requires prompt and resolute measures—in personnel policy and in new approaches and norms of party, state and public life.

The drive for renewal has scored an ideological and moral victory; it is spreading and penetrating deeper.

But as we make such a responsible evaluation we should not allow exaggerations nor, worse yet, complacency. We actually now are only on the first wave of the restructuring. This wave has sent ripples through stagnant water.

We must not allow readjustment in the party to lag behind the economic, social and spiritual processes that are taking place. We cannot allow a situation where changes in life, in the moods of people would outpace the understanding of these processes in the party, and even more so in its guiding bodies.

The leadership of the party and the country has a unity of views on the fundamental questions of the restructuring effort, of domestic and foreign policy. This unity makes it possible to adopt and to implement confidently decisions dictated by the times.

I think this is always important but especially so at crucial periods of development.

Desire for Prosperity

The radical economic reforms in the USSR are not based on fantasy. They reflect the aspirations of millions of Soviet people who demand that the Communist Party continue its broad compaign to transform all spheres of the country's life. In this lies the main potential of the restructuring. . . .

Fundamental reforms are going on in the areas of economic management, planning, price formation, financing, crediting and the guidance of scientific and technological progress. These measures should open up vast prospects for the initiative and creative endeavors of millions of working people and turn the economic improvement program into a vital cause of every Soviet citizen. The desire of the Soviet people for prosperity will provide the basis for major breakthroughs.

E. Ryabtsev, *People's Daily World*, July 7, 1987.

Few notable improvements are occurring in such a major regional party organization as that of Gorky Region. The departments of the CPSU [Communist Party of the Soviet Union] Central Committee are called upon to act in a new way in the new situation, exerting deeper influence on the state of affairs in the republican, territorial, and regional party organizations, and ensuring control over the implementation of the decision of the CPSU Central Committee.

Improve Performance

[We] need to strengthen discipline, to raise the degree of organization, to enhance responsibility and to improve performance everywhere at all levels. . . .

On behalf of the Politburo and the Ministry of Defense, I firmly state that there should be no doubt either in the party or among the people about the ability of the armed forces of the USSR to defend the country. . . .

In the existing conditions we should consider the establishment, on the basis of the people's control committee, of a single and integral system of control that would have a wide range of powers throughout the country, that would rely on a maximum of openness in its work and that would discharge its important functions in a comprehensive fashion, proceeding from the point of view of the entire people and in a broad sociopolitical context.

[Restructuring] arouses immense interest throughout the world. We believe that our problems are understood not only by the working people in the socialist countries, but also by broad sections of the world public, and we feel their sympathies.

Toward Reorganization

The course toward reorganization has been taken seriously by very different political forces. That course substantially increased the weight, influence and authority of our country, and it is convincingly demonstrating the sincerity and peaceful nature of our intentions on the international scene.

That very policy does not suit influential groups in the West, especially in the United States. Some members of America's ruling group are arguing that *glasnost* is a challenge to American diplomacy, imperiling the spirit of the free world, its life today and the prospects for its security tomorrow. They understand that it is difficult to find convincing arguments against the course of our party toward reorganization.

This is why their main stake is on using the process of democratization and openness for prompting us to develop false aims and defective values, for sowing doubt among our people concerning the correctness and sincerity of the party's policy, its course toward reorganization and improvement of the situation in the country. There is nothing new for us here. That was to be expected, and we foresaw that it would be so. Soviet people know well the real worth of such an 'interest' in our affairs.

We are conducting the reorganization—extending democracy and consolidating the intrinsic values of socialism—not for the purpose of appealing to some other group but so that our society, through reorganization and democracy, can reach new heights in the process of socioeconomic and spiritual advancement. And we shall not steer away from the road of reorganization.

It will be appropriate if the course of reorganization is the focus of attention at the meetings of communists, if they consider the participation of communists—workers, farmers, intellectuals and our leading cadres—in that great undertaking of the entire people. The forthcoming report and election meetings in the party should appraise what has been done and decide what should be done to deepen and accelerate the process of reorganization.

Serious changes were needed in structural policy, in the direction of capital investments. But they were not made.

150

The desire to slow down the declining growth rates by extensive methods caused exorbitant outlays for building up the fuel and energy branches and excessive growth in demand for additional labor, which caused an acute shortage in the national economy and a decline of the output-per-asset ratio. Natural resources were hastily brought into production and used irrationally.

Getting our economy out of the pre-crisis situation in which it has found itself calls for in-depth, truly revolutionary transformations. Over the past two years, the first steps have been made toward mastering new methods of management worked out on the basis of an analysis of the situation around 1980 and a series of large-scale economic experiments.

Reform Strategy

The current transformations in the economy are not being carried out in isolation. They are a component of the overall strategy of perestroika, and this can produce results only if it embraces all aspects of life and aims at making our political system more democratic, adopting a new approach to the solution of social problems, enlivening the situation in the cultural and ideological sphere and making the climate there healthier.

Leonid Abalkin, *New Times*, no. 28, July 20, 1987.

[The aim is to] reorient economic growth from intermediary to final, socially significant results and to satisfying public needs, promoting an all-round development of the individual, making scientific and technological progress the main factor for economic growth, and creating a reliable input-restricting mechanism.

Broad Democratization

To achieve all this, it is essential to change over from predominantly administrative to predominantly economic methods of management at every level, to broad democratization in administration, and to activating the human factor in every way.

This changeover involves:

First, drastically extending the margins of independence for amalgamations and factories, converting these facilities to full-scale profit-and-loss accounting and self-financing, increasing responsibility for achieving the highest results, fulfillment of obligations to clients, directly linking the collective's income level and its work performance, and using the team contract extensively in labor relations;

Second, radically transforming centralized economic management, raising its qualitative level and focusing it on the main issues determining the strategy, quality, pace and proportions of development of the national economy as a whole and its balance, while at the same time decisively relieving the center from interference in the day-to-day activities of subordinate economic bodies;

Third, moving ahead with reform in planning, pricing, financing and credit, with transition to wholesale trade in productive goods, and reorganized management over scientific and technological progress, foreign economic activities, labor and social processes;

New Organizational Structures

Fourth, creating new organizational structures to ensure deeper specialization and more reliable coproduction schemes, the direct involvement of science in production and, on this basis, a breakthrough to world standards in quality;

Fifth, completing the transition from the excessively centralized command system of management to a democratic method, promoting self-administration, creating a mechanism for activating the individual's potential, clearly delimiting the functions and fundamentally changing the style and methods of work of party, local government and economic bodies. . . .

A radical reform of the pricing system is a most important part of the economic overhaul. We are faced with the need to carry out not just a partial improvement in the system of pricing, but a radical reform of pricing and interconnected restructuring of our entire price system—wholesale, purchase, retail prices and tariffs.

The overhaul of the system of the material and technical supply of the national economy is closely linked with the reform in pricing. Its main direction is a decisive transition to wholesale trade in means of production both through direct contacts between suppliers and consumers and through self-sustained wholesale bases. . . .

Improving Management

The measures for improving the management of external economic relations taken now are aimed specifically at deepening the Soviet Union's participation in the international division of labor, which becomes an ever more important factor in the development of the Soviet national economy.

Not only we and our allies, but also all who are interested in cooperation with our country in new, more favorable conditions would gain from the successful implementation of the plans for the reorganization in our country, from the modernization of our economy.

The overhaul of the economic mechanism is called upon to create favorable economic, organizational and legal conditions for deep integration of our national economy with the national economies of fraternal countries.

The system of pay and labor incentive must be arranged in a new way. It is particularly important that the actual pay of every worker be closely linked to his personal contribution to the end result, and that no limit be set on it. There is only one criterion of justice: whether or not it is earned.

The intensification of social production, the creation of a corresponding economic mechanism encourages us to appraise in a new way the problems of effective employment in our society.

Labor Resources

The extent to which the excessive workforce will be trimmed will increase considerably as scientific and technological progress accelerates. The need in labor resources for public services, culture, education, health services and recreation will increase at the same time. Such a rearrangement of the workforce requires close attention and carefully considered organizational measures.

The Concept of Reform

The economic reform now under way in the U.S.S.R. is the focus of attention of scientists and businessmen, statisticians and housewives. Judging from numerous press comments and our readers' numerous letters to the editor, world public opinion has taken due account of the boldness and consistency of the reform that began with the main link of the economy, the industrial plant, and therefore assigns the leading role to the workingman, that is to the working class.

What does the radical restructuring of economic management consist of?

It consists of a resolute changeover from predominantly administrative to predominantly economic methods of management, and taking the interests of all the parties concerned into account, in a broad democratization of economic management. It also consists of shifting the emphasis from extensive to intensive methods, from quantity to quality.

Yuri Shevchenko, *New Times*, no. 27, July 13, 1987.

We must ensure social guarantees for the employment of the working people, their constitutional right to work. The socialist system has such opportunities. . . .

The restructuring drive under way across the land is directly continuing the cause of the October Revolution and consistently projecting the ideals inscribed on the banner of our revolution.

*"Stalinist economics binds the empire together
and keeps power firmly in the hands of the
Communist aristocracy, but it freezes economic
progress."*

Soviet Economic Reform
Is a Myth

Lawrence Minard, Peter Brimelow, and Seweryn Bialer

Lawrence Minard and Peter Brimelow both contribute to *Forbes,* a
monthly business magazine. Seweryn Bialer is a Soviet expert at Columbia University who taught for several years in Warsaw, Poland.
Minard and Brimelow wrote the following viewpoint after interview-
ing Bialer. The authors argue that there are no reforms occurring
in the Soviet Union. Gorbachev's economic restructuring is the same
useless system that Stalin promoted, they conclude.

As you read, consider the following questions:

1. How do the authors characterize Gorbachev's proposals for
   restructuring the economy?
2. What does Bialer say are the basic problems with the Soviet
   system and what effect do the problems have on the Soviet
   economy?
3. According to the authors, what hinders Gorbachev's
   proposals from effectively changing the Soviet economy?

Lawrence Minard and Peter Brimelow, "The Legacy of Stalin—A Chat with Seweryn
Bialer." Excerpted by permission of *Forbes* magazine, December 1, 1986. © Forbes Inc.,
1986.

There are no fundamental changes currently under way in the Soviet Union. Says [Seweryn] Bialer: "The mass terror is abolished. Personal dictatorship was abolished. But in the economic field, the Stalinist system is completely in command of Russia today."

By Stalinism, Bialer means centralization of power in Moscow, with scarcely any real decision making left to individuals anywhere in the vast country. Continuation of the system dooms the Soviets to backwardness but any real change threatens the power of the ruling elite. So clumsy is the system that even when its spies steal industrial secrets from the U.S., its industry cannot easily absorb what it steals.

"The Chinese adapt from America whatever they want and still think they're superior to us," says Bialer. "But the greatest thing with the Russian leaders, when they meet our leaders, is to say they should be equal with us because they have equal strategic power. But in all other aspects they are unequal. This makes them feel internally insecure, which was always the situation in Russia."

We ask Bialer: How do we know how weak the Soviet economy is? Can you get any kind of GNP numbers at all on the Soviet economy? "That is a wonderful question," says Bialer. "In my opinion, one can't. And I must tell you that most of the Soviet economists rely on the American calculations of the GNP made by the CIA that are presented every two years to the Congress in two green volumes."

Soviet Secretiveness

Such is the secretiveness that grips the Soviet Union: Even its own economists must look outside for believable statistics.

"You have a situation," says Bialer, "where secrecy, underdevelopment of the infrastructure, the fear of risk, lack of entrepreneurship and lack of rewards all combine to make the Soviet Union—in the civilian sector, not the military sector—fall more and more behind the U.S. and other industrial countries."

Stalin's methods did work once. Look at any Soviet city: The major building seems to date from Stalin's time and just after. Even after Stalin's death in 1953 Khrushchev and then Brezhnev were able to claim that Russia could catch up with the West.

Today, however, the cheap resources have been depleted, the sheer energy that rebuilt the country has been dissipated. The Soviet economy is like a great beast that exhausted itself in a fight for survival and now sprawls, energyless and panting. To close the gap with the West, the Soviets must shift from extensive growth based on cheap natural resources and starvable human labor, to intensive growth based on microchips, information and human ingenuity—a shift, says Bialer, that has not been made and perhaps cannot be made.

Says Bialer: "There is no question that the Soviet system does not fit the third industrial revolution. Here, the Soviet system possesses all the characteristics that work against development. It is a secretive nation, where information is compartmentalized."

Centralization, repression—Stalinism—has enabled the leaders to mobilize enough resources to become a world military power. But down the Stalinist road lies economic stagnation. And with stagnation the struggle to retain military parity becomes harder and harder. With stagnation, too, the Soviet Union becomes a laughingstock, not the proud model for the future its founders dreamed about. The Soviet economy has become what a recent writer in *The American Spectator* aptly called "an overgrown Bulgaria."

No Real Reforms

Uncertainty plagues Western efforts to understand what is happening now in the Soviet Union. Gorbachev's obvious dissatisfaction with the performance of the system and his frequent speeches calling forcefully for reforms all testify to a determination to take a dramatically new approach to economic affairs. But declarations of intent mean little unless they are translated into policy, and policy that is made to stick. And it is here, on the various battlefields that determine the actual fate of an economic reform, that a picture, admittedly very fuzzy, is beginning to emerge. That image shows an approach to the Soviet economy that is far more traditional than Gorbachev's speeches would suggest and well short of the radical reforms he says he wants.

Ed A. Hewett, *Current*, March/April 1987.

The problem is not essentially a military one. "People who know," says Bialer, "are telling me that with regard to airplanes and missiles, the Russians are four years behind (the West). I think they are six years behind. Maybe they are eight years behind. But so what? The Russians are always behind, but they catch up—with enormous sacrifices—in the military field. It will cost them more. So what? They have a population that is ten times as hard in terms of sacrifices and is ten times more controlled by their government than America's."

But the sacrifices get harder and harder as the economy falls further and further behind. The ruling elite begins to suffer, not so much from fear of popular discontent but for reasons of security and prestige. The people may want consumer goods, but, says Bialer, "The elite think in different terms. Their standard of living is not stagnating. But they look at the situation where, for the first time in Soviet history, the Soviet Union, far from closing the gap with developed capitalist countries, is falling behind.

"The point is that the whole ideology and the whole sense of the Soviet Union as a global power is based on the assumption that this gap will be closing. And it is not. This is a major change. And a major crisis. And from this point of view, the reserves of growth that Gorbachev wants to exploit are totally insufficient."

Thus far Gorbachev has tinkered and temporized, hoping he can save the Stalinist system by squeezing more growth from it.

Work harder, drink less. Don't steal state property for private use. There are new incentives for research institutes to be more productive. There is a crackdown on drinking—"this in itself is probably worth 1% of labor productivity increase a year," says Bialer, "if you knew how Soviet workers and engineers were drinking at work."

But nowhere has Gorbachev gone further than his predecessors. Says Bialer: "You know, every year since Stalin's death (in 1953) there have been dozens of reforms, which I compare to elections. They try to fight the worst irrationalities of the economic system. But they do not change the basic structural characteristics of the system, which I describe in my current book: centralized planning, centralized command, the stress on quantity as opposed to quality, the passive role of money and credit, profits being really an accounting device rather than a measurement of effectiveness."

Arthur Hartman, the U.S. ambassador to the Soviet Union, once observed to a FORBES reporter that whereas the West was going through a technological revolution based largely on the free flow of information, the Soviet system presumes that information should be kept under lock and key and doled out only to a few.

Information Is Power

Bialer nods. "Information," he says, "is a part of power. A bureaucrat who has a particular knowledge of something will not part with this knowledge, because this knowledge is his leverage, his instrument of power.

"The photocopy machine, for example. You go to an institute of the Academy of Science and try to make a copy. Try to get a copy of anything. The machine is somewhere in a special room. Somebody is always there. You have to have a signature of somebody who is entitled to give a signature for making a copy. And you will wait quite a time until it is made.

"Let's take another example. Computers do not make sense unless connected with communications. All right, now look at the Moscow telephone net. Look how difficult it is to make a call. And this is in Moscow. Try to go to a small town and call up Moscow. You will wait two, three hours. Can you imagine those computers talking to each other in such a situation?

"Or take the question of software. I would be surprised if less than 90% of software in America comes from individual entrepreneurs and from small firms. In the Soviet Union—well, first of all, a man who would have the initiative to write a software program would have to have the computer. And there are no computers privately owned in the Soviet Union, not even word processors."

Don't Soviet managers ask for productivity-enhancing equipment, to help fulfill the ambitious planning targets set for them in Moscow? That, says Bialer, is to misunderstand entirely Soviet incentives.

Good Managers, Bad System

"Suppose that you are the director of the factory of nails. Instead of producing your plan of 10,000 tons of nails, you produce 10,300 tons. Next year you will receive a new plan that will be based on your overfulfillment of the plan this year. You are punished because you have overproduced.

"Now, one must be an idiot, in this situation, to be interested in overfulfillment of the plan or new technology. If a first-rate American manager were transferred to Moscow, within two weeks he would figure out what is good for him and would act exactly as the Soviet managers are acting. It is not that they steal or are uneducated or untalented. They are simply working within a system that does not reward talent and devotion and technological progress."

Economic Incompetence

In domestic policy, despite a blistering attack on Soviet economic incompetence and a call for "profound restructuring" of the economy, [Gorbachev's] campaign is against waste and inefficiency, and not for dismantling the deeply entrenched socialist infrastructure.

John Hughes, *The Christian Science Monitor*, June 21, 1985.

Stalinism is the cause of the problem, but to discard economic Stalinism after 60 years risks the disintegration of the modern Soviet empire, which has been held together only by force and centralized power. The Soviet Union is really a Russian empire ruling subject peoples. "A decentralization," explains Bialer, "would not be a devolution of power only among the Russians. It would be a devolution of power to ethnic groups, which compose 49% of the Soviet population, and this will encourage, if not secessionist, then at least centrifugal forces within the society."

Besides the empire, there are the tributary states in Eastern Europe. Recalling the direct link between Khrushchev's anti-Stalin speech to the Politburo in February 1956 and the Hungarian uprising later that year, Bialer asks: "If you have liberalization of the system in Russia, what conclusions will the people who want liberalization in Eastern Europe reach? They will take it to the nth degree."

Stalinist economics binds the empire together and keeps power firmly in the hands of the Communist aristocracy, but it freezes economic progress. Gorbachev has listened attentively to his economists' pleas to introduce market prices into the Soviet economy. . . .

"[Gorbachev] doesn't have the power to make the (really important) decisions. And he has still, in my opinion, illusions that lesser reforms can repair the system. In my opinion, they will improve, slightly, the economy's performance, but they will not repair its basic backwardness compared to us."

A Prisoner of Russian History

Gorbachev, then, is not so much a dictator as he is a prisoner of the Stalinist system. And not only of the system but of Russian history as well. Says Bialer: "My proposition is that the autocratic, nondemocratic, centralized type of Soviet system did not go against the Russian tradition. Very simply, in the entire Russian history, from the beginning until today, there was not one day that they had a democratic regime. Not one day."

Hoping the system will magically rejuvenate but probably aware that it cannot, Gorbachev needs to deliver something. Freezing the arms race would take pressure off the economy, buy time for the system he represents. It would also enable the Red Army's generals to sleep more soundly. All of which means that an arms deal may be in the offing—one that the U.S. can accept. Says Bialer: "The Soviets have found out that, despite all their strategic parity with the U.S., we are on the verge of a new arms race where technology will play a higher role. Their (military) security will be in danger. Never in the past 20 years did they want arms control as badly as today."

Distinguishing Between Fact And Opinion

This activity is designed to help develop the basic reading and thinking skill of distinguishing between fact and opinion. Consider the following statement as an example: "The USSR's average annual national income increased between 1951 and 1981 by 7.1 percent." This statement is a fact that can be confirmed by comparing the data on national incomes over a 30-year period. But consider this statement: "The essential goal of the Soviet economy is not economic growth, not a general increase in production, not even a rise in productivity or profit, but the functioning of a mighty military machine." This statement is clearly an expressed opinion. Many people who see the economic imbalance weighted in favor of the military would agree, but others may not.

When investigating controversial issues it is important that one be able to distinguish between statements of fact and statements of opinion. It is also important to recognize that not all statements of fact are true. They may appear to be true, but some are based on inaccurate or false information. For this activity, however, we are concerned with understanding the difference between those statements which appear to be factual and those which appear to be based primarily on opinion.

Most of the following statements are taken from the viewpoints in this chapter. Consider each statement carefully. *Mark O for any statement you believe is an opinion or interpretation of facts. Mark F for any statement you believe is a fact.*

If you are doing this activity as a member of a class or group, compare your answers with those of other class or group members. Be able to defend your answers. You may discover that others will come to different conclusions than you. Listening to the reasons others present for their answers may give you valuable insights in distinguishing between fact and opinion.

1. Soviet fixed production rates grew sevenfold in the last 25 years.

2. The Soviet Union can no longer depend on using additional natural resources to sustain high growth rates.

3. The primary causes for negative economic trends result from mistakes and flawed economic management.

4. In 1985 alone, 23,000 new inventions were put into use in the Soviet economy.

5. Reforms in Soviet agriculture would reduce the power of bureaucrats and agricultural managers.

6. It is safer for the USSR to maintain socialist farming than to admit the failure of the communist system.

7. The Soviet man can expect to live only 60 years, six years less than in the mid 1960s.

8. The USSR is responsible for only 12 or 13 percent of the world's GNP.

9. The growth rates of Soviet labor productivity have increased over the past two years.

10. Glasnost will imperil the spirit of the free world.

11. Radical reformation of the pricing system is the most important part of the economic restructuring.

12. The standard of living of the Soviet elite is not declining.

13. **Cracking down on alcoholism would increase Soviet labor productivity by about one percent per year.**

14. There are no privately-owned computers in the USSR.

15. Gorbachev is a prisoner of the Stalinist system.

16. Lack of high technology will endanger the USSR's military security.

17. In 1965 only four percent of the Soviet population earned more than 100 rubles per month.

Periodical Bibliography

The following articles have been selected to supplement the diverse views expressed in this chapter.

Seweryn Bialer and Joan Afferica
"The Genesis of Gorbachev's World," *Foreign Affairs*, special issue, vol. 64, no. 3, 1986.

Igor Birman
"Soviet Bluster Stems from Economic Decay," *The Wall Street Journal*, December 23, 1983.

Pavel Bunich
"Economy: Total Reconstruction," *Soviet Life*, November 1986.

Charles Gati
"Soviet Empire: Alive but Not Well," *Problems of Communism*, March/April 1985.

Marshall I. Goldman
"Gorbachev's Risk in Reforming the Soviet Economy," *Technology Review*, April 1986.

Alice C. Gorlin
"The Soviet Economy," *Current History*, October 1986.

Vladimir Gurevich
"Reform and Law," *Soviet Life*, June 1987.

Ed A. Hewett
"Is It Reform or Rhetoric? Gorbachev and the Soviet Economy," *Current*, March/April 1987.

David Ignatius
"He's Young, Gifted and Wants To Get the Country Moving Again," *The Washington Post National Weekly Edition*, May 4, 1987.

Mark Isaacs
"Genuine Reform, or Superficial PR?" *The New American*, August 3, 1987.

Bill Keller
"In Soviet, Capitalism," *The New York Times*, May 1, 1987.

John Pearson
"Gorbachev's Russia," *Business Week*, November 11, 1985.

Vladimir Shlapentokh
"Fewer Rubles Under the Table," *The New York Times*, June 18, 1986.

Russell Watson
"Gorbachev's Opposition," *Newsweek*, May 18, 1987.

Reiner Weichhardt
"The Soviet Economy—A New Course?" *NATO Review*, June 1987.

What Is the Soviet Union's Role in Eastern Europe?

the
SOVIET
UNION

Chapter Preface

The Soviet Union began a reform period in 1956 when the new
Soviet Premier Nikita Khrushchev spoke at the twentieth Congress
of the Soviet Communist Party. He denounced the excesses of former
leader Josef Stalin. Khrushchev's speech led to reforms in Soviet
policy that were echoed in communist Eastern Europe. But Eastern
Europe's liberalization had unforeseen consequences. That year
witnessed a major disturbance in Hungary, where rioting for more
reforms led to a Soviet invasion to counter this trend. The Hungarian
invasion precipitated a continuing debate on the Soviet role in the
Eastern bloc. Western observers point to it and subsequent upris-
ings in Czechoslovakia in 1968 and Poland in 1980 as proof that the
Soviets control a captive yet rebellious population in Eastern Europe.
Dissidents in Eastern Europe and in exile argue that their countries
would have democratic, popular governments were it not for Soviet
domination. Soviet and Eastern European leaders disagree; they
believe that the Soviets deserve gratitude for the help they extended in rebuilding Eastern Europe's war-damaged economies. They
argue further that these are independent countries that have chosen
to emulate the Soviet model of socialism.

Viewpoints from communist party officials, opposition leaders,
Western and Soviet scholars, and journalists are included in the
following chapter. They have very different interpretations of recent
events in Eastern Europe. These differing views are indicative of
the controversy surrounding Soviet influence in Eastern Europe.

"Friendship with the Soviet Union meets with the vital interests of each socialist country."

The Soviet Union Has Been a Model for Eastern Europe

Marian Orzechowski

Marian Orzechowski writes in the following viewpoint that since liberating Eastern Europe from the Nazis, the Soviets have continued to play a positive role there. Alliance with the Soviets, solidified in the Warsaw Pact, has helped socialist countries develop and has maintained peace in Europe. Orzechowski has been a history professor and a member of the Central Committee of the Polish United Workers Party. In 1985, he became Poland's foreign minister.

As you read, consider the following questions:

1. What factors led to the alliance of Central and Southeastern Europe with the Soviets after World War II, according to the author?
2. Why does the author believe the disarmament efforts of Warsaw Treaty nations are important?
3. According to Orzechowski, how has friendship with the Soviets helped Poland?

Marian Orzechowski, "Warsaw Treaty in the European Context," *World Marxist Review*, Vol. 30, No. 3 March 1987. Reprinted with permission.

The European socialist countries signed the Treaty of Friendship, Cooperation and Mutual Assistance, known as the Warsaw Treaty, in Poland's capital on May 14, 1955. This inaugurated the military-political organisation which has since then been a dependable instrument safeguarding the national and collective security of the fraternal countries against the threat of imperialist aggression. Moreover, it has become the vehicle strengthening peace in Europe....

Our interaction was initiated and grew strong in the struggle against fascism, when the forces championing national liberation relied on the assistance of the Red Army and cooperated with it. This cooperation enabled countries of Central and Southeastern Europe to restore their independence and then begin a wide-ranging transformation of their political and socio-economic structures.

As it became increasingly clear that the people's democratic states had external and domestic aims in common, cooperation among them took shape in defence, which was institutionalised by bilateral treaties of friendship, cooperation and mutual assistance (more than 30 of these treaties were signed in the period up to the close of the 1940s). These allow identifying two phases in the process of forming the defensive system of the countries of Central and Southeastern Europe. In the period from 1943 to the beginning of 1947 allied relations took shape among a group of states (the Soviet Union, Poland, Yugoslavia, and Czechoslovakia) that belonged to the Anti-Hitlerite Coalition and were members of the United Nations. In the second phase (end of 1947-beginning of 1949), these relations spread to Bulgaria, Romania, and Hungary that by then had embarked upon revolutionary transformations.

Soviet Help

The system of bilateral treaties was given colossal international weight by the participation in it of the Soviet Union, a socialist state whose might was already then a major material factor countering imperialism's aggressive designs.

In the life of peoples and states no issue is more crucial than security. It is the cornerstone of their existence. Experience has shown that *solid foundations of national security can only be built by a progressive social system with a high level of economic development and civilisation dependably backed up by a system of international alliances consistent with the interests of the member-countries.* The consolidation of our people's independence, our society's development, and the maintenance of our territorial integrity and state sovereignty have been and remain among the cardinal concerns of Poland's domestic and foreign policies.

Prior to and during the Second World War the nation's left-wing forces formulated the basic principles of its postwar policy. Conspicuous among these principles were those that provided for restoring independence and ensuring abiding security. Moreover, the Polish Communists advocated the formation of new international alliances, notably with the USSR. The 42 years that have elapsed since the victory over Nazi Germany have shown that the successful fulfillment of Poland's development plans and the strengthening of its international positions depend to a very large extent on the solidity of its fraternal links and on mutually beneficial cooperation with the Soviet Union and the other countries of our community.

Poland is situated between Western and Eastern Europe. Winds of war have blown across our country time and again, and the specificity of defence in this situation is that our national security is linked firmly to European security. The Soviet Union was interested in seeing a strong, independent, and democratic Polish state. The conclusion of military-political alliances between the USSR and its closest neighbours was regarded by it as a means of erecting a barrier to aggression and the outbreak of another war in that part of Europe. . . .

A Peaceful Continent

Europe has been living at peace [for] over four decades. For more than 40 years our planet hasn't seen the nightmare of a global war. Much of the credit must go to the Warsaw Treaty. The Warsaw Treaty secures the post-war frontiers of the European continent, preserves the constructive civilian labour of the fraternal socialist countries' peoples, and bolsters their international prestige. The member-states of this defensive alliance have put forward outstanding peace initiatives to strengthen international security, avert nuclear war and see the world disarm.

Ivan Lyutov, *Soviet Military Review,* May 1987.

The signing of the Warsaw Treaty gave a fresh impetus to the socialist community's peace strategy. The member-states concentrated their joint actions, coordinated in the Political Consultative Committee, in the main areas of international relations and sought to put them into effect through the United Nations, the Disarmament Committee, and various forms of socio-economic and cultural contacts. As soon as it was set up the Warsaw Treaty Organisation began pressing for recognition of peaceful coexistence as the basic principle regulating relations between states. Here special significance was and still is attached to Soviet-US relations. The principle of peaceful coexistence was included in the Basic Principles of Relations Between the USA and the USSR signed in May 1972. Further, the Warsaw Treaty member-states worked for détente in Europe based on recognition of political realities: the immutability of postwar frontiers and the existence of two equal German states.

Multiple efforts have been made by our community to achieve disarmament. In keeping with socialism's ideals, the fraternal countries are endeavouring to exclude war from the arsenal of means for settling disputes. *Today, when science used for military purposes has developed pre-eminently accurate weapons of enormous destructive power, general disarmament and equal security for all are the only reasonable alternatives to war....*

An extremely promising way to scale down the arms race and eliminate nuclear weapons is to create nuclear-free zones. The socialist countries have been consistently urging this in the course of the past 30 years. Poland, in particular, has put forward many initiatives aimed at normalising the political situation and downgrading the military confrontation level in Europe. The idea of creating a nuclear-free zone in Central Europe was suggested as early as 1957 by the Rapacki Plan. Although the idea was not accepted at the time there was a wide response and it later crystallised in other regions of the world. Lastly, in 1963 Poland came forward with a proposal known as the Gomulka Plan, which called for a freeze on nuclear armaments in Central Europe in order to avert the build up of a nuclear potential in this most vulnerable part of the continent.

Constructive Initiatives

At its meeting in 1986 the Warsaw Treaty Committee of Foreign Ministers called for the creation of nuclear-free zones in various regions in Europe and a nuclear-free corridor along the line of contact between NATO and the Warsaw Treaty Organisation. This idea thus continues to live and its realisation may become the first major step towards the total elimination of nuclear stockpiles.

At the different ongoing and future forums, for instance, the Conference on European Security and Cooperation, People's Poland will, in line with the traditions of its foreign policy, continue advancing constructive initiatives to remove the threat overhanging humanity.

In the 1970s the Warsaw Treaty member-states focused their coordinated foreign policy efforts mainly on convening a conference on security and cooperation in Europe. Poland was one of the initiators of the epoch-making meeting in Helsinki. That conference adopted most of the theses and concepts worked out and put forward by the socialist countries. While we assess the Helsinki results as a success, we consider that further collective efforts are needed to augment political détente with military détente so as to make the impulse towards improving the situation in Europe irreversible....

The Congress of the fraternal parties, including the Tenth Congress of the [Polish United Workers Party] PUWP (1986), made a large contribution to blueprinting the socialist community's programme for cutting short the negative trends in international relations and restoring détente. The actions of the socialist countries are motivated by their sincere desire to settle European problems through the dismantling, not strengthening, of military blocs, through the consolidation of peaceful cooperation among all the nations of the continent.

A Unified Community

The European socialist countries attach considerable significance to their political cooperation, to their multilateral efforts to ensure security and peace. This was what led to the formation in 1976 of a new body of the Warsaw Treaty Organisation, the Committee of Foreign Ministers, in which the allies consider the international situation and work out the political ways and means of attaining their aims. The mechanism of cooperation is being upgraded: the Political Consultative Committee is meeting more often, consultations and working meetings of Foreign Ministers are held, working groups are set up to consider specific issues, and so on.

The undeviating striving of the Warsaw Treaty member-states to reinforce the community's unity and cohesion is of no little importance for the steadfast implementation of the principles of peaceful coexistence of countries with different social systems. Today, when the situation in the world has deteriorated perceptibly, interaction within the Warsaw Treaty Organisation is an essential condition for attaining the alliance's principal objective, that of ensuring world peace.

Socialism's Appeal

Since the second world war decisive changes in the world balance of forces have been brought about by the fact that the socialist system, first established in the U.S.S.R., has become a world system. . . .

The social and economic progress of the Soviet Union and the other socialist countries, and the international authority of our community add to the appeal of socialism and provide a reliable bulwark for every progressive and peace-loving movement. I believe therefore that the most important thing for the socialist community at present is that our countries, separately and together, should further reveal the advantages of the socialist system.

Janos Kadar, *New Times*, no. 41, October 20, 1986.

The period of more than 30 years that has elapsed since the Warsaw Treaty Organisation was formed has forcefully shown that it has an immense role to play in building unshakable foundations of peace and security. The influence of the Warsaw Treaty Organisation is seen in the work of its leading bodies and also in the work of the United Nations, the Disarmament Committee, and other international agencies.

The socialist community took shape on the durable foundation of Marxism-Leninism and internationalism, and of the common basic aims of the fraternal countries. *The strengthening of the unity and solidarity of the members of our military-political alliance, particularly friendship with the Soviet Union, meets with the vital interests of each socialist country and is the condition for their successful development.* The fact that peace has reigned in Europe for more than 40 years and the recognition in international law of the postwar territorial and political realities in Europe show the effectiveness of the Warsaw Treaty.

A Reliable Member

We have always declared that Poland is a reliable member of the Warsaw Treaty Organisation. This has been further reaffirmed in the decisions of the PUWP's Tenth Congress: "Poland's membership in the military-political Warsaw Treaty Organisation is of fundamental significance for Polish state interests. The Polish People's Armed Forces will continue to contribute to the aggregate defensive potential of the Warsaw Treaty. The Polish state will participate actively in coordinating foreign policy within the framework of this alliance and in collective actions on the international scene."

*"The intervention of a victorious Soviet Union...
effectively checked and halted the evolution of
democracy in central and eastern Europe."*

The Soviet Union Has Stifled Eastern Europe

Ladislav Hejdánek

Ladislav Hejdánek was an activist during the Prague Spring—a period
of liberalization and reform in Czechoslovakia in 1968. In August
1968, the Soviet Union and other Warsaw Pact countries invaded
Czechoslovakia. Shortly after, when an orthodox communist government came to power, Hejdánek lost his position at the Philosophical
Institute of the Czechoslovak Academy of Sciences. Since then he
has worked as a nightwatchman, a porter, and a clerk, while continuing to be a leader in the human rights movement. In the following viewpoint, Hejdánek argues that Soviet socialism has become
a system that justifies expansionism and dictates people's lives. He
concludes that a unified human rights movement is necessary to
transform Soviet-style socialism to a more democratic system that
respects individual freedom.

As you read, consider the following questions:

1. What group of people does the author mean when he refers
   to "democratic forces" in Eastern bloc countries?
2. How has socialism deviated from its roots, according to
   Hejdánek?

Excerpts from "Prospects for Democracy and Socialism in Eastern Europe," by Ladislav
Hejdánek, in *The Power of the Powerless: Citizens Against the State in Central-Eastern Europe.*
Reprinted by permission of M.E. Sharpe, Inc., Armonk, New York 10504.

The intervention of a victorious Soviet Union at the end of the Second World War, during which it had been transformed into a world power, effectively checked and halted the evolution of democracy in central and eastern Europe; this region now found itself part of a widened Soviet sphere of influence as a result of the new political settlement in Europe. Czechoslovakia was arguably the worst hit, after having remained a firm bastion of democracy in central Europe throughout both the inter-war decades. During the last quarter of a century, however, the political, cultural, social and even economic situations in the European countries of the Soviet bloc have grown to resemble each other to such a degree that, for the foreseeable future, the trend towards convergence seems likely to prevail over tendencies to assert national peculiarities. This represents a significant change. Until now, all attempts to counteract the compulsory Soviet archetype and assert a degree of autonomy have based themselves on the specific conditions of the individual national societies. Henceforth, they will be in a position to refer to generalized conditions when confronting directives rooted in the remnants of the political and social anomaly of Russian autocracy. It is high time to jettison, once and for all, the idea that the democratic forces in the individual Soviet bloc countries should concentrate on asssserting some sort of independent path, some kind of 'private' emancipation from the Kremlin's economic and political control and governance. It is necessary to examine the issue in terms of political power, and to concentrate on co-operation between the democratic forces of all the countries concerned. It must be absolutely plain that it is not the goal of the democratic forces to destroy the bloc (or socialism, for that matter) but, rather, to achieve democratic transformations in the social, economic and political life of all countries of so-called 'existing socialism'. And in support of this goal, it is essential to unite the democratic forces in the individual countries on a genuinely democratic footing and, if possible, by democratic means. . . .

If our countries are to count on a future better than their past and their present, thought must be given to more than mere methods of political conflict. The greatest failure of socialist programmes to date, and particularly of the Bolshevik revolution, was that they did not tackle the question of what the new society was to look like and, above all, what sort of person was going to feel at home in it (nor, for that matter, did they do anything to ensure that anyone could feel at home in it).

Socialist Deviations

This is all linked to the need to re-evaluate the roots of the socialist movement and to seek the reasons for its numerous failures and cases of outright deviation. By now, it must be obvious to all thinking people that socialism is the offspring of liberal-democratic tradi-

KAL. 1987 Cartoonists & Writers Syndicate.

tions and is far from capable of prefiguring, or of even presenting itself as, a new historical epoch or, as Marx and his supporters thought, a new socio-economic system. Socialism's historical justification is its extrapolation of democratic principles into social and economic realms and its practical implementation of them. Socialism is democracy taken to all its conclusions in every field. Whenever the settlement of social demands has been violently divorced from its democratic roots, and whenever democratic structures have been abolished in the name of social progress, or deprived of any real meaning, socialism has entered a historical blind alley and become a negative example to all who might seek to follow in its footsteps. In order to conceal the true facts about such deviant socialism, the socialist programme was transformed into an ideology capable of acting as a cover even for expansionism, using socialism and socialist feelings as a strategic weapon, i.e., as an instrument. At the same time, the social realities of so-called 'existing socialism' had to be hidden as far as possible from view, so as to minimize control and inspection. This was the principal motivation behind drawing the so-called iron curtain (which was not at all a defence against subversion or espionage). And even after so many appalling revelations, the fear that the veil might be lifted on the internal social and political situation in extensive areas of the Soviet Union constitutes the chief obstacle to extending economic and cultural ties beyond a strictly official and narrowly selective minimum.

It will therefore be necessary to subject socialist ideology to the severest and most open criticism from within in order to expose its fraudulent and mendacious pretentions and, instead, rehabilitate its genuine roots and the true core of socialism as the social implementation of democracy's political principles. There must be a radical effort to take the ideology out of socialism. And, of course, this must not fail to tackle the democratic programme and its fundamental principles, for democracy as well as socialism has failed on many occasions. . . .

Economic Liberation

In the countries of so-called 'existing socialism' (and not only there), the state has taken over the entire economic life of the nation and, in so doing, has forced every individual and the whole of society into a state of dependence and subjection. The purpose of human rights campaigns was, at the outset, to establish the bounds beyond which all state and government intervention ceases to be legitimate and legal: in short, to prevent the political enslavement of the citizen. It has turned out that the defence of civil and human rights must be looked at in a much wider sense: the citizen is also in need of economic liberation. So-called 'existing socialism' may well have freed citizens from want, but it did so by increasing their economic and, therefore, their general social dependence. The root cause of this failure and deviation of socialism was the linking of the machinery of state and its political structures with a country's economic structures. In accordance with the trend towards total control over society at every level, the state also gained ascendancy in other major fields, such as culture, scientific and technical research, the media, education, such that it now increasingly penetrates the private lives of citizens through every channel. There is only one way to right this: by emancipating civil society from domination by the state and its machinery. And this can only be achieved by completely emancipating every main area of civil society, starting with the workplace. As a complement to the old and, in general, well-tested separation of powers and the decentralization of the state machine, it is necessary to separate culture, information and communication media, education, etc., from the state, on the same lines as the church/state separation. A consequence of this will be that the economic organization of a country will assume greater importance, since it is a task which is impossible without a certain degree of central control; the dangers inherent in this can only be avoided by means of thorough-going democratization, i.e., the establishment of self-managing bodies at every level, and the systematic separation of all economic structures from the field of government control. . . .

Democracy and socialism both have their roots in Europe, and not only in its political, but above all in its spiritual and moral traditions. There are hopeful signs that as a result of the progressive decline of these traditions (a phenomenon which can be explained partly as a temporary outcome of social and historical upheavals and shifts), Europe will be the first to realize the need to move into a new phase of the centuries-old struggle for basic human freedom and inalienable human rights. And since it is immediately obvious that in the course of this continuing fight the existing states will look on the defenders of these rights and freedoms as a threat to their power, there will be a vital need to make every effort to achieve understanding between groups and movements of this type across state frontiers and, above all, beyond the blocs. If the trend towards international *détente* can be maintained, and progress can be made in talks about European security and co-operation, and if, in other parts of the world, the forces of peace succeed in isolating and extinguishing the hotbeds of tension and conflict, perhaps we can look forward with hope to the day when, in Europe itself, we witness the liberation of society from total state domination and the emergence of a situation precluding the centralization of the means of production, which have for so long been kept out of people's hands and removed from human ends by governments. Perhaps then we would see the end of the division of Europe. This could in turn set an example to other parts of the world of how to construct a society in which peace will not only be preserved superficially but also inwardly, on the basis of the thorough-going democratization of all aspects of life, not only in political terms, but also in the broadest economic and social sense. This will be inconceivable without the emancipation of the overwhelming majority of the lives of societies and individuals from the clutches of *dirigisme* and control by the machinery of state. Furthermore, this will not be achieved without the patient struggle of creative people and defenders of fundamental human values, a process that can only be jeopardized by political agitation, organization, coercion and violence. These human values, and these values alone, justify the battle for human freedoms and rights. Democratic political, social and economic structures have as their highest purpose the creation of a space in which to bring these values to life and introduce and assert them in the lives of individuals and societies alike: in the lives of free individuals and free societies.

*"The basic Soviet command economy model,
with central planning and party control,...
continues to prevail in Eastern Europe."*

Soviet Domination Harms Eastern Europe's Economies

Herbert J. Ellison

Economic problems have often been cited as a cause of discontent in Eastern Europe. In the following viewpoint, Herbert J. Ellison argues that Eastern European economies depend on Western technology and Soviet subsidies to function. Improving the economies, however, requires wide-ranging economic reforms, according to Ellison. The Soviet Union will not allow reforms, he contends, which means that Eastern Europe's economies will continue to suffer from the failings of Soviet socialism. Ellison is a professor of history and Russian and Eastern European studies at the University of Washington in Seattle.

As you read, consider the following questions:

1. How have economic reforms threatened the political system in Eastern Europe, according to the author?
2. How does Ellison believe Soviet subsidies will affect the Soviet-Eastern European alliance in the long-run?

"On Eastern Europe: The Economics of Power" by Herbert J. Ellison, reprinted from *Parameters*, Vol. XIV, No. 2 (June 1984), pp. 15-23. Reprinted with the author's permission.

The period from the Soviet invasion of Czechoslovakia in 1968 to the Polish revolution and counterrevolution of 1980-81 contains some of the most dramatic and important political developments in the history of postwar Eastern Europe. The entry of Soviet troops into Prague shattered the hopes that the Czech "Spring" had nurtured for a comprehensive transformation of political and economic institutions in that country, one which would create a new order that the Czechs longingly described as "socialism with a human face." Curious as it seems, the Czechs and Slovaks genuinely believed that they would succeed where the Hungarians had failed, that the Soviets would accept their peaceful transformation of Czechoslovak institutions precisely because it would be peaceful and because the reformed state would remain loyal to the Warsaw Pact. Similar illusions reappeared in Poland in 1980-81. It was thought that by not challenging the primacy of the party, but rather reforming (i.e. "democratizing") the party internally, one could achieve a peaceful transformation of Polish socialism and avoid Czechoslovakia's failure.

The shattering of such illusions, whether by direct external military intervention or by internal declaration of martial law, is one of the most important consequences of the tumultuous events of the past 15 years. In one sense these events represent a victory for communism on the Soviet model and for Soviet power in Eastern Europe. It is an uncertain victory, and it remains to be seen whether political stability can be reestablished in Poland. But at least for the moment, it appears that fundamental change will not be accomplished by political revolution, peaceful or violent, and that the familiar systems are again intact.

Yet it is precisely these systems that generated the political crises, and will do so again and again until fundamental changes are made. The central questions, therefore, as much for internal leaders as for external observers, are: what are the fundamental changes needed to avert future crises and what evidence is there of them being made?

Basic Economic Changes Needed

The most essential of those needed changes are in economic organization and policy. This may seem too obvious a proposition, yet much of the political analysis of East European events, both in Eastern Europe and outside, gives scant attention to the precise interaction of economics and politics, and Western economic analysis justifiably limits its concern with politics to the direct effect of political developments upon economic change. It is the argument of the present essay that the experience of postwar Eastern Europe, particularly the recent years, demonstrates a repetitive pattern of weakness in basic economic institutions which is ultimately the most important ingredient in the recurrent political crisis. It is further argued that with the notable exception of Hungary none of these states has made significant progress toward a solution to the prob-

177

lem, that the reasons are to be found in political institutions and policies, and that the problem has reached a new and more dangerous form, particularly for the more industrially advanced countries, because rapid changes in the world economy, into which they have been progressively and disruptively integrated, have gravely aggravated existing internal weaknesses.

The past 10 to 12 years have been a period of severe trial for the economies of Eastern Europe—not the first such period since the introduction of the Soviet model of socialist command economy, and probably not the last—but among the most complex and difficult to manage. Economic crisis has, of course, been a recurrent theme in East European life for the past three decades, and often with momentous political consequences. Behind each of the recurrent political explosions—in East Germany, Czechoslovakia, Hungary, and Poland—lay an economic crisis, one that played either a primary or a supplementary role in a major political eruption....

The Paradox of Soviet Aid

Soviet relations with the empire in Eastern Europe have experienced a number of ironic developments over the past two decades. First, the Soviets established political and economic dominance in the region by creating derivative regimes headed by externally dependent elites; as a result, the Soviet role within the bloc has eventually evolved from one of coercion to one of captivity....The Soviets faced an intractable dilemma. The absence of Soviet aid would mean certain political instability and economic deterioration throughout the system, which would harm the Soviet economy, perhaps undercut Soviet domestic political stability, and certainly spell the end of the empire as East Germany, Poland, and Czechoslovakia faced mass unrest. On the other hand, Soviet aid merely whetted appetites in the periphery for more rubles and linked political stability even more closely to consumption and growth—and therefore to infusions of Soviet aid.

Valerie Bunce, *International Organization,* Winter 1985.

As in the Soviet Union, the kinds of East European economic reform proposed in the early 1960s came to be seen as carrying with them unacceptable political implications. The economic decentralization recommended by reformers meant more than simply a rational scheme of economic management; it meant the loss to central party and government authorities of decisive powers in production planning and resource allocation and challenged a wide range of vested interests in the main economic ministries. The resistance to reform was therefore very strong, and the main objective of the leadership was to find means of extracting greater production from the existing economic system.

The search for a means to restore economic growth without structural changes in the economy led to formation of the main program of the 1970s—massive importation of Western technology financed by borrowing from Western banks and governments. The intention was to raise the level of efficiency of the East European economies by improving capital stock and productivity and then to repay the accumulated indebtedness from export earnings. The availability of funds for borrowing vastly exceeded expectations, thanks to large loanable reserves in Western banks created by the OPEC quadrupling of oil prices in 1974. The result was a massive growth of the East European debt to the West, rising from $6 billion in 1970 to $55.8 billion in 1980. But in several important ways the scheme of the East European economic planners failed to work out, and the eventual consequences were extremely grave.

The new technology imported from the West did not provide the expected rapid rise in productive efficiency, as the factors supporting productivity rises from technological innovation in Western market economies were absent. And meanwhile the imported technology imposed new costs in hard currency for Western raw materials and semi-manufactures, costs which it became increasingly hard to meet as the decade and the indebtedness advanced. Complicating these problems, the Western economic recession from 1975 on reduced markets for East European exports, exports which were already often insufficiently competitive because of production costs or quality.

The Soviet Price Increase

In this context, when all factors seemed to move against the East European economic position, a further complication was added by the Soviet decision to raise prices of crude oil and other key raw materials exported to Eastern Europe, beginning in 1975. The long-term price contracts were replaced with annual price agreements, and oil prices were more than doubled. As East European terms of trade with the West and with Third World countries had already deteriorated, the cumulative effect of these negative changes was immensely damaging. East European political leaders were, however, slow to change their economic policies in response to the negative trends, choosing to rely on Soviet trade subsidies and Western credits to meet current needs rather than risking the political costs of lowering growth rates. But the USSR, drawn by rising world market prices, sought to ship increasing quantities of fuels and nonfood raw materials to hard currency markets, reducing the supplies available to Eastern Europe and forcing East European leaders to make hard currency purchases at high prices on world markets.

Over the course of the period from 1972 to 1981 the Soviets and the Western countries provided enormous sums of money to the East European economies—approximately $162.5 billion. The Western share of this sum was $51.7 billion accumulated as debt by the latter year, while the Soviets provided nearly $102 billion in implicit subsidies (goods provided at below world market values) and an additional $6.9 billion in ruble credits.

Soviet Subsidies

The willingness of the USSR to provide enormously expanded economic subsidies to the East European economies during this period is an important point for analysis. The expansion was a direct function of rising Soviet prices charged to East European purchasers, prices which lagged far behind world oil prices, so that implicit subsidies rose with each jump in world oil prices. Thus the subsidies rose nearly fourfold between 1973 and 1974, and then nearly trebled between 1978 and 1980. Accounting for 2.8 percent of the East European GNP, the subsidies were provided mainly as crucial shipments of energy and key raw materials. . . .

Clearly the subsidies represented (and represent) an enormous cost to the Soviet economy. But the pressures upon the East European economies in that period were heavy, and their potential political impact great. Soviet leaders were well aware of past political consequences of serious economic failure in Eastern Europe, and therefore were willing to pay a heavy price to avoid it. Strategically, the East European glacis was the foundation of Soviet strategic power in Europe—a broad territorial buffer, a location of Soviet forward

Dick Locher. Reprinted by permission: Tribune Media Services.

military bases, and an important source of military manpower. Politically, the East European ruling party leaderships remained dutifully accepting of Soviet international policy, and their heavy economic dependence upon the USSR—for imports of energy and nonfood raw materials and for receipt of East European exports—helped greatly to ensure their acceptance of Soviet leadership among communist parties, governing and nongoverning.

Future Prospects

The long-term effect of Soviet trade subsidy policy has been to sustain East European economic dependence upon the Soviet Union. The foundation of that dependence is, in the first instance, Soviet insistence upon retention of a fundamentally inefficient economic system built upon the Soviet model. But the problem has been further complicated by Soviet trade subsidies which provided oil and gas, even at the beginning of the 1980s, at prices lower than world levels, thus encouraging continued inefficient use of energy and the dependence which went with it. . . .

What are the future prospects for Eastern Europe and the Soviet-East European relationship? To find an answer to this question one must go again to the heart of the matter—the close tie between politics and economics in the East European system. Economic failures have engendered repeated crises which have in turn brought political crises. In the crises of 1956, 1968, and 1980-81 the opposition, within and outside the communist party, insisted on both political *and* economic reform. In each case the Soviets used direct and/or indirect intervention to control the process, seeking mainly to prevent change in the structure of the communist party (replacement of democratic centralism by authentic democracy) and to retain party control of power over the main institutions and activities of economic, social, and cultural life.

From the mid-1950s to the present the Soviets have demonstrated willingness to tolerate extensive changes in economic organization—from decollectivization of management and restoration of profit and markets in Hungary. They have not tolerated changes in the fundamental political system. It was the threat to party dictatorship under Imre Nagy and Alexander Dubcek, in Hungary and Czechoslovakia, and the acceptance of democratic elections and free industrial and agricultural unions in Poland that brought Soviet military intervention in the first two cases and internal declaration of martial law in the third. The leadership of Solidarity and the reformist wing of the Polish United Workers' Party (PUWP) were no less naive than Dubcek and Nagy in their estimate of the degree of change the Soviets would tolerate. And it was not just the Soviets. In each situation there remained at least a significant core of their own party leadership supporting the Soviet view and prepared to collaborate with the Kremlin (though not for some months in the

Czech case), not to mention the cooperation of fellow Warsaw Pact leaders who feared as much as the Soviets the challenge of the political changes their neighbors were undertaking.

The Wrong Structure

When the structural flaws of the social system have become obvious, it is becoming increasingly clear how wrong it was to impose an economic and political system molded under the specific conditions of post-czarist Russia upon the countries of Eastern Europe, with their completely different structures. . . .

Soviet authorities have never permitted the central powers to lose control of the economy. Although planning techniques and the organization of administration have improved considerably over the course of time, the economic system itself has not changed. A few countries with planned economies have dared to undertake radical changes in the economic steering system, under pressure of mass movements, but they have never been able to "maintain order in the midst of change, and change in the midst of order." This applies both to the revolutionary movement in Poland and Hungary in 1956, to Czechoslovakia in 1968, and, especially, to events in Poland in 1980 and 1981. The geopolitical factor has played a decisive role in the suppression of these revolutionary movements, for the Soviet leadership is convinced that the maintenance of "universally valid rules of order" is an indispensable precondition for Eastern integration.

Adam Zwass, *The Economies of Eastern Europe in a Time of Change,* 1984.

In effect, then, the Soviet position—and that of the dominant communist leaderships throughout Eastern Europe—has been that economic reform was acceptable and political reform was not. The Polish experience in 1980-81 was only the latest in a long series of demonstrations of that crucial point. The question often posed in the past was whether it was possible to have economic reform without political reform. Since with the partial exception of Hungary the repudiation of political reform has been followed by the abandonment of economic reform, the answer appears to be no. The economic system is not a separable component of a larger economic and political/administrative structure. It is an integral part of it—in structure and in policy. The bureaucratic structure that controls and regulates the economy is a party-dominated structure. The bureaucratic vested interests and ideologically founded policies have their nerve center in the party apparatus, and since significant reform must challenge such interests and policies it is virtually certain to be resisted or repudiated. Thus the basic Soviet command economy model, with central planning and party control of economic power

182

levers, continues to prevail in Eastern Europe, not just because the Soviets favor it but also because it has a powerful structure of internal administrative vested interests to defend it . . . .

The Soviets are faced with the enormous cost of subsidizing the East European economies. It is impressive to observe how much they have had to pay to absorb the enormous costs of Eastern Europe's economic crisis as it developed in the 1970s. Measured in implicit subsidies and trade surpluses, Soviet support of East European economies grew from $500 million in 1972 to $15 billion in 1982. During 1980-82, Poland alone cost $7 billion, and even the latest rise in intra-CMEA oil prices in 1982-83 left the Soviets with a huge annual subsidy to Eastern Europe. Combined with a $6 billion annual subsidy to Cuba and Vietnam, the total Soviet subsidy to these allied communist states represents a formidable expense. And the expense is incurred at precisely the time when the Soviets are experiencing severe capital shortages. Oil and gas exports to Eastern Europe represent not only subsidies, but also hard currency earnings forfeited. Meanwhile, the pressure upon Soviet economic planners to find investment capital for all needs, to maintain hard currency earnings, and also to meet the huge cost of subsidizing the economies of Eastern Europe poses a formidable challenge.

Politically Necessary Subsidies

The changing pattern of subsidies since the advent of the Polish crisis shows a clear Soviet appreciation of the political necessity of those subsidies. Poland was a relatively low-priority recipient before 1980 and it is one of the highest-priority recipients now. The more efficient Hungarian economy is meanwhile required to carry a heavier burden—a paradoxical reward/penalty for more competent management . . . .

For all of Eastern Europe a renewed and increased economic dependency upon the Soviet Union is the price of failure. Yet it is a Soviet price too, and the steady rise of prices of Soviet exports to Eastern Europe toward world market levels, and the efforts to contain or reduce exports of fuel and vital raw materials, demonstrate that even Soviet policy presses Eastern Europe toward integration with the global economy. Hence the persistent dilemma. Eastern Europe is pressed toward the global economy, but bearing a legacy of economic institutions and policies which must be radically changed if it is to cope. The instruments of political repression can compensate for many of the internal consequences of a weak economy; they are of no use in dealing with the consequences of weakness in a global economy to which both Eastern Europe and the Soviet Union are inexorably drawn.

*"Unanimity and comradely mutual assistance...
are not just words, but reflect the actual state of
relations between the CMEA members."*

The Soviets Do Not Dominate
Eastern Europe's Economies

Vyacheslav Sychev, interviewed by Vladimir Ganin

Soviet Professor Vyacheslav Sychev is the secretary of the Council
for Mutual Economic Assistance (CMEA), an organization of socialist
countries. While the Soviet Union is the largest single country in
the CMEA, the majority of its members are Eastern European
countries. The following viewpoint is an interview with Sychev conducted by Soviet correspondent Vladimir Ganin. Sychev disputes
the contention that the Soviets subsidize Eastern Europe. According
to Sychev, this is Western propaganda that is meant to obscure the
mutually beneficial relations between socialist states.

As you read, consider the following questions:

1. What contrast does Sychev see between the scientific
   capacity of socialist countries and the scientific capacity of
   the capitalist West?
2. What does Sychev mean by "socialist integration"?
3. How does the Soviet Union benefit by providing energy to
   Eastern Europe, according to the author?

Vyacheslav Sychev, interviewed by Vladimir Ganin, *Expert Opinion: The Prospects for Our
Cooperation Are Good*. Moscow: Novosti Press Agency Publishing House, 1986.

Ganin: More and more people in the world are interested in the work of the Council for Mutual Economic Assistance. How did this organization come into being? What kind of work is it engaged in and what are the goals of the CMEA?

Sychev: In January 1949 representatives of Bulgaria, Czechoslovakia, Hungary, Poland, Romania and the USSR met in Moscow to discuss the setting up of a basically new type of international economic organization, the Council for Mutual Economic Assistance. The need for such an organization was dictated by concrete historical circumstances.

After the Second World War (1939-1945) a system of socialist countries emerged. In these countries radical socio-economic changes were being carried out which led to the establishment of socialist production relations on a uniform economic basis. These countries shared the same ideology and had the same objective—that of building a new, socialist society. In the matter of international economic cooperation they relied above all on one another, concentrating on the development of commercial, economic, scientific and production links among themselves. It then became necessary to coordinate their economic development within the framework of the entire community of socialist countries.

Unified Against the West

Another reason why an economic organization of the socialist states was set up is that soon after the war ended the Western countries pursued a policy of aggravating the international situation, of isolating socialism politically and economically in the international arena. It was only by uniting their efforts that the socialist countries could counter this policy, strengthen their independence and ensure their social and economic progress. Thus the CMEA came into being. . . .

Ganin: Critics of the CMEA in the West say that in order to carry out the various tasks set by the Comprehensive Programme the socialist community countries will need outside help, and that the CMEA countries are trying to build up their scientific and technological capability primarily by importing Western technologies and equipment.

Sychev: Many people in the West indeed seem to believe that the socialist economy is modernized only thanks to the machines and technologies imported from capitalist countries.

In some instances socialist countries do buy equipment and technological processes from developed capitalist countries. But this is part of the international division of labour in which all developed states are interested.

The CMEA countries not only import but also export various modern goods and ideas, from research and development projects and processes to finished products, including machines and equip-

185

ment. For instance, during the last five years the Soviet Union sold the United States three and a half times more licenses than it bought from it. To date the USSR has purchased 1,600 US patents as against more than 5,500 Soviet patents purchased by the United States.

Of the more than five million people working in the field of science in the socialist community countries, one-third are engaged in research. The CMEA states now own 20 per cent of the world's patents for new technologies and equipment.

Thanks to their scientific and technological cooperation the socialist countries can cope with nearly all their economic problems without outside help. . . .

Relying on the CMEA

The bitter truth is that we Poles are still living on credit. . . . But in our plans we rely on the international cooperation of CMEA countries. . . . I should like to stress once again that joint enterprises are of mutual benefit. . . . The profit we shall draw along with the U.S.S.R. and other CMEA member countries is to go into the strengthening of our economy, clearing our foreign debt and, hence, to consolidate Poland's independence.

Wlodzimierz Natorf, quoted in *New Times*, no. 45, November 17, 1986.

Ganin: It is often said in the West that the CMEA countries are unable to withstand the economic crises that hit the world economy from time to time. As an example, it is pointed out that the economic growth rates of the CMEA states dropped in the early 80s. How would you account for such a situation?

Sychev: It is true that the negative processes in the capitalist economy affected the economy of the socialist countries. But the problems that faced these countries on the threshold of the 80s did not constitute a crisis.

Restructuring To Increase Growth

The CMEA countries' economic growth rates slowed down in the early 80s because they were going over to intensive economic development. At that point the possibilities of extensive growth had been exhausted, at least in the European CMEA countries. The changeover to intensification meant corresponding changes in planning and management. Economic reforms and large-scale experiments are now being carried out in several CMEA countries, with each country taking into account the specific needs of its development. These measures are designed to restructure all branches of the national economy, to increase the rates of economic growth and raise people's living standards.

Another reason for the economic slowdown in the early 80s was the considerable rise in the cost of production of raw materials in the preceding years.

Incidentally, even in the worst period the economic growth rates of the CMEA member countries were twice as high as those of Western countries.

And while talking about an alleged crisis in the socialist community our critics have nothing to say about its achievements and the basic differences between the CMEA and the international economic organizations in the West, for example, the European Economic Community (EEC).

Ganin: In what ways do these two organizations—the CMEA and the EEC—differ?

Sychev: Outwardly they are similar: both coordinate their member countries' interests and seek mutually acceptable solutions. But the EEC is unable to prevent economic crises or to eliminate the effect of such crises on the capitalist economy.

Trade Wars and Selfish Interests

Integration within the EEC is marked by rivalry between the member countries. The outcome of such rivalry is predictable: the stronger countries gain the upper hand. Each of them tries to occupy leading positions in the organization. They are waging all kinds of trade wars: lamb, wine, steel wars, etc. Their aim is to secure the best possible conditions of production and trade for their own monopolies and thus enable the latter to obtain maximum profits. Former Chancellor of the Federal Republic of Germany Helmut Schmidt noted, for instance, that the community lacked solidarity. The EEC partners were chiefly concerned about their own selfish interests, he said.

Ganin: And what are the distinctive features of socialist integration?

Sychev: Its foundation is public ownership of the basic means of production, and it takes into account both the national and international interests of each participating country and of the community as a whole.

Integration links within the CMEA are very important for the economic growth of many states of the community. For them, work for the common socialist market and production cooperation with partners within the community are in effect the only way of specializing production and putting it on a large-scale basis. And this is essential for achieving production efficiency in modern conditions.

Mass Production

Take the following example. Not a single motor works in Western Europe makes more than 20,000-30,000 rear axles for buses in a year, and the reason for this is market instability. Now the RABA plant in Hungary turns out more than 100,000 rear axles annually. They are in great demand in countries of the socialist community and so

Real incomes of the population of CMEA member countries

(1970 = 100)

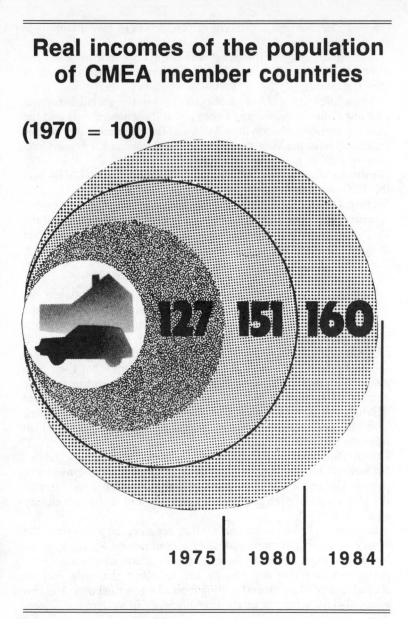

127 151 160

1975 1980 1984

they find ready buyers. The same can be said about Bulgarian lift trucks, Czechoslovak tram cars and railway coaches built in the German Democratic Republic.

There is ample evidence that the industry of CMEA member countries is developing successfully thanks to socialist economic integration. Suffice it to say that Hungary, Bulgaria, the GDR and

Czechoslovakia sell 30 to 40 per cent of their machines and equipment on CMEA markets.

Ganin: But to develop their industry most CMEA countries rely on the supply of fuel and energy from the USSR. . . .

Sychev: The Soviet Union has been supplying fuel and energy to these countries on a stable basis already for many years. In 1981-1983 it exported to these countries 264 million tons of oil and petroleum products and 92,000 million cubic metres of natural gas. In the current five-year period (1986-1990) a main gas pipeline running from West Siberia to the Western border of the USSR—a distance of more than 4,500 kilometres—will be built with the participation of the European CMEA countries. This will increase the delivery of Soviet natural gas to fraternal countries.

The supply of fuel and energy is part of the whole complex of mutually advantageous economic relations between CMEA partners. Thus, the Soviet Union buys two-thirds of all the machines and equipment it imports from other CMEA countries. In the last five years it imported consumer goods from its CMEA partners worth 40,000 million roubles.

Mutual Benefits

The point is that in providing fuel primarily to other CMEA countries the Soviet Union in turn receives the goods it needs from them.

Ganin: How do CMEA member countries pay for fuel and energy supplies from the USSR?

Sychev: The basic principle of price setting in trade between the socialist community countries is as follows. Prices for mutually delivered goods are set each year on the basis of the average world prices for the preceding five years. Here is an example. When oil prices rose sharply on the world market in the early 70s, the Soviet Union's CMEA partners felt the impact gradually, and somewhat later. Should the CMEA countries have bought Soviet oil at world prices in the 1976-1980 period they would have had to pay an additional 15,000 million roubles.

Now that world oil prices are falling the reduction of oil prices in trade between CMEA countries will also be gradual. It should be noted, however, that it is cheaper to deliver oil by pipeline, as is done by the Soviet Union when supplying oil to its CMEA partners, than by tanker. This substantially reduces the difference which now exists between world prices and those on the CMEA market. Besides, accounts for the sale of Soviet oil to CMEA countries are settled in transfer roubles or by deliveries of goods.

Ganin: When discussing problems faced by the CMEA, Western commentators usually resort to the following stereotypes: one, the Soviet Union is said to sacrifice its own interests in order to help its allies; and two, the CMEA is allegedly an instrument with the help of which the USSR "fleeces" its friends. One of these mutually exclusive allegations must be false....

Sychev: In fact, both are false. Article 1 of the CMEA Charter says that economic and scientific and technical cooperation of the Council's members shall be carried out in accordance with the principles of socialist internationalism on the basis of respect for state sovereignty, independence and national interests, non-interference in the internal affairs of countries, full equality, mutual advantage and comradely mutual assistance. Each of these principles is strictly observed.

Equal Representation

Of course, socialist internationalism does not rule out differences of opinion on ways of solving various problems or non-antagonistic contradictions within the community. However, when it comes to matters of principle, the positions of the CMEA countries are the same, and this enables them to solve the problems facing them.

Ganin: How is this done?

Sychev: Each member country, irrespective of its economic capacity, national income, population, contribution to the organization's budget or any other conditions, has one vote at negotiations at all levels held within the CMEA framework and in any of the CMEA representative bodies....

Bourgeois Sneers Wrong Again

Bourgeois propaganda sneered at the CMEA, referring to it as a "joint-stock company for beggars" and predicting its inevitable collapse. Socialism's "grave-diggers," however, miscalculated once again. Whereas initially the Council comprised only European socialist states, today it unites 10 European, Asian and American countries, with a territory as large as 19 per cent of the globe's surface and a population of 450 million. Although this is no more than 10 per cent of the world's population, the CMEA countries account for 25 per cent of the global national income, over 30 per cent of industrial output, 20 per cent of agricultural produce and 30 per cent of scientific and technological potential.

Yuri Pevnev, *Soviet Military Review,* June 1986.

Socialist economic integration does not call for the establishment of supranational bodies whose decisions all member countries must accept. In the CMEA no one forces any decisions on anyone. Decisions are taken not by a majority vote but by the consent of the countries concerned. The fact that one or several member countries do not take part in a given project does not prevent others from carrying it out.

This procedure of decision-making in CMEA bodies means that no decisions can be passed by the Council which are detrimental to the interests of or which give unilateral advantages to any member country. . . .

Ganin: Granting privileges to economically less developed countries of the socialist community means that the stronger partners have to make certain sacrifices.

Sychev: Yes, but they stand to gain in the long run. For the evening out of the development levels of all CMEA countries adds to the economic potential of the community.

Economic Growth in the CMEA

That this long-term policy is a sound one is confirmed by the fact that the CMEA is today one of the world's most powerful economic organizations. This is largely due to the high growth rates of the national economies. Naturally, these rates differ from one member country to another, depending on the specific conditions of the given country.

So, unanimity and comradely mutual assistance, which are often mentioned in CMEA documents, are not just words, but reflect the actual state of relations between the CMEA members.

Ganin: Is there any truth in the assertion that some countries of the socialist community prefer to broaden cooperation with the West instead of expanding it within the CMEA framework?

Sychev: CMEA member states do not regard their organization as an autarchic one. They have always expressed a desire to establish mutually advantageous trade and economic relations with the West and have repeatedly called for their more active development. Anti-communist circles in some Western countries try to use this circumstance to promote their selfish ends. They quite often resort to outright blackmail, including in the sphere of credit. They would cast doubt on the credit-worthiness of the countries of the socialist community, referring to these countries' allegedly colossal debts to Western banks and governments. . . .

Ganin: What will the CMEA inherit from the 20th century and what will it bring to the new century?

Sychev: The socialist community will enter the next century with good prospects for promoting cooperation between the member countries. Integration will embrace all sectors of their economy—from direct links between individual enterprises and industrial amalgamations to the formation of large international firms. The CMEA's role in the world economy will grow further.

"There was no society in eastern Europe less prepared [than Poland] . . . to accept Soviet socialism, imposed by Russian bayonets."

The Soviets Have Destroyed Polish Freedom

Timothy Garton Ash

British Writer Timothy Garton Ash is a well-known expert on Central and Eastern Europe whose articles have been published in the *Spectator, The London Times,* and *The New York Review of Books.* He begins the following viewpoint by tracing the historical animosity between the Soviet Union and Poland to explain the unpopularity of Soviet-style communism. Ash argues that the Polish political system, modeled after the Soviet Union's, provides privileges for Communist Party members and their families. When an economic crisis struck Poland in the late 1970s under the rule of Edward Gierek, members of the young working class protested and supported the Solidarity trade union. Ash concludes that Solidarity set an example that will not be forgotten as the Polish people continue to struggle against Soviet domination.

As you read, consider the following questions:

1. What three lessons about Polish-Soviet relations does Ash draw from his brief survey of Polish history?
2. What examples does the author cite of privileges the *nomenklatura* has?

When I first came to Poland I kept hearing a very strange word. 'Yowta', my new acquaintances sighed, 'yowta!' and conversation ebbed into melancholy silence. Did 'yowta' mean fate, I wondered, was it an expression like 'that's life'?

'Yalta' (Polish pronunciation 'yowta') is the first fact of life in contemporary Poland. 'Yalta' is where the story of Solidarity begins. 'Yalta' for the Poles means that, after their army had been the first to resist Hitler, after Britain had gone to war in defence of Poland's independence and Polish servicemen had fought courageously in defence of Britain, after some six million of their compatriots (one in every five citizens of the pre-war Polish Republic) had died in the war—after all this, their country was delivered up by their western allies, Britain and America, into the famously tender care of 'Uncle Joe' Stalin.

While it can be argued that Churchill and Roosevelt had no alternative, since when the Big Three met at Yalta in the Crimea in February 1945 the Red Army already occupied the territory of the former Polish Republic, and while in the final communiqué of that meeting Stalin solemnly promised 'the holding of free and unfettered elections as soon as possible on the basis of universal suffrage and secret ballot', such a deliverance was an equivocal blessing, for anyone. But to understand why it was in Poland that the first workers' revolution against a 'Workers' State' erupted in August 1980, you must understand why the prospect of Soviet 'liberation' was so particularly appalling to the great majority of Poles in 1945.

A History of Resistance

To understand this you must [consider]...Poland's recorded history....Poland lay on the open plains between two hungry autocracies, Russia and Prussia.

Despite last-minute efforts to reform and strengthen the [Polish] kingdom, culminating in the famous liberal Constitution of 3 May 1791, Poland was simply carved up by her neighbours, Russia, Prussia and Austria, in the 'Partitions' of 1772, 1793 and 1795. Poland disappeared from the map of Europe as an independent state for the next one hundred and twenty-three years. But it refused to disappear as a nation.

Though in the 'Golden Century' of Noble Democracy Poland had been known as the 'paradise of heretics', a haven of religious tolerance and diversity, the Poles' fervent patriotism was now expressed through an ever closer identification of the nation with the Roman Catholic Church, against the creeds of their oppressors, German Protestantism and Russian Orthodoxy. Again and again, in 1794, and 1830-1, and 1863-4, and 1905, they expressed their longing for freedom through heroic insurrections, which were crushed with habitual brutality by Tsarist Russia....

This whistle-stop tour through...history must serve to establish three points which are as important as they are basic: the Poles are an old European people with an unquenchable thirst for freedom; freedom in Polish means, in the first place, national independence; the Polish national identity is historically defined in opposition to Russia....

Power for Power's Sake

Half of Europe, including Poland, was given a new regime quite simply because a conquering army was occupying these countries, pushing the frontiers of the Soviet Empire further towards the West....

We may finally have the answer to the question of what happens if the real will of the people—10 million members of an independent trade union—turns against the monopoly of power, and demands *some* of the rights that their rulers enjoy *(only some*, for the Poles have displayed too much realism and self-discipline to be suspected of trying to get rid of the Party as the spokesman for their membership in the Soviet bloc). The exposure of the military junta's actions in the name of the Party introduces a new element only because it reveals the essence of any system whose goal is power for power's sake.

Czeslaw Milosz in *Poland Under Jaruzelski: A Comprehensive Sourcebook of Poland*, 1983.

The Poles remember 17 September 1939, when Soviet troops invaded eastern Poland. More than one million Poles (roughly one-tenth of the population of Soviet-occupied Poland) were deported eastward by the Soviet authorities—fewer than half of them returned, carrying children who would not forget Siberia. One such child was Andrzej Gwiazda, later to become a leader of Solidarity. His tender feelings towards the Soviet Union may be imagined. It is now established beyond any reasonable doubt that thousands of Polish officers were murdered on Stalin's orders at Katyn in 1940. The Warsaw Uprising, launched by the underground Home Army (AK) in 1944 as a last desperate attempt to keep control of Poland's liberation in non-communist Polish hands, was crushed with unsurpassed brutality by the Germans, while the Red Army held back just a few miles away on the left bank of the Vistula, and Stalin for weeks refused to allow American aircraft carrying supplies to refuel on Soviet airfields.

And so to 'Yalta'....

There was no society in eastern Europe *less* prepared voluntarily to accept *Soviet* socialism, imposed by Russian bayonets. Soviet socialism did not start from scratch in Poland; it started with a huge political and moral debit. Stalin himself said that introducing communism to Poland was like putting a saddle on a cow; the Poles thought it was like putting a yoke on a stallion. This fundamental, historic opposition and incompatibility is the most basic cause of the Polish revolt against 'Yalta' and Soviet socialism in 1980. For thirty-five years Poland's communist rulers tried either to break the stallion to the yoke or to mould the saddle to the cow. It was always probable that they would fail.

The Sovietisation of Poland

'Yalta', then, means the way in which Stalin broke the promises he made at Yalta, as he was bound to if he wished to impose Soviet socialism on Poland. For in a genuinely 'free and unfettered election' the puppet communist party, formed in Russia in 1942 (since the pre-war Polish communist party had been dissolved and its leaders murdered on Stalin's orders) did not stand a chance. The advance of the Soviet liberators was therefore closely followed by a second army of NKVD [Soviet secret police] men, arresting and deporting leaders of the non-communist resistance to Hitler. As early as 8 March 1945 Winston Churchill wrote despairingly to Roosevelt about

> the liquidations and deportations. . .and all the rest of the game of setting up a totalitarian regime. . .if we do not get things right now [he went on] it will soon be seen by the world that you and I by putting our signatures to the Crimea settlement have underwritten a fraudulent prospectus.

In the 'election' finally held in January 1947 a million voters were summarily disenfranchised, thousands of Peasant Party members and 142 candidates were simply arrested, the vote count was rigged. . . .

[By 1954] the Leninist-Stalinist political system had been installed in Poland which, in essentials, was still in place in 1980. The nature of this system has been well characterised by the former East German dissident Rudolf Bahro as a 'politbureaucratic dictatorship'. Supreme power is normally concentrated (barring direct intervention by the Soviet Union) in the Party's Politburo, a body with ten to twenty members, chaired by the Party leader (formally, Party First Secretary). Historically, as in the Soviet Union, the personality of the Party leader has marked the 'eras' in a fashion typical of a dictatorship. The Politburo's decisions are transmitted to society through two linked pyramids of political bureaucracy, the Party and the state administration, the latter being in practice subordinate.

The security of the regime depends at all times on the potential coercive power of the security and armed forces (with the ultimate threat of the Red Army, two divisions of which are permanently stationed on Polish soil). . . .

The Party controls not only the appointment of its own full-time officials, known collectively as the *apparat*, but also all the most important appointments in almost every walk of life: central and local government officials, managers in industry and commerce, publishers, newspaper editors, senior army officers, judges, trades union leaders, university rectors, headmasters, leaders of youth and women's organisations, bankers, fire brigade commanders. . . . For this purpose, the Party's Central, regional and local committees maintain lists of positions, and of people judged fit to fill them. The Soviet term for these lists, *nomenklatura*, has come to be applied by extension to the class of people holding such positions. In 1972 the *nomenklatura* was expanded to increase the Party's central control, so that by 1980 there were probably some 200,000 to 300,000 *nomenklatura* jobs.

A Hard Lesson

There are many lessons to be learned from the Polish events. But, I would maintain, the principal lesson to be learned is the lesson of the failure of Communism, the utter villainy of the Communist system. It has been a hard lesson to learn. And I am struck by how long it has taken us to learn it. I say we—and of course I include myself. I can remember reading a chapter of Czeslaw Milosz's *The Captive Mind* in *Partisan Review*. When it came out in 1953, I bought the book—a passionate account of the dishonesty and coerciveness of intellectual and cultural life in Poland in the first years of Communism, which troubled me but which I also regarded as an instrument of cold war propaganda, giving aid and comfort to McCarthyism. I put it on my student's bookshelf. Still a student (though an unofficial one) twenty-seven years later, in 1980, on the eve of my first visit to Poland, I took down my old copy of *The Captive Mind* from the shelf, re-read it (for the first time) and thought, and thought only: But it's all true. And in Poland, I was to learn that Milosz had, if anything, underestimated the disgrace of the Communist regime installed by force in his country.

Susan Sontag, *The Nation*, February 27, 1982.

The *nomenklatura* can accurately be described as a client ruling class. Its members enjoy power, status and privileges (in varying degrees) by virtue simply of belonging to it. They may not individually own the means of production, but they do collectively control them. In the 1970s they were popularly known as 'the owners of People's Poland'. By contract with other class systems, economic and political power are concentrated permanently in the same hands. Neither is this a purely functional élite. The children of the *nomenklatura* enjoy automatic advantages, so long as they remain loyal to the system. In the 1970s these advantages were comparable with hereditary privilege in the West: if you were the son of a senior apparatchik you had a much higher standard of living, better education and career chances than your contemporary, the son of a worker. If one includes families, perhaps 1-1½ million people depend directly on the continuance of Party monopolies for their jobs, powers or privileges. . . .

The Power of Youth

Poland was by [1979] an exceptionally youthful country: nearly one-third of the industrial working class was under twenty-five. . . .Their material expectations had been dramatically raised by [Polish ruler Edward] Gierek's great leap [during the 1970s]. In their early teens they had experienced a dizzy increase in their standard of living; after the puritan stagnation of the late Gomulka years [in the 1960s], the shops had been suddenly filled with food, jeans, transistor radios and cassette players from the West; new buildings had shot up around them; they had been told they might reasonably expect to move into a new flat in a few years—and even, if they were very lucky, to acquire a car. Moreover, they had been able—for the first time ever—to take a holiday in the West. The little Polski Fiat, piled high with provisions and children, became a familiar sight in Vienna and West Berlin. They had seen with their own eyes the noxious evil of the capitalist West—and they rather liked it.

Now these raised expectations were being disappointed. Everywhere they looked they saw standards falling. As the economy broke down, the shortages became ever more frequent and infuriating: this week there was no shaving cream, next week the shelves were spilling over with shaving cream but there were no razor blades; this week there was meat but no cooking oil, next week cooking oil but no meat. The queues lengthened. As in Gomulka's last years, working conditions in the factories and mines actually deteriorated: according to official statistics there were more deaths per thousand workers in 1979 than in 1970. . . .

Moreover, it was characteristic of the Gierek boom that the gains were unevenly distributed. Relatively speaking, the rich got richer and the poor got poorer. . . .Many members of the communist ruling class appropriated state funds to build themselves luxurious villas: corruption on an unprecedented scale spread from the top down. . . .

All these symptoms of growing inequality offended deeply against the egalitarianism which this generation of workers and students had imbibed with their socialist education at school. The propaganda which continued vaingloriously to proclaim 'you've never had it so good!', when any fool could see they had had it better, was simply an insult to their intelligence. What is more, there was absolutely no secular institution through which they felt they could express their discontent. . . .

This was the generation which would flock to the Solidarity stan-

197

dards and give the mass movement its youthful dynamism. Solidarity filled that yawning gap between the family and the nation; Solidarity was the first secular organisation which had ever spoken for them; it was their movement, their generation's bid for political participation. . . .

Solidarity was the most infectiously hopeful movement in the history of contemporary Europe, and its long-term legacy is one of hope.

A Struggle for Democratic Values

While the fog was dispersed we were privileged to watch the Poles fighting, with extraordinary courage, dignity and self-restraint, for values which most of us can hardly fail to recognise as our own—individual freedom, democratic government, the rule of law, free speech—values born from the common culture of old Europe. . . .

They did not, however, merely reassert old values. Solidarity was not just what Poland was for G.K. Chesterton: the bulwark of Christian civilisation against the diabolical materialism of the East. Young Poles measured their rulers' conduct both against traditional, European and Christian standards, and against some of the socialist values which those rulers had preached. They found the regime wanting by the standards of equality and full employment (which means more than everyone having a nominal workplace) as well as by the standards of free speech, freedom of worship or political pluralism. . . .

One thing at least is certain: [the Poles] will not forget. Though Solidarity's cells fade away even in the industrial strongholds, though the Solidarity badges, the photos and the tapes are pushed to the back of the bottommost drawer, the dramas, the ideals and the political methods of the Polish revolution will live on, in this most tenacious of national memories, as myth—and as precedent. This simple statement 'They will not forget' is a statement of the first political importance. As Milan Kundera writes, out of the bitter experience of Czechoslovakia's 'normalisation', in the Soviet world 'The struggle of man against power is the struggle of memory against forgetting.'

They will not forget, as the world will forget, and the Soviet masters of forgetting want us to forget. And just because they will not forget, there will certainly come a day, sooner or later, when we, and the masters of forgetting, will again be reminded that the Poles are still waiting, impatiently, for freedom. As the call of the bugle sounds every hour from the tower of St. Mary's Cathedral across the great square of Kraków, so their call will sound once more, across the world.

"The 40 years of peace and friendship with the USSR . . . have given Poland the kind of independence and security it never before enjoyed."

The Soviets Have Protected Polish Freedom

Mike Davidow

Mike Davidow is the Moscow correspondent for the *People's Daily World*, the newspaper of the Communist Party USA. The following viewpoint was written shortly after Davidow returned from a trip to Poland. He examines the progress socialist Poland has made since World War II. As Poland's wealth has increased, he contends, the lives of its people have improved. Davidow argues that alliance with the Soviet Union has kept Poland secure and at peace, despite the attempts of the anti-Soviet agitators in the Solidarity movement who worked with Western capitalist powers to try and destroy Poland.

As you read, consider the following questions:

1. What historical events does Davidow cite to support his argument that the Soviets have supported Polish independence?
2. What role does Davidow believe the church has played in Poland?
3. According to the author, what does the 1980-81 crisis in Poland prove about the influence of the Soviet Union and other socialist states?

Mike Davidow, "Poland Tackles Its Problems," *Daily World*, October 31, 1985 and "Polish-Soviet Relations," *Daily World*, November 27, 1985.

The People's Republic of Poland faces serious and complex problems. The crisis of 1980-82 was a hard school of economics and politics for the Polish people, especially for workers and farmers. Problems and solutions are still being probed, even as steps are being taken to overcome the problems.

On a recent trip to Poland, I talked with leaders of the Polish United Workers Party, coal miners, farmers, youth. I was impressed by the frank, sober discussion of their difficulties.

The people seem determined not only to learn from them, but to use them to strengthen socialism in Poland, to provide themselves with an adequate and stable supply of food, and to increase the supply of consumer goods.

Poland's History

Poland became socialist with a heritage of social and economic backwardness.

Pre-war, pre-socialist Poland had the most anti-Soviet, anti-Communist ruling class in Europe. It had a per capita national income in 1939 that was five to eight times lower than that of the highly developed countries. Its industry was poor, its agriculture primitive, its infrastructure acutely inadequate.

In the immediate postwar years of 1946-47, former big landowners and capitalists led an armed struggle against the redistribution of land among the peasants and the nationalization and workers' takeover of the factories. Thousands of peasants and workers, especially Communists, were killed.

Poland also had to expend vast resources to rebuild after the terrible destruction of the war.

Considerable Progress

Nevertheless, socialist Poland has achieved considerable progress in the past 40 years of its development.

Before the war, Poland had been primarily an agricultural country. In 1946, two-thirds of the population lived in the countryside. The 40 years following World War II saw great urbanization. Housing in the cities had increased from 2 million to 6.5 million by 1983; in the country as a whole, housing was 10,310,900 in 1983.

Urbanization of the country reflected changes in the social and economic structure. In the pre-war years, half of the population lived off agriculture. Today, farming is the direct source of income for only 20% full-time farmers. (Some are part-time farmers as well.)

Intensive industrialization has been the main trend in Poland's economy. New branches of industry were developed, among them electronics, transistors, automotive, shipbuilding, copper mining and processing. The average annual economic growth rate was 10%. Poland's net industrial production is 20 times higher now than in 1946.

In calories consumed per day, the average Pole eats as well as people in any other developed country. However, meat, dairy and protein-rich products still form too small a share of the average diet. For this reason, the food program is the most important in the government's socio-economic policy.

Poland has a modern, efficient transportation system, with excellent roads.

Better Education

Before the war, about 25% of the Polish population was illiterate, with very few people having a higher education. In 1946, just one year after Poland's liberation, there were 86,000 students receiving a higher education—more than twice as many as in 1939. The number of people with higher education has risen from 30,000 before the war to 1.6 million today; and for secondary education, from 500,000 to 6.5 million. In education, Poland today is on the highest world level.

Living Among Friends

Poland at loggerheads with her neighbours, entangled in "exotic alliances", banking naively on the good will of the Western powers, is a thing of the far distant past. Today, Poland's place is unambiguously and enduringly defined. Her international position depends directly on her significance in the socialist community. . . .

To live among friends, to enjoy their joint guarantees and to be at the same time an underwriter of the post-war territorial and political order in Europe—this is the essence of the Polish *raison d'état*.

The foundation of our foreign and defence policies is our unshakeable alliance and fraternal friendship with the Soviet Union. Both past history and the present day confirm its importance for the Polish nation.

Wojciech Jaruzelski, speech to the Sejm (Parliament), July 21, 1984.

As in other socialist countries, Poland has a comprehensive, almost free, health care system. In 1946 there were 7,700 physicians; in 1983, there were 69,300. For dentists, the figures are 1,600 and 17,300 respectively.

Taking the year 1960 as 100%, Poland's national income in 1946 was 27.4 and in 1983 it was 266.8. It went up nearly 10 times. Using the same yardstick, gross industrial production (which includes material costs) was 13.2 in 1946 and 426.8 in 1983. The figures for net industrial production were 19.6 in 1946 and 360.2 in 1983 (which indicates production consumed too much material).

Income in socialized production industry was 36.7 in 1950 (with

1960 as 100) and 361.9 in 1983. In socialized construction it was 42.2 in 1950 and 318.4 in 1983.

In agriculture the situation is more complex and the rate of growth much slower. With 1961-65 as 100, in 1946 it was 34.8 and in 1983, 134.6. In 1970 the socialized sector of the economy provided 74.9% of the national income and the private sector, 25.1%. In 1983, 79.5% was provided by the socialized sector and 20.5% (mainly in farming) by the nonsocialized sector. A total of 4.9 million are employed in industry—4.6 million in socialized industry and 370,000 in private, largely in services and crafts.

Socialism's Deep Roots

The progress achieved in four decades does not mean that the difficult problems will be automatically resolved. No one in Poland's leadership has such illusions. But it reveals that socialism has struck deep roots in Poland, both in the material life of the country and in the minds and hearts of the people. It is on the basis of this solid foundation that Poland, led by the Polish United Workers Party, is creatively and with its eyes wide open tackling its complex problems. . . .

Before the establishment of socialism, Poland was the most anti-Soviet, anti-Communist state in Europe. Dr. Boleslaw Borysuik, secretary of the Polish-Soviet Friendship Society, told me in an interview that Poland's leaders were so rabidly anti-Soviet that, rather than accept the Soviet offer in August 1939 that year for collective security against the impending invasion by Nazi Germany, they led the Polish people into the catastrophe that cost Poland six million lives.

This anti-Sovietism and anti-Russianism has historical roots in the czarist occupation of part of Poland. Today it is used by enemies of socialism in Poland, both inside and outside the country.

Anti-Sovietism

What must also be grasped, however, Dr. Borysuik said, is that though still widespread and a powerful influence, this anti-Sovietism was deeply challenged by Poland's liberation by the Soviet Red Army and the Polish Army of Liberation, at the cost of more than 600,000 Soviet lives, and by 40 years of subsequent mutually beneficial Polish-Soviet relations.

The liberation of Poland by the Soviet armed forces in World War II had a profound impact on the Polish people. For many, it was their first contact with the Soviet people. It shattered the distorted image of the enemy to the East, which had long been portrayed as the main threat to Poland's existence.

It was out of this personal contact with thousands of Soviet soldiers and officers who liberated hundreds of towns and villages and helped feed, clothe and provide medical care to the Polish people, that the

Polish-Soviet Friendship Society developed.

From the start, however, proponents of Soviet-Polish friendship had to engage in sharp ideological struggle against anti-Soviet slanders and distortions promoted by the West as well as internal foes. The movement for friendship had to contend from the very beginning with resistance from the forces of reaction, who took up armed and terrorist struggle against new Poland in 1946-47. Activists and leaders of the movement were threatened and physically attacked.

The Society Grows

The Polish-Soviet Friendship Society grew, nevertheless. There were 10,000 members of the Polish-Soviet Friendship movement in 1945, and 360,000 in 1947. Membership rose steadily until it reached 3.5 million members in 1974.

By 1983, membership in the Society had decreased to 2.6 million, largely as a result of ideological confusion created by Solidarity as well as the terror tactics it used, particularly against members of the Polish-Soviet Friendship Society. Dr. Borysuik said that Solidarity even demanded to take over the modern headquarters of the Society.

A Helping Hand

It would have been hard for Poland to economically survive so serious an ordeal without the Soviet Union's substantial and effective assistance....In our darkest hour it extended a helping hand. It agreed to step up deliveries of vital commodities and raw materials, though this had not been planned. It has now agreed to a temporary upset in the balance of trade. It has granted Poland the biggest credits ever in the history of our relations....

We shall never forget the help our Soviet comrades, the Soviet people gave us. It has enabled us to survive the worst, while today it enables us to view the future without anxiety.

Wojciech Jaruzelski, quoted in *New Times*, no. 29, July 28, 1986.

Anti-Sovietism has been steadily nourished by the slanders, lies and distortions of a well-financed anti-Soviet apparatus operating from the U.S. and countries of the West, particularly the Federal Republic of Germany and France, and by the internal enemies of Poland. Anti-Soviet slander was one of the main weapons of the anti-socialist forces who dominated Solidarity in 1980-82.

This was made worse by serious weaknesses in the teaching of the history of Soviet-Polish relations, which in some schools of higher learning was taught from a bourgeois rather than a Marxist viewpoint.

The 1920 invasion of the young Soviet state by the reactionary Pilsudski regime, for example, which took advantage of the civil war, counterrevolution and intervention by 14 Western powers, was presented to students as a struggle for Polish independence. Overlooked was the fact that Poland had invaded Kiev.

The Soviet moves to check Hitler's push toward its borders and to liberate Byelorussia and the western Ukraine from Nazi domination were presented as a stab in the back to Poland. Not mentioned was Poland's refusal to accept Soviet aid in August 1939 to stop Hitler's invasion of its land.

The lie spread by Goebbels, Hitler's chief propagandist, about the so-called murder of 12,000 Polish officers at Khatyn was revived. Yet, the best proof of who actually committed this atrocity is furnished by the Nazis themselves. Among the first victims of Nazi genocide were 183 Polish professors of the famous Jagellionian University in Cracow, who were invited to a meeting at the university and then transported to their death in Germany.

Overlooked, too, was the Nazi aim to exterminate the Polish nation.

The Western Threat

But Poland's experience in 1981-82 exploded the anti-Soviet myths. It showed that the threat to Poland's independence and security came not from the Soviet Union, but from the West. The Soviet Union and other socialist countries came to Poland's aid.

Sanctions imposed by the U.S. and Western countries, particularly on grain exports, in contrast, deprived Polish livestock and chickens of fodder and feed. The Polish people were hit hard economically. As a result, the U.S., once popular among the Polish people, is now regarded by them as a prime enemy.

Today, the Soviet-Polish Friendship Society is on a more solid basis. It has about 14,000 branches in cities, towns and villages throughout Poland, and a force of 110,000 activists. It has a core of 1,200-1,300 lecturers who have a broad knowledge of Soviet life, and a school where potential lecturers and activists study various aspects of Soviet society both in the classroom and through visits to the USSR.

There are many exchange visits with Soviet trade unionists, cultural workers, scientists, youth, women, artists and athletes. During my visit I saw the enthusiastic reception accorded the Bolshoi and Moscow Art Theater during the Days of Russian Culture in Poland.

The Polish-Soviet Friendship Society has a national council that includes prominent writers and artists, and leaders of the Catholic organization PAX, the United Peasants Party, the Democratic Party, the trade unions, and youth and women's organizations.

It would be wrong, however, to underestimate the danger still coming from the anti-Soviet enemies of socialist Poland. They have demonstrated they know well how to play on deeply rooted prejudices in times of difficulties.

The chief organizers of this resistance are the descendants of the former landowners and capitalists whose big landed estates and factories were taken over and given to the farmers and run for the benefit of the people. They are aided by the most reactionary elements in the Catholic Church.

The struggle against anti-Sovietism in Poland is a struggle against reaction. It is a struggle for a democratic, socialist Poland.

Poland lies in the very center of Europe and therefore plays a very important role in European affairs. The revanchist forces, prodded by U.S. imperialism, want to return to the pre-war borders in Poland and throughout Europe. However, the 40 years of peace and friendship with the USSR and other socialist countries have given Poland the kind of independence and security it never before enjoyed.

Evaluating Sources of Information

A critical thinker must always question sources of information. Historians, for example, distinguish between *primary sources* (eyewitness accounts) and *secondary sources* (writings or statements based on primary or eyewitness accounts or on other secondary sources). The diary of an East Berlin citizen describing the construction of the Berlin Wall is an example of a primary source. A historian evaluating the incident by using the citizen's account is an example of a secondary source.

To read and think critically, one must be able to recognize primary sources. This is not enough, however, because eyewitness accounts do not always provide accurate descriptions. Berlin residents and Soviet soldiers remembering the Wall's construction may differ in their reports of what happened. The historian must decide which account seems most accurate, keeping in mind the potential biases of the eyewitnesses.

Test your skill in evaluating sources of information by completing the following exercise. Listed below are a number of sources which may be useful in a report on Eastern Europe. *Place a P next to those descriptions you believe are primary sources.* Second, *rank the primary sources* assigning the number (1) to what appears to be the most accurate and fair primary source, the number (2) to the next most accurate, and so on until the ranking is finished. *Next, place an S next to those descriptions you believe are secondary sources and rank them also, using the same criteria.*

If you are doing this activity as a member of a class or group, discuss and compare your evaluation with other members of the group. Others may come to different conclusions than you. Listening to their reasons may give you valuable insights in evaluating sources of information.

$$P = primary$$
$$S = secondary$$

206

_____ 1. A book by an exiled Polish dissident describing the effects of Soviet domination.   _____

_____ 2. A five-year economic plan for Warsaw Pact countries written by the Soviet Central Committee.   _____

_____ 3. A *Los Angeles Times* editorial explaining how the Soviet economy could be improved.   _____

_____ 4. A professor's lecture on Eastern Europe and international relations.   _____

_____ 5. An interview in *Die Zeit* of an East German political leader.   _____

_____ 6. The account of a Western journalist's travels through Warsaw Pact nations.   _____

_____ 7. A Tass feature citing the improvements of life in Eastern Europe since World War II.   _____

_____ 8. A published address by Pope John Paul II to striking Polish workers.   _____

_____ 9. An American documentary on the history of the Berlin Wall.   _____

_____ 10. A speech printed in *Pravda* by Mikhail Gorbachev on the importance of Eastern Europe.   _____

_____ 11. The transcript of a clandestine Polish radio broadcast calling for an end to Soviet involvement in Poland.   _____

_____ 12. A chronology in a history book of wars fought in Eastern Europe.   _____

_____ 13. A made-for-TV movie about the 1917 communist revolution in the USSR.   _____

_____ 14. A Soviet soldier's letter to his parents which is reprinted in a book about Soviet-occupied countries.   _____

Periodical Bibliography

The following articles have been selected to supplement the diverse views expressed in this chapter.

Oleg Bogomolov — "Prospects for Economic Cooperation," *New Times*, no. 8, February 1986.

Wiktor Borcuch — "Gdansk Shipyard: Why the Workers Turned away from 'Solidarity,'" *World Marxist Review*, April 1987.

Charles Gati — "Gorbachev and Eastern Europe," *Foreign Affairs*, Summer 1987.

Václav Havel — "Interview: Living the Truth in Prague," *New Politics*, Summer 1987.

Zdenek Horeni — "Taking up a Point: This Is a Real Revolution," *New Times*, no. 17, May 4, 1987.

Jan Kavan — "Prague's Kamikaze Icebreakers," *The Nation*, January 24, 1987.

Yuri Kazakov — "Thirty Years of Service to the Cause of Peace," *Soviet Life*, June 1985.

B. Kozlov — "Turning Point," *New Times*, no. 28, July 21, 1986.

A. James McAdams — "A New Deal for Eastern Europe," *The Nation*, June 13, 1987.

Adam Michnik — "A Pole's Appeal for an Open Trial," *The New York Times*, May 21, 1985.

Jerzy Milewski, Krzysztof Pomian, and Jan Zielonka — "Poland: Four Years After," *Foreign Affairs*, Winter 1985/86.

The New Republic — "Solidarity Forsaken," January 5 & 12, 1987.

Stefan Opara — "Criticism Under Socialism," *World Marxist Review*, March 1987.

Miklos Ovari — "Taking up a Point: If an Enterprise Is Losing Money," *New Times*, no. 5, February 9, 1987.

Zbigniew Pudysz — "Who Stands To Gain?" *New Times*, no. 12, March 30, 1987.

Douglas Stanglin — "Eastern Europe Rattles the Yoke," *U.S. News & World Report*, June 2, 1986.

World Press Review — "Europe's Yalta Legacy," April 1985.

5 CHAPTER

Is Glasnost Genuine?

the SOVIET UNION

Chapter Preface

Since Mikhail Gorbachev became Soviet premier in 1985, glasnost has become a catch-phrase in the Soviet Union and around the world. Gorbachev's policies to reinvigorate the economy and to inspire reforms in Soviet society became known as glasnost, meaning "openness." As a result of these policies, Gorbachev asserts, official newspapers such as *Pravda* now print articles on formerly taboo topics, alcoholism and corruption are the focus of government campaigns, and economic ties with the West are being cultivated.

Many critics contend that Gorbachev's glasnost is simply a superficial maneuver to gain favorable trade with the West while the worst aspects of the USSR remain unchanged. Some of the critics concede that Soviet attempts at change may be genuine, but they argue that glasnost cannot overcome the inherently oppressive structure of the communist system.

Supporters of glasnost believe any positive changes in the Soviet Union, however small, should be welcomed and encouraged. They cite Gorbachev's call for arms control, the release of dissidents such as Andrei Sakharov, and the printing of formerly objectionable literature such as Boris Pasternak's *Dr. Zhivago* as positive signs of reform.

Whether or not glasnost is a genuine effort by the Soviets to improve East-West relations will be known in time. The authors in this chapter debate whether glasnost is a fraud, is well-intended but ill-fated, or is destined to bring new vitality to the Soviet Union.

"We have the necessary political experience and theoretical potential to carry out the tasks facing society."

The Soviet System Embraces Glasnost

Mikhail Gorbachev

Since becoming the leader of the Soviet Union in 1985, Mikhail Gorbachev has worked to rejuvenate his nation's economy. These reforms, along with Gorbachev's emphasis on "openness," have met with some resistance within the Soviet Union. In the following viewpoint, taken from a speech before the Trade Unions of the USSR, Gorbachev contends that resistance to glasnost can be overcome. The Soviet system, in Gorbachev's opinion, is amenable to change. With the dedicated support of workers, intellectuals, and professionals, Gorbachev believes that economic reform and glasnost can become reality.

As you read, consider the following questions:

1. Why does Gorbachev stress the importance of the worker in making glasnost succeed?
2. According to Gorbachev, how can opposition to restructuring the economy be overcome?
3. Why does the author think democracy will advance glasnost?

Mikhail Gorbachev, "Restructuring—A Vital Concern of the People," a speech presented to the 18th Congress of the Trade Unions of the USSR, February 25, 1987.

A year is a brief period. But much took place in [1986] which is of great social significance. And at the same time we realize now that only the very first steps have been made.

The main thing, and hence the most difficult, still lies ahead. Up to now we have been mostly preparing for restructuring: we have been working out the strategy of restructuring, mapping out the main ways, identifying everything that is a hindrance and calls for adjustment, and determining the points of departure.

It is now time to get the actual work of restructuring under way. . . .The fate of the restructuring is being in fact decided now and the foundation for acceleration is being laid.

The restructuring, as was emphasized at the January, [1987] Plenary Meeting of the Central Committee, is a reality, and no longer a mere idea. It is getting hold of the minds of people and that means that it works. It works for socialism, for the renewal of our society.

Building Socialism

We are not building from scratch, and one cannot build anything worthwhile if he has nothing to start with. We have got something to be proud of and to rely upon. We have great values which we place above everything else.

Our country had carried out the greatest of revolutions, one which drastically changed the course of events in our country and in the world and made an indelible imprint on the destinies of mankind. We already have a vast and rich experience, which has not yet been assessed to the full, in building socialism, an experience which one must constantly turn to as we learn to solve in the Leninist way problems that arise.

We already have a tremendous economic, scientific, technical and intellectual potential created and multiplied by the energy and talents of all the peoples of our great country.

Yes, comrades, we have traversed a long path, a difficult and heroic one. But in all the ordeals we have upheld the revolutionary spirit of the people, faith in socialism and its supreme justice.

We have coped with and overcome all difficulties. We have been able to make an unprecedented advance from the wooden plough and the light-giving splinter to space flights, and we have experienced an incomparable joy—the joy of great accomplishments.

The Great Gains

The indissoluble link between work and civic concern for the common good, which unites all generations of Soviet people, our patriotism, working-class pride, labour enthusiasm, and the sacred feeling of belonging to the great cause of the October Revolution— all these are the great gains of our system without which it is simply inconceivable.

It is precisely the working people, and first of all the working class

212

with its devotion to revolutionary traditions, who are the main motive force in today's transformations. Industriousness has always been the supreme moral value of our people, and mastery of one's profession or trade has always been among man's chief virtues....

We all want changes for the better, and as soon as possible. The great goals which the Party has put forward and the increasing

From *The Wall Street Journal*—Permission, Cartoon Features Syndicate.

changes in the economic, social and political spheres have resulted in what may be called a "revolution of expectations". Many want quick social and material returns. This I can tell also from my meetings with the working people of Latvia and Estonia.

Let us be frank, comrades, there is only one way whereby we can achieve acceleration and improve the quality of our entire life: through efficient and highly productive work. No mechanisms of distribution or redistribution can create anything by themselves. . . .

Positive Changes

When evaluating at the January Plenary Meeting of the Central Committee the positive changes that have taken place, we said that they reflected the Soviet people's powerful support for the Party's policy and for the Party's course towards restructuring. But the state of affairs at the beginning of this year shows that the positive changes have not become a steady trend of economic development. There were growing difficulties in iron-and-steel industry, in the chemical and electronic industries, but the relevant ministries, the USSR State Planning Committee and the USSR State Committee for Material and Technical Supply did not pay proper attention to this. People at many enterprises in these industries did not set about correcting the situation in time.

The results showed that both in the centre and in the localities many people were not properly prepared for work in conditions in which increased demands are made on the activity of enterprises and production associations as a result of full-scale transition to new methods of economic management.

The situation is improving now, but the process is too slow. The Central Committee of the Party is counting on the working class and all working people to show understanding of the significance of the present moment, of the importance of the successful implementation of the projected plans for the cause of acceleration, and on their growing contribution to economic development.

Today we want radically to change the atmosphere in our society, for we cannot be satisfied with the way we lived and worked previously. But we will achieve nothing if we do not completely do away with the forces of inertia and deceleration which are dangerous in that they can draw the country back again into stagnation and dormancy, threatening us with the ossification of society and social corrosion. . . .

Now the process of restructuring is deepening; it is being carried out in practice. And it turns out that it is affecting the interests of many: first, through product acceptance by state-appointed inspectors; second, through the introduction of a system of self-repayment and self-financing; third, through the implementation of the principle of elective office; and fourth, through control, openness, criticism and so on.

There is nothing surprising here. The process of restructuring affects more and more spheres of the life of society and the interests of all social groups. And as in the case of truly revolutionary changes, restructuring encourages and imparts fresh vigour to some, while others are perplexed, still others simply do not like the ongoing changes. These changes are particularly resented by those who got used to working without much effort, to doing everything haphazardly, who are indifferent to things and inert. These changes are also resented by those who until now ran the affairs of an enterprise, district, city or laboratory as if it were their own private domain, without the slightest regard for the opinion of the collective, of the working people. Among them are also people who took advantage of the atmosphere of total licence for embezzling public funds and self-enrichment, cynically disregarding our laws and moral principles. Here lie the sources of resistance to restructuring, of sluggishness and a desire to sit things out.

Restructuring

More than two years have passed since the concept of restructuring tempestuously and firmly entered the life of the Soviet people. With it are associated dramatic changes in the economy and in management, in social policy and democracy. Restructuring has virtually encompassed our entire society and all regions of the country....

The people are the ones to decide the success of reform. The healthy young forces that are replacing corrupt officials should ensure and consolidate this success.

Soviet Life, September 1987.

Let me say once again: in principle, there is nothing surprising here. On the contrary, it would be strange if the work of restructuring suited everybody—honest and dishonest, hard-working and lazy people, activists, people of principle, and high-handed functionaries. This would mean that there is something in our policy that is not well-thought-out, that does not work and is faulty. However, here is a political nuance which should not be disregarded. I have just spoken of those who oppose restructuring for selfish reasons. There is, however, dramatism in a situation, where selfless, honest people who have so far remained captives of outdated notions, are among its opponents. These are people who have not realized the acute and critical nature of the problems facing our society.

We ought to persuade them and win their confidence on the basis of the correctness of our cause, of the success of the work of restructuring. It is our duty to help such people understand where their true interests lie and find their place in the common ranks.

In general, restructuring is affecting everybody: Political Bureau members, Central Committee secretaries, government officials, workers, farmers and members of the intelligentsia. It is affecting the whole of society, the interests of all and everyone. At this point I would like to recall what Lenin said concerning the need to distinguish between the short-term and vital interests of the working class.

Long-Term Interest

Yes, indeed, restructuring is affecting our short-time interests. But it meets the vital long-term interests of the working people. We ought to understand that. Such an understanding is of fundamental significance.

This is a very important principle.

Restructuring should reveal socialism's potential, enable our society to advance to new frontiers, ensure a new quality of life in all spheres—economic, social and intellectual—and strengthen socialism. As I have already said, it meets the vital interests of the working people. And if it is affecting us in some way today, we should consider everything calmly, objectively assess the situation and adopt practical measures to deal with acute problems that arise.

We have the necessary political experience and theoretical potential to carry out the tasks facing society. One thing is clear: we should advance without fail along the path of restructuring. If the work of restructuring fades out, the consequences will be very serious indeed for society as a whole and for every Soviet person in particular.

Our choice of the path is a correct one. We are not moving away from socialism; we are developing the potential of the socialist system through restructuring. We are not moving away from democracy, but towards greater democracy in the interests of the working people. . . .

The system of socialism is a working people's system. Everything that takes place in a socialist state is a concern of the people. That is why we stand for openness. It should be normal practice rather than a short-term campaign. We stand for criticism and self-criticism, which should also be normal practice in our life. We need such powerful forms of democracy as openness, criticism and self-criticism in order radically to change every sphere of our social life.

Herein lies a guarantee against the repetition of past errors, and consequently a guarantee that the restructuring process is irreversible.

The People and Democracy

Further democratization might lead some people to ask if we are not disorganizing society, if we will not weaken control and lower standards with regard to discipline, order and responsibility. This is an extremely important question, and we should be quite clear as to where we stand on it.

I will put it frankly: those who have doubts about the desirability of further democratization apparently suffer from a serious shortcoming, one that is of great political significance—they do not believe in our people. They say that democracy will be used by people to disorganize society and undermine discipline, to weaken the system. I think we cannot agree to that.

Democracy is not the opposite of order. It is order on a higher level, being based not on unquestioning obedience, mindless execution of instructions, but on the active equal participation by all members of society in all its affairs.

Democracy is not the opposite of discipline. It is conscious discipline and organization of working people based on a sense of really being the master of the country, on collectivism, and solidarity of interests and efforts of all citizens.

Democracy is not the opposite of responsibility. It does not mean absence of control or an attitude that everything goes. Democracy means society exercising self-control, based on the confidence in the civic maturity and awareness of social duty on the part of Soviet people. Democracy is unity of rights and duties.

Advancing Through Democracy

The deepening of democracy is certainly no easy task. And there is no need to get alarmed if things do not proceed smoothly at once, if there are potholes here and there, if not deep gullies. But our society is mature, our Party is strong. The socialist system rests on the firmest foundation—the support of the people—and draws strength precisely from our democratic way of life. The more democracy we have, the faster we shall advance along the road of restructuring and social renewal, and the more order and discipline we shall have in our socialist home.

So, it is either democracy or social inertia and conservatism. There is no other way, comrades.

I have said that we need democracy not so that we can show off and so that we can play democracy. We need democracy so that we can reorganize many things in our life, give greater scope to the creative abilities of people, to new ideas and initiative.

"It should be evident that, even if he wished, Gorbachev could not radically transform the vast Soviet state."

The Soviet System Will Not Allow Glasnost

Robert L. Pfaltzgraff Jr.

Though the Soviet Union has shown signs of change since 1985, many Soviet critics do not think the USSR is capable of true reform. They assert that the Soviets are making only minor changes to encourage much-needed Western trade and technology transfer. In the following viewpoint, Robert L. Pfaltzgraff Jr. writes that though Gorbachev's intentions are good, he cannot change the entrenched Soviet system. Pfaltzgraff is president of the Institute for Foreign Policy Analysis and a professor of law and diplomacy at Tufts University.

As you read, consider the following questions:

1. Why does the author think that Gorbachev cannot succeed in reforming Soviet society?
2. According to Pfaltzgraff, does the release of a few political prisoners mean the Soviets have changed?
3. In the author's opinion, why should people not be lulled into thinking glasnost has changed the USSR?

Robert L. Pfaltzgraff Jr., "Glasnost: Gorbachev and the 'New Millennium.'" This article first appeared in the June 1987 issue of *The World & I* and is reprinted with permission from *The World & I* magazine, a publication of the Washington Times Corporation.

In the nearly 70 years since its founding, the Soviet Union has had fewer leaders than any other major power in the twentieth century. Until the present decade only four men had reached the pinnacle of power in the Soviet Union, including its founder, Vladimir I. Lenin himself, and Nikita Khrushchev, whose tenure, important as it was, in retrospect stands as a period of transition between the long Stalinist era and the ascension of Leonid Brezhnev. Between them, Stalin and Brezhnev ruled for a total of 47 years—two-thirds of the history of the Soviet state.

The death of the enfeebled Brezhnev in 1982, followed by the gerontocracy represented successively by Yuri Andropov and Konstantin Chernenko, formed the leadership setting for the emergence of Mikhail Gorbachev in 1985.

Among other things, Gorbachev stands apart from his two immediate predecessors in vigor and comparative age. Gorbachev reached the leadership of the Soviet Union at age 54, just several years older than Stalin at a similar point in his career, and four years younger than Brezhnev when he came to power as general secretary of the Communist Party of the Soviet Union. Thus, from an actuarial perspective, Gorbachev has the potential to lead the Soviet Union into what he has termed the "new millennium," provided he can consolidate his position and avoid the fate that befell Khrushchev, who was ousted in October 1964.

Moscow's Influence

The Soviet state that Gorbachev inherited possesses unprecedented military capabilities amassed under Brezhnev, together with the projection of Moscow's influence into regions as distant from the Soviet Union as Southeast Asia and Central America, as well as the empire that was Stalin's legacy from the Soviet victories in World War II and the consolidation of communist power in Eastern Europe in the years that followed.

Yet Gorbachev presides over a Soviet state that, in all sectors except the military, has failed its own ideology and stated programs. As Gorbachev well knows, the Soviet Union has long since fallen far short of the goals set by the 21st Party Congress in 1961—that within a decade Soviet industrial and agricultural output would surpass that of the United States and "socialism will inevitably succeed capitalism everywhere" in accordance with the "objective law of social development."

For Gorbachev, the evidence is abundant that such expansive ideological rhetoric cannot mask the inefficiency of a stagnating economy, laggard growth rates, and a poorly motivated labor force. Hence, the only alternative is seen as *glasnost* (openness) about the nature, extent, and implications of the malaise, together with a program based on *perestroika* (restructuring) as the prerequisite for breathing new life into the Soviet system at all levels.

In his speech to the Central Committee Plenum on January 27, 1987, Gorbachev set the tone for this discussion:

> No accomplishments, even the most impressive ones, should obscure either contradictions in societal development or our mistakes and failings. . . . At some point the country began to lose momentum, difficulties and unresolved problems started to pile up, and there appeared elements of stagnation and other phenomena alien to socialism. All that badly affected the economy and social, cultural, and intellectual life.

Blaming the Past

Although he has yet to attribute the failures of the past to his predecessor by name, the implication of Gorbachev's indictment is clear: The formidable problems confronting the Soviet state form a bitter legacy of the Brezhnev years. In this respect, Gorbachev has stopped one step short of a full-scale denunciation of Brezhnev comparable to Khrushchev's momentous address to the 20th Party Congress in 1956, during which the brutal dictatorship of the Stalin era was exposed for all the world to see.

Reforms Will Not Change System

Nearly seventy years of ruthless and unscrupulous Communist rule have destroyed the trust which may have existed originally between the Soviet rulers and the people. The people can hardly expect significant improvements as a result of any within-the-system reforms because the very idea of this system has outlived itself. But even if the system is dismantled, it could take a couple of generations before the people recover completely. Collectivized farmers have to learn how to be peasants, "proletarians" have to learn how to be workers, surviving craftsmen have to teach their skills to new generations.

Vladimir Bukovsky, *Commentary*, September 1986.

More in keeping with Gorbachev's tone is Khrushchev's statement, if his memoirs are to be believed, concerning the plight of the Soviet consumer, that "when the state mismanages agriculture, the average Soviet citizen suffers. How do we know when the state is mismanaging agriculture? I believe the food counters more than I believe the statistics I read." Thus the economic problems that Gorbachev seeks to address are those that Khrushchev attempted but failed to resolve.

In place of Khrushchev's bombast and optimism, Gorbachev's pronouncements reflect a more somber assessment of the magnitude of the problem: "The tremendous scale and volume of the work ahead is coming to light more fully, and it is becoming clearer to what extent many conceptions of the economy and management, of social issues, of the state system . . . still lag behind the tasks of further development."

It would be tempting, but misguided, to read into Gorbachev's policies a radical departure from the Soviet past, the cumulative effect of which will somehow be a new era of political pluralism. A careful analysis of Gorbachev's pronouncements and a focus on his actions, as well as the human and structural obstacles that he would face even if he wanted to effect such a radical transformation, should dispel such an illusion.

He speaks of the "renovation of socialism" and of the need to "revive in modern conditions and to revive to the fullest extent possible the spirit of Leninism, to assert in our life the Leninist demands on cadres." Ritualistically genuflective though they may be, as a necessary act of obeisance to Leninist principles, these are not the words of a bourgeois reformer. Instead, Gorbachev has taken upon himself the task, ambitious as it may be, of eradicating the harmful practices of drunkenness and sloth, reversing decay and corruption, and adapting the Soviet system to the needs of a new era. In this respect, like Czar Peter the Great, he feels compelled to borrow what is deemed appropriate for the Russian setting from the West and to increase contacts at various levels, while maintaining as absolute a degree of control over the political system as possible.

It should be evident that, even if he wished, Gorbachev could not radically transform the vast Soviet state with its entrenched governing apparatus—short of destroying the foundations on which his rule is based. When he speaks of the need for decentralization, Gorbachev means not the dismantling of the monopoly of the party but instead its reinvigoration with new people and ideas.

Election "Changes"

The much-touted proposal unveiled by Gorbachev in his party plenum speech of January 27, 1987—for the election of party chiefs from the local district to the republic, or state, level—is illustrative. What this means is that, in place of one candidate, two or more names would be placed in nomination for selection, not by the entire electorate but instead by the appropriate party committee voting by secret ballot. The Leninist principle of "democratic centralization" would remain intact, with the upper levels of the party able to overrule those below them. The Soviet Union would continue to be a one-party state with multicandidate lists chosen by the Communist Party.

If such proposed minuscule change met with opposition, as has been reported, it is not difficult to imagine what the response would be to genuine reform in which the Communist Party became but one of two or more parties, each of whose leaders was elected by secret ballot on the basis of universal suffrage. Long before any such transformation had been achieved, it is likely that Gorbachev would have been packed off to one of the psychiatric hospitals used by the

KGB for the incarceration of political dissidents.

Among the other manifestations of *glasnost* is the dramatic decision in December 1986 to permit the Sakharovs to return to Moscow after seven years in enforced internal exile in the city of Gorky. This was followed by the release of a number of political prisoners, some of whom have been forced to emigrate from the Soviet Union as a condition for being let out of Soviet jails and labor camps—undoubtedly a humanitarian gesture but hardly a decision to allow unfettered debate in the Soviet Union. As long as several thousand Soviet prisoners of conscience remain in detention in degrading circumstances, Gorbachev's reforms will have a hollow ring.

Difficult Emigration

While some who disagree with the regime are forced to emigrate, others continue to be denied the right to do so. Gorbachev's new emigration law, which took effect on January 1, 1987, was lauded in the Soviet Union as a step toward simplifying the process by clarifying the procedures. In fact, in several respects, including family reunification, it makes the process more difficult because only the closest of relatives are to be counted as family members eligible for emigrating. Clearly, the Soviet openness policy has far to go if it is to affect the prospects for the hundreds of thousands of Jews and

J.D. Crowe, reprinted with permission.

others who, if permitted to do so, would leave the Soviet Union.

There is abundant evidence that, under Gorbachev, the Soviet intellectual and literary-artistic scene has shed at least some of the drabness and abject conformity symbolized by "socialist realism." The stultifying hand of censorship has been lightened—but not lifted—to permit the publication of long-banned works such as Boris Pasternak's *Doctor Zhivago*, as well as Anatoly Rybakov's *Children of the Arbat*, whose focus is the terror of the Stalin era.

Of more immediate significance, the Soviet media under Gorbachev, as might be expected, have been enlisted to help stimulate discussion and even intense debate about those areas in which the leadership seeks reform. However, when the regime decides to do so, such debate can be cut off as easily as it was turned on. There is no part of Gorbachev's life experience that would lead him inevitably to favor openness of discussion as an end in itself. A party line of *glasnost* could be superseded by an equally dramatic change in course, as has happened before in Soviet history.

Media Manipulation

If Gorbachev is determined to expose and eliminate misconduct, it follows that the press and television can form powerful tools, provided they remain, as they will in the Soviet Union, faithful instruments under state control. Thus *Pravda* plays a useful role when it exposes the illegal arrest by the KGB of a reporter who had attempted to focus public attention on corruption in the coal-mining industry in the Ukraine. If Gorbachev has concluded that the Soviet Union has much to learn from the West and if its economy is to gain needed efficiency, the media become the indispensable vehicle for disseminating such information, even to the extent of reporting favorably on those conditions in the United States and elsewhere from which the Soviet Union can learn something of value.

Because nothing ranks higher on Gorbachev's domestic agenda than the reform of the Soviet economy and the reversal of its decline, *glasnost* has emerged not as a manifestation of Gorbachev as an out-of-the-closet liberal but for the purpose of providing for the influx of new ideas in order to revitalize the economy. Gorbachev's openness extends to somewhat greater flexibility for state enterprises in negotiating with foreign companies but obviously not to the establishment of a capitalist private sector, although farm workers will be encouraged to cultivate private plots and collective farms to sell extra production on the open market.

At the present time only 1.5 percent of farmland in the Soviet Union is under private cultivation, yet it is said to account for as much as half of all food available to the consumer. Thus, what Gorbachev proposes for Soviet agriculture is hardly an innovation of dramatic proportions.

Another important dimension of considerable consequence both for Gorbachev's policy and for the West is the use *glasnost* has as an instrument of Moscow's foreign policy. Gorbachev plays host to visiting delegations of eminent political figures, as well as scientists, artists, writers, and academics from the United States and elsewhere, with whom he engages in what is termed learned dialogue. Such an educational experience itself is designed to enhance Gorbachev's *glasnost* image, aside from what it may actually yield in the form of new ideas and information for the Soviet leader.

The Dangers of Glasnost

To the extent that Western expectations of beneficial change are raised, *glasnost* helps to pave the way for needed Soviet acquisition of what will be required if even a modicum of the economic advance decreed by Gorbachev is to be registered. In this sense, openness becomes the latter-day manifestation of the detente policy that, in the United States at least, came to be discredited in the 1970s as a basis for relations with the Soviet Union.

It remains to be seen whether Gorbachev's emphasis on the deeply rooted domestic problems of the Soviet Union will produce a lessening of those expansionist tendencies that have pushed the tentacles of Soviet power into remote regions and continents. Whatever the opportunities for the West that may arise from *glasnost*, the dangers are numerous. They include the prospect that, once again, the West will be lulled into an expectation of fundamental Soviet change, only to realize that the basic interests of the Soviet state transcend specific leaders and to discover that, with or without the economic changes proposed by Gorbachev, the Soviet Union will remain a formidable military superpower at odds with the United States on fundamental security issues in a world fraught with conflict potential as we approach the "new millennium" of the twenty-first century.

"All these so-called changes in the Soviet Union are rather contrived....What they are doing is a huge propaganda campaign."

Glasnost Is a Public Relations Ploy

Vladimir Bukovsky

Vladimir Bukovsky emigrated from the Soviet Union in 1976 after spending 12 years in Soviet prisons, labor camps, and psychiatric hospitals for his dissident political activities. In the following viewpoint, Bukovsky warns that people should not believe that Soviet society has become any more open or any less repressive. He maintains that glasnost is only a public relations campaign to improve the Soviet Union's worldwide image.

As you read, consider the following questions:

1. According to Bukovsky, why did the Soviet press need to start publishing the truth?
2. How does the author support his argument that glasnost is just a public relations campaign?
3. Why does the author argue that glasnost is merely a pragmatic move?

Vladimir Bukovsky, "Glasnost: Genuine Change or Illusion?" a speech addressed to The Heritage Foundation, March 11, 1987. Reprinted with permission.

I am very sure that you all care about the news from the Soviet Union. It is very confusing to many people. Even some of our more experienced compatriots have lost touch, after hearing this campaign of 'glasnost', or cultural openness, or whatever the current term might be. Indeed the signals are very contradictory. And it is mainly because so many people want to see changes in the Soviet Union.

A few dozen prisoners get released, and of course it is very pleasant, a very good thought for all of us, but it is important to remember that the main reason that they were released was to get the prisoners to maximize the public impression with immediate concessions. But if we really had a change of heart, because of the way the Soviet Union works, we would not release one by one the most prominent dissidents over the duration of a year, we would simply declare amnesty. And we would not demand that these prisoners sign a statement that they would not continue anti-Soviet activity.

We also hear now and then of Gorbachev speaking, the press tells me, of the necessity for radical economic reforms in the Soviet Union. It is, of course, very pleasant to hear. Unfortunately, though it remains on paper or in words, to date, there are no reforms in the Soviet economy. . . .

The Confusion of Glasnost

But I tell you, the most confusing and the most objectionable maneuver is the current policy of so-called 'glasnost'. Indeed, I cannot imagine that many people believe it when they read in the Soviet Union, in *Pravda*, statements and facts that only a few years ago would have been branded as anti-Soviet slander and for which people could have been imprisoned for up to several years. However, these policies make virtue of necessity because the Soviet propaganda machinery is built entirely on lies, it seems to be accepted. At least people have started reading the newspapers in the Soviet Union. Before, they didn't. Now you can come across, in one of the articles in TASS or *Pravda*, facts which previously you had obtained only from Voice of America or Radio Liberty.

And a person may be frustrated. It is even dangerous to rely on a huge propaganda machine that does not charm anybody any more. More or less could be said about the so-called cultural show. A few writers who died long ago have finally been published in the Soviet Union, and they of course, can be read. But we should remember always—be aware—that they are already dead, and therefore cannot do anything unexpected, and that we have a very long line of these dead writers who are waiting for the next cultural thaw to come around so they can be legalized.

That is, in a way, a sad thing. That is the tragedy of Russian culture, because in order to become known to readers and viewers, Soviet writers, musicians, dancers, or film producers have to become either dead physically or dead spiritually to become a part of the propaganda machine in order to be allowed to show their art in the Soviet Union. We hear, of course, that emigre cultural figures were invited secretly to come back and be pardoned, but that is the most ridiculous proposition. I know most of them, and I can assure you that none of them will go back. They are not that stupid. After living in the West and breathing the air of freedom it would be impossible for these people to live under the constant threat of KGB control. That is senseless to them.

Deceptive Promotion

Is 'glasnost' truth-in-packaging, or deceptive promotion? We suspect the latter. Why, you say? Let me ask you. . . .

Is it 'glasnost' when the Soviets falsely accuse the CIA of the Jim Jones massacre in Guyana, or when they publicly accuse the U.S. Army of creating and spreading the AIDS virus to Africa, while admitting in private that this is not so? It is 'glasnost' when the Soviets forge documents and deliberately distort the nature and purpose of our Strategic Defense Initiative—cynically playing on the passions of innocent men and women who hope and pray for a better, more peaceful world? Is it 'glasnost' when the Soviets won't allow American bookstores in the Soviet Union, yet Soviet bookstores are easily found here?

Charles Z. Wick, *Vital Speeches of the Day,* May 1, 1987.

If the Soviets really wanted to liberalize the access to their culture, they should have started by allowing the works of prominent writers, musicians, and film makers to be available to the Soviet readers, viewers, listeners, and then there would be no need for these so-called backdoor negotiations. In that case, we would return with pleasure.

A Public Relations Ploy

So, as you can see, all these so-called changes in the Soviet Union are rather contrived and not formal. The first impression you get from what they are doing is of a huge propaganda campaign, a huge public relations campaign calculated primarily for the consumption in the West, but partly also to encourage, to invigorate people, who stopped paying attention. We simply forget that the Soviet regime is excessively repressive and restrictive. And that even with much bigger changes, its essence, its nature will not change. Indeed they can release all the prisoners they have right now, they can allow emigration, they can publish the work of many writers, and they even can publish *The Gulag Archipelago* by Alexander Solzhenitsyn, and the Soviet system will not be destroyed.

They might become free and capitalistic and operate as they did in Hungary and Poland, but only for a short duration of time, much shorter than they did in Hungary or Poland, or even China. Because unlike Hungary and Poland, they do not have a big brother looking over their shoulders, always ready to come up and pull them back. And unlike China, there are a host of small brothers to look after. So, the question right now is not how far these so-called changes of Gorbachev have gone, but how long will they continue. For instance, if you take the smallest change, and imagine its continuing for five years, you immediately see that it might make some irreversible changes.

In five years, those who are fourteen years old right now will become nineteen, as we used to be during Khrushchev's time and his efforts at some liberalization. Five years later, the KGB did not know what to do with us. The same with the liberation of Sakharov and his return to Moscow. Right now, it is probably a big advantage to the Soviet leaders, because no matter what he said, the impression he produces is that Gorbachev is really a liberator, because he has allowed Sakharov to speak. But five years from now, if he were still allowed to speak what he speaks, it would create a tremendous problem, because naturally, a lot of people would come in contact with him, and a network of contacts and connections would organize itself around him all through the country, as it used to be in the 1960s and 1970s when we had just started the movement for human rights. And then, it would be an alternative structure—something the Soviet Union would not and could not tolerate.

Short-Lived Changes

We are so used to the Soviet system being absolutely unmovable and unchangeable that the smallest deviation is considered radical and almost revolutionary. Let us consider the most daring, the most courageous of Gorbachev's suggestions—namely, to liberalize the election rules within the party. Now if that were allowed to happen, the people of the Soviet Union would get somewhat closer to the situation that black people have in South Africa, with our "whites" being only 7 percent of the population having free elections for themselves. But if that continued for more than five or ten years, it would be very serious, and maybe it would lead to irreversible changes. It might actually lead to a split in the ruling party and that would be serious.

Now the impression that I get is that the campaign is not calculated to continue very long, and the Soviet rulers know it very well. It is just a short and very intensive effort. Another confusing part of what is happening right now, which is confusing primarily in the West, among the specialists, the Kremlinologists or whatever, is how to define this new Soviet leadership. Some assessments call them the new Stalinists, others have called them liberal and pragmatic. And frankly, I do not see much of a contradiction in these, if there is such a thing. Because, after all, Stalin could be very pragmatic and liberal when he needed. For example, when he wanted, very quickly, to have nuclear weapons created in the Soviet Union, he allowed the scientific community in the Soviet Union much more freedom than anyone else enjoyed. And was very pragmatic about that. Or during World War II, in the most difficult times, the most dark times when the Germans were advancing to Moscow, Stalin was pragmatic and liberal enough to address his nation as brothers and sisters, and not as comrades. And throughout the duration of World War II, he never mentioned socialism or communism, he just mentioned the great Russian tradition. And a lot of people at that time and after the war, were bought by this change in Soviet policy. Some old emigres from Paris went back to the Soviet Union believing that the system had changed, simply because Stalin had opened the churches, only to find themselves very quickly in jail in the Soviet Union.

KAL. 1987 Cartoonists & Writers Syndicate.

So, what we are dealing with is these typical, goal-oriented people, people who are revolutionaries. I have been reading a book about economic policy, and I discovered, among the memoirs of some communist people of that time, a very interesting detail, a very interesting fact. Apparently, even Felix Dzerzhinsky, the founder of the Cheka, the original KGB, became incredibly liberal and pragmatic when he was appointed by Lenin to chair the group directing Soviet industry, while, at the same time, remaining at the head of the secret police. Now, those who worked with Dzerzhinsky at that time say that he was incredibly liberal with the so-called bourgeois specialists, the scientists and engineers, who were working in Soviet industry. As long as he remained in charge of Soviet industry, none of them was arrested or harassed by the secret police. He was a great liberal figure to them, so much so that they would exchange anti-Soviet jokes while working and he would not as much as notice it. He would be embarrassed when he came into a room and a number of professors would rise. He would beg them not to rise, to remain seated. But at the same time, at exactly the same time, working for the secret police, he would be killing and torturing virtually millions of people. How can one explain?

It is a very simple scenario of goal-oriented people. If they need, in order to reach their goals, to kill millions of people, they will do that. If they need, to reach their goals, to become very liberal and pragmatic, they will do exactly that—as long as they can achieve their purpose. Current Soviet leaders are direct descendants of Lenin; they are his peers and students. Not only because the proportion of KGB in the Politburo right now is probably higher than at any time in Soviet history, and not only because it was the chief objective of Andropov himself as the head of the KGB for fifteen years, but mostly because psychologically they are goal-oriented. They will do anything to reach their goals....

Not a New Concept

I myself find it bizarre to talk about the current campaign of 'glasnost'. I was imprisoned in 1965 for demanding 'glasnost' and in 1967 for the review of the articles of the penal code, which used to imprison people on political grounds, Articles 17 and 190. And now Gorbachev says that he is going to review them. What Gorbachev did was quite skillful. He actually hijacked our slogans. But he still does what he wants to. For example, I believe that 'glasnost'...is something that the public does, not the government. Now, in my view, the interests of 'glasnost' would be much better served if the Soviets were to allow free access to Xerox machines rather than to conduct all this criticism of operations directed from the top. The Party still maintains a monopoly on the truth. And tomorrow, after all, the truth might be different.

230

"We dismiss the interpretation that reforms and changes are merely 'cosmetic,' a public relations gimmick."

Glasnost Is Not a Public Relations Ploy

Julius Jacobson

Many experts on the Soviet Union have been surprised by the appearance of articles critical of the Soviet system in official newspapers such as *Pravda*. Supporters of glasnost point to these candid articles as an indication that Soviet society is truly becoming more open. In the following viewpoint, Julius Jacobson writes that the Soviets are indeed reforming their society to spur the economy and motivate workers to improve production. Jacobson is an editor for *New Politics*, a journal that supports socialism.

As you read, consider the following questions:

1. Why does the author disagree with the theory that glasnost is only a cosmetic change?
2. What cultural and artistic proof does Jacobson present to support his belief in the change in Soviet attitude?
3. According to the author, why must the Soviet Union reform?

Julius Jacobson, "Glasnost and the Cult of Gorbachev," *New Politics*, Volume I, No. 3, Summer 1987. ©1987 New Politics Associates, Brooklyn, NY.

"A bloodless revolution" and a "revolution by culture" (as distinct from "a cultural revolution"). A revolution in process that is "a fight to the death" against the active opposition of conservatives and the silent resistance of inertia and apathy. That is how Andrei Voznesensky, one of the Soviet Union's leading, spirited poets of the post-Stalin thaw, described the unfolding drama of change and reform in his country since Mikhail S. Gorbachev succeeded the aging Soviet President and Party General Secretary, Konstantin Chernenko. Perhaps Voznesensky's hopes soar somewhat higher than most with a similar history and background, but it is clear enough that many victims of Soviet repression, dissidents in general, and perhaps the bulk of the Soviet intelligentsia, some more skeptically than others, endorse the reforms as genuine changes improving the quality of life in the USSR; and, also on varying levels, are convinced that Gorbachev is determined to democratize Soviet society.

Are we witnessing a "revolution," as Voznesenky believes? Are political, economic and social relations in the Soviet Union undergoing a fundamental transformation? Or do the reforms have a more limited intent? Are the reforms reversible? Do they pose a threat to the Communist system? Are Gorbachev and his supporters in the upper echelons of the Communist Party prepared to dismantle the repressive institutions of a one-party state for the sake of democratizing Soviet society? If social revolution from above is not possible, do the reforms and changes open new possibilities in the USSR (and in Soviet bloc nations) for the flowering of movements from below for democratic social change and peace? These are among the questions to be touched upon in this commentary.

The Reforms Are Real

First, we must make clear that we dismiss the interpretation that reforms and changes are merely "cosmetic," a public relations gimmick, a propaganda device to give the Kremlin an ideological advantage in the Cold War, etc. That Gorbachev seeks to improve the Soviet image and to project the persona of a man of peace shaping a society committed to detente and self-improvement should be self-evident. But to reduce the drama of reform and change to tactical machinations in the Cold War or to a kind of vanity is to trivialize and misunderstand what is happening, and why. We cannot ignore or dismiss Gorbachev's peace initiatives. No matter his motives, the proposals were a positive contribution to de-escalating the arms race, met with hostility and cynicism by the Reagan Administration.

Had just one or two or a dozen political prisoners been freed and only a few modest reforms carried out, one might make a case for the "cosmetic" interpretation. But in the past year [1986], the most prominent dissidents and prisoners of conscience have been released from the camps and permitted to return from exile. Sharansky, Orlov, Koryagin, Sakharov, just to mention a few of the approximately 100

(140 if the Soviet authorities are to be believed) who have been freed. And there has been a remarkable change in the cultural atmosphere. Consider that the banned *Doctor Zhivago* is to be printed officially, its author, Boris Pasternak, rehabilitated, his house in a Moscow suburb to become a museum, his grave a place for pilgrimages and poetry readings. Anna Akhmatova's *Requiem,* a collection of poems describing the personal torment of waiting outside a prison for news of loved ones during Stalin's terror, will be published. Anatoly Rybakov's *Children of the Arbat,* a novel about Stalin's terror turned down for publication more than 20 years ago, will also be published. Vladimir Nabokov's novels will be permitted for the first time. So will the poetry of Nikolai S. Gumilev (Akhmatova's husband), executed by the Bolsheviks in 1921. Novels by Vladimir Dudintsev and Aleksandr Bek will once again surface.

Not Mere Propaganda

[Our] skepticism shouldn't be seen as backing us into the Reaganaut corner where the Gorbachev reforms are condemned as mere propaganda. Andrei Sakharov himself said of the *glasnost* policy, "It's not right to say that it's only propaganda or window-dressing. It's not a matter of helping Gorbachev but of helping ourselves."

Danny Collum, *Sojourners,* June 1987.

The reforms are reflected in Soviet cinema as well. A film, *Repentance,* dealing with Stalin's terror has opened, playing first in Stalin's native Georgia. On view is the film, *Is It Easy to be Young?* that revolves around the problems of disturbed Soviet veterans of the Afghan war. Gosinko, Soviet film censors, sent flowers to the funeral services for Andre Tarkovsky, the noted film director it had persecuted, who emigrated to Paris in 1984. The censors have removed any number of banned films from their shelves. Glasnost has also benefitted the theater. Yuri Lyubimov, former director of the avant garde Taganka Theater has been invited to return from emigration. There are now many plays dealing, at least obliquely, with the Stalin terror. Ovechin's "Say It!" criticizes the past performance of the Party and urges the people to speak out—to "Say It!" (Of course, not to say too much.) There is much more openness on television, in cultural and political programming. The Soviet public was treated to a debate between American and Soviet personalities about human rights and the war in Vietnam. There is a visible attempt to accommodate the youth culture. Heavy metal groups perform aboveground, and break dancing can be viewed on television. The press, too, is more open in its reportage of disasters and even informed the public of the riots in Alma-Ata.

Official historiography has also been touched by glasnost. In a March [1987] issue of *Argumenty i Fakty*, a weekly which provides Party publicists with the approved political line of the moment, the historian, Aleksander Samsonov, holds Stalin responsible for the military blunders that cost the Soviet Union so dearly just before and after the German armies attacked in June 1941. In Shatrov's *The Dictatorship of Conscience*, there is a debate between Lenin and the characters in the play, and the distinctions are made between Lenin's conceptions and what followed after his death in 1924.

There are also reforms which permit public pressure to change government policy. For example, government-initiated construction projects, such as dams, have been abandoned in response to objections by environmentalists and protests in the press.

There is no reason to believe that the reforms have peaked. On the contrary, we expect the public will be allowed even more space. Likely, there will be liberal revisions in criminal law to protect the rights of defendants and to reduce the sweeping nature of statutes against "anti-Soviet agitation and propaganda," which have provided the "legal" basis for condemning so many to prisons, labor camps, and exile. There is even talk of granting citizens the right to sue officials.

Further Improvements

There has been an easing of restrictions against Jewish emigration. Approximately 500 Jews were allowed to leave in March [1987]. Reportedly, a number of restrictions against the right of Jews to practice their religion will be lifted. And possibly Gorbachev will make a more serious effort to extricate the Soviet Union from *its* Vietnam—Afghanistan.

It is even possible that a number of prominent victims of the Stalin purges will be rehabilitated; perhaps Bukharin, Zinoviev and others of similar stature. What else can one make of Gorbachev's speech to media dignitaries, in which he said that ". . .there should be no blank pages in history and literature. . ." "We should not move into the shade those who made the revolution" and "We must not forget the names, and even more immoral is to forget or to keep silent about whole periods in the life of the people who lived, believed and worked under the party in the name of socialism."

There may be more than one candidate for offices in lower levels of Party and State organs. That would be a novelty few if any living Soviet citizens have ever experienced.

This internal relaxation is inseparable from the Gorbachev peace offensive; the emphasis placed on detente and the initiatives undertaken by the Kremlin to reduce the nuclear arsenal of the two great powers.

The Soviet Union is beset by a social and economic crisis which has no chance of resolution in the context of the Cold War and an

234

economically exhausting arms race. In a speech to the Writers Union in July 1986, Gorbachev candidly described the state of the Soviet economy with special anguish and glasnost. "The whole of society is in a state of flux, the economy is in disarray. . . ." He amends this to "Our economy is in *great* disarray. We lag behind in every sphere." As an example: "In 1969 in Stavropol, we had a problem: what to do with meat and milk. And we had butter—lots of it. . . . And today we have nothing. The relationship between money and goods, income and goods, has been distorted." Another example is the extraordinary fact that the Ukraine, the breadbasket of the USSR, has become an importer of grain.

Sincere Change

Mr. Gorbachev is asking for no less than radical change. Lenin's utopian and violent revolution sought to destroy Czarist Russia and to build a new, world society, no less. Stalin's brutal revolution sought to concentrate all power in the Kremlin in order to force industrialization and to consolidate control over the empire. Mr. Gorbachev's more humane revolution seeks to make the Soviet Union a more efficient and productive society and a superpower that can better balance political and economic strength with military might.

William H. Luers, *The New York Times*, July 7, 1987.

Soviet industry is a disaster. Its plants and machinery are aging and its technology lags grievously. Labor productivity is declining. Machinery production for the first 2 months of [1987] was 3.6 percent less than Jan.-Feb., 1986. After 60 years of bureaucratic nationalization, the average industrial wage is estimated at about 200 rubles a month (about $300 dollars). In a speech delivered to a special conference on agriculture, Gorbachev passed judgment on Soviet economic performance for the first half of the eighties: "The whole of the Eleventh Five Year Plan was a wheelspin."

Fighting Crippling Corruption

The Soviet economy is also crippled by the debilitating effects of pervasive corruption and the indifference of the working class to quality standards or production goals; by absenteeism, labor indiscipline and, in the General Secretary's words, "our national tragedy—drunkenness." Gorbachev unburdened himself to the Writers Union: "There are many people who are drunkards, thieves and embezzlers. But of course, first and foremost, we have loads of bureaucrats who do not wish to part with their privileges. Why do I sit all the time surrounded by Lenin's works? I leaf through them, I look for solutions. . . . Because it is never too late to consult Lenin."

Gorbachev is making an effort to directly invigorate the faltering economy through methods he never learned by consulting Lenin. He recognizes the adverse effects of a stifling cultural atmosphere and political repression on economic development. Relaxation becomes an economic necessity, particularly to catch up in the area of high technology. The Party needs the support of professionals and intellectuals, all those subsumed under that broad category, the intelligentsia. For the intelligentsia to contribute their intelligence and skills most productively means to contribute them willingly. And that requires a freer, more congenial cultural and political atmosphere. But the cooperation of the intelligentsia will not be of much value if bureaucratic mismanagement and corruption is countenanced. And glasnost aims to make it more difficult for the purveyors of corruption to hide their misdeeds and escape justice; and easier for honest people to come forward and expose the miscreants without fear of reprisal from corrupt personnel.

Seeking Economic Salvation

Glasnost and "democratization" are also designed to arouse the enthusiasm and consciousness of the working class, to turn them from vodka to churning out high quality products. Without this participation by the working class, there will be no economic salvation. But to achieve this objective, glasnost is not enough. Gorbachev has additional ideas about how to involve the working class in his "revolution.". . .

Without any equivocation, I welcome the reforms initiated by Mikhail Gorbachev. But support for these reforms no more implies support for Gorbachev, or a benign tolerance of the Soviet system, than support for reforms initiated by or acceded to by U.S. administrations implies support for those administrations or muting our opposition to the capitalist society they serve and seek to make more stable and acceptable via social reform.

Recognizing Statements That Are Provable

From various sources of information we are constantly confronted with statements and generalizations about social and moral problems. In order to think clearly about these problems, it is useful if one can make a basic distinction between statements for which evidence can be found and other statements which cannot be verified or proved because evidence is not available, or the issue is so controversial that it cannot be definitely proved.

Readers should constantly be aware that magazines, newspapers, and other sources often contain statements of a controversial nature. The following activity is designed to allow experimentation with statements that are provable and those that are not.

The following statements are taken from the viewpoints in the fifth chapter of this book. Consider each statement carefully. *Mark P for any statement you believe is provable. Mark U for any statement you feel is unprovable because of the lack of evidence. Mark C for any statements you think are too controversial to be proved to everyone's satisfaction.*

If you are doing this activity as a member of a class or group, compare your answers with those of other class or group members. Be able to defend your answers. You may discover that others will come to different conclusions than you. Listening to the reasons others present for their answers may give you valuable insights in recognizing statements that are provable.

1. There is only one way the Soviet Union can improve its quality of life: through efficient and highly productive work.

2. Glasnost will reveal socialism's potential and will allow our society to advance to new frontiers.

3. In the nearly 70 years since its founding, the Soviet Union has had fewer leaders than any other major power in the twentieth century.

4. As Gorbachev knows, the Soviet Union has fallen far short of the goals set by the 21st Party Congress in 1961.

5. It is evident that Gorbachev could not radically transform the vast Soviet state even if he wanted to.

6. Only 1.5 percent of farmland in the Soviet Union is under private cultivation.

7. Strong leadership by determined men at the top would never be enough to get the Soviet Union moving again.

8. Glasnost continues to be manipulated by the Kremlin to assist it in ousting a long string of Brezhnev appointees.

9. If only the Soviet people knew how bad things were, they would move to correct them.

10. Soviet censorship has lightened to permit the publication of long-banned works such as Boris Pasternak's *Doctor Zhivago*.

11. There has been an easing of restrictions against Jewish emigration. Five hundred Jews were allowed to leave the Soviet Union in one month.

12. The main reason the Soviets release political prisoners is to maximize on positive public opinion.

13. If communist leaders need to kill millions of people to reach their goals, they will do it.

14. The average industrial wage in the Soviet Union is about 200 rubles a month, or about $300.

Periodical Bibliography

The following articles have been selected to supplement the diverse views expressed in this chapter.

Vassily Aksyonov	"Through the Glasnost, Darkly," *Harper's Magazine*, April 1987.
Archie Brown	"A Reformer in the Kremlin," *The Nation*, June 13, 1987.
Archie Brown	"What's Happening in Moscow?" *The National Interest*, Summer 1987.
Silviu Brucan	"Political Reform in the Socialist System," *World Policy Journal*, Summer 1987.
Stephen F. Cohen	"Sovieticus," *The Nation*, June 13, 1987.
John Greenwald	"Wooing the West," *Time*, March 2, 1987.
Robert G. Kaiser	"Okay, Comrades, Let's Take It from the Top," *The Washington Post National Weekly Edition*, January 26, 1987.
The Nation	"*Glasnost* and Us," June 13, 1987.
Richard Pipes	"The 'Glasnost' Test," *The New Republic*, February 2, 1987.
Andrei Sakharov	"Gorbachev's 'Courageous' Reform Plan," *U.S. News & World Report*, February 16, 1987.
Stephen Sestanovich	"What Gorbachev Wants," *The New Republic*, May 25, 1987.
Natan (Anatoly) Shcharansky	"Gorbachev Plays a 'Liberator' Game," *The New York Times*, February 8, 1987.
Daniel Singer	"Top Down or Bottom Up?" *The Nation*, June 6, 1987.
Robert C. Tucker	"Gorbachev and the Fight for Soviet Reform," *World Policy Journal*, Spring 1987.
Russell Watson	"Gorbachev's Opposition," *Newsweek*, May 18, 1987.
Tom Wicker	"In the West's Interest," *The New York Times*, February 18, 1987.
George F. Will	"The Sickening Soviet Reality," *Newsweek*, January 19, 1987.
James H. Wolfe	"Reluctant Reform in the Communist World," *USA Today*, May 1987.

Organizations To Contact

The editors have compiled the following list of organizations concerned with the issues debated in this book. All of them have publications available for interested readers. The descriptions are derived from materials provided by the organizations themselves.

American Committee on US-Soviet Relations
109 11th St. SE
Washington, DC 20003
(202) 546-1700

The Committee includes members of the academic and business communities, former ambassadors, labor leaders, and public interest spokespersons. Its purpose is to reduce tensions between East and West by encouraging support for strategic arms agreements and mutually beneficial programs in science, trade, and culture. The Committee publishes the *East/West Outlook*, as well as books and occasional papers.

American Security Council
499 S. Capitol St., Suite 500
Washington, DC 20003
(202) 484-1676

The Council sponsors the Coalition for Peace Through Strength, a bipartisan alliance of organizations, pro-defense lawmakers and American citizens. It works for the adoption of a strong defense policy and resistance to Soviet influence around the world. The Council recently published the booklet *A Strategy for Peace Through Strength*, and publishes the monthly *National Security Report*.

Amnesty International (AI)
322 8th Ave.
New York, NY 10001
(212) 807-8400

Amnesty International monitors human rights throughout the world, including in the USSR. AI is independent of any government, political faction, ideology, economic interest, or religious creed. It publishes an annual report on human rights conditions worldwide, and has published several reports specifically on the Soviet Union, covering such topics as the treatment of dissidents and prison conditions.

Cardinal Mindszenty Foundation
PO Box 11321
St. Louis, MO 63105
(314) 991-2939

The Foundation is a worldwide, non-profit educational organization offering information on the nature, propaganda, and goals of atheistic communism. It sponsors conferences and radio broadcasts. The Foundation publishes a monthly newsletter, *The Mindszenty Report*, and *The Red Line*, an analysis of official communist publications.

Citizen Exchange Commission (CEC)
18 E. 41st St.
New York, NY 10017
(212) 889-7960

The CEC promotes mutual understanding between American and Soviet citizens. The Commission organizes cultural, educational, and professional travel programs for Americans in the USSR and provides programs and hospitality for Soviet visitors in the US. It publishes pamphlets and the quarterly *Communique*.

Committee for National Security
1601 Connecticut Ave. NW, Suite 301
Washington, DC 20009
(202) 745-2450

The goal of the Committee is to promote informed public debate on national security issues, and to encourage arms control and improved US-Soviet relations. It recently published *The Other Side*, the first in a series of illustrated books on the Soviet Union and US-Soviet relations.

Communist Party of the United States of America (CPUSA)
235 W. 23rd St., 7th Floor
New York, NY 10011
(212) 989-4994

The Communist Party works to create a socialist society. It promotes a more realistic view of the Soviet Union than is given in the media and works for improved relations between the US and the USSR. It publishes the *People's Daily World* and the monthly *Political Affairs*.

Council for the Defense of Freedom
1275 K St. NW, Suite 1160
Washington, DC 20005
(202) 789-4294

The Council disseminates information on communism in order to combat it and to protect national security. The Council's weekly paper, *The Washington Inquirer*, reports on the arms race, US lack of preparedness versus the Soviet Union, and human rights abuses in the Soviet Union.

Department of State
Correspondence Management Division
PA/PC Room 5819
Washington, DC 20520

The Department of State publishes speeches and testimony by State Department officials and US government leaders concerning US-Soviet relations and arms control.

Fellowship of Reconciliation
Box 271
Nyack, NY 10960
(914) 358-4601

The Fellowship sponsors US-USSR Reconciliation Projects. These are various personal activities, such as sending poems for peace on postcards to people in the Soviet Union. The Fellowship publishes a variety of books, pamphlets, and audio-visual presentations encouraging peaceful relations with the Soviet Union, and a monthly magazine, *Fellowship*.

Freedom Federation
300 I St. NW, Suite 2
Washington, DC 20002
(202) 546-7440

The Federation is a formal coalition of members of 25 ethnic groups who have fled takeovers by the Soviet Union or Soviet proxies in Europe, Africa, Latin America, and Asia. It provides support for anti-Soviet resistance movements and promotes broadcasting to Soviet-dominated areas. It publishes a quarterly newsletter, *Update*.

Ground Zero Pairing Project
PO Box 19049
Portland, OR 97219
(503) 245-3403

The Ground Zero Pairing Project pairs American and Soviet cities so that citizens in both countries may learn more about each other. It publishes and distributes educational materials on the Soviet Union and US-Soviet relations. The Project also publishes the bi-annual newsletter, *Linkages*.

The Heritage Foundation
214 Massachusetts Ave.
Washington, DC 20002
(202) 546-4400

The Heritage Foundation is a conservative think tank that examines the Soviet challenge to Western nations and institutions and encourages the West to resist this challenge. The Foundation looks at military, political, economic, and cultural dimensions of the East-West relationship. It publishes position papers, newsletters, and the quarterly *Policy Review*.

Institute for Policy Studies (IPS)
1901 Q St. NW
Washington, DC 20009
(202) 234-9382

The Institute's program on national security provides both factual analysis and critiques of foreign and military policy. Its goal has been to unravel the myths of the Cold War and provide a more balanced view of relations. The IPS has a joint exchange with the Institute for the Study of the USA of the USSR Academy of Sciences. With the Academy, it has developed a model treaty on general disarmament. The Institute publishes several books on these subjects, including *The Rise and Fall of the Soviet Threat*, and *Soviet Policy in the Arc of Crisis*.

National Council for American-Soviet Friendship
162 Madison Ave.
New York, NY 10016
(212) 679-4577

The Council encourages better relations between the US and the USSR through cultural and scientific exchange and increased trade. It publishes pamphlets, pictorial exhibits, and the quarterly *Friendship News*.

National Conference on Soviet Jewry
10 E. 40th St., Suite 907
New York, NY 10016
(212) 679-6122

The Conference is a coalition of major Jewish organizations and councils that works for the emigration of Jews from the Soviet Union and for the right of Jews in the Soviet Union to have the same rights as other ethnic and religious minorities. It publishes pamphlets, reports, and the weekly *Newsbreak*. A list of publications will be provided on request.

Soviet Embassy
Information Department
1706 18th St. NW
Washington, DC 20009

The Soviet Embassy distributes speeches by Mikhail Gorbachev and other Soviet leaders on topics including disarmament, energy, and the development of the Soviet economy. Among the publications available are *Yearbook USSR*, an annual review of events; *Soviet Life*, a monthly photo feature news magazine; and *USSR, 100 Questions and Answers*.

Bibliography of Books

Anatole Alexandrov — *Possessing Energy Resources Is Not Enough.* Moscow: Novosti Press Agency, 1986.

Georgi Arbatov and Willem Oltmans — *The Soviet Viewpoint.* New York: Dodd, Mead & Co., 1981.

Mark Azbel — *Refusenik: Trapped in the Soviet Union.* Boston: Houghton Mifflin Co., 1981.

Seweryn Bialer — *The Soviet Paradox: External Expansion, Internal Decline.* New York: Alfred A. Knopf, 1986.

Michael Binyon — *Life in Russia.* New York: Pantheon Books, 1983.

Elena Bonner — *Alone Together.* New York: Alfred A. Knopf, 1986.

Alan Bookbinder, Olivia Lichtenstein, and Richard Denton — *Comrades: Portraits of Soviet Life.* New York: Plume Books, 1985.

Zbigniew Brzezinski — *Game Plan: How To Conduct the US-Soviet Contest.* Boston: The Atlantic Monthly Press, 1986.

Michael Charlton — *The Eagle and the Small Birds: Crisis in the Soviet Empire.* Chicago: University of Chicago Press, 1984.

Stephen F. Cohen — *Sovieticus: American Perceptions and Soviet Realities.* New York: W.W. Norton, 1986.

Timothy J. Colton — *The Dilemma of Reform in the Soviet Union.* Washington, DC: Council on Foreign Relations, 1986.

Brian D. Daily and Patrick J. Parker, eds. — *Soviet Strategic Deception.* Lexington, MA: Lexington Books, 1986.

Alexander Dallin and Condoleeza Rice, eds. — *The Gorbachev Era.* Stanford, CA: Stanford Alumni Association, 1986.

Paul Dibb — *The Soviet Union: The Incomplete Superpower.* London: Macmillan Publishers for the International Institute for Strategic Studies, 1986.

Milovan Djilas — *Of Prisons and Ideas.* San Diego: Harcourt Brace Jovanovich, 1986.

Dusko Doder — *Shadows and Whispers: Power Politics Inside the Kremlin from Brezhnev to Gorbachev.* New York: Random House, 1986.

Florence Fox — *Poland Answers.* Gravenhurst, Ontario: Northern Book House, 1984.

Mark Garrison and Abbott Gleason — *Shared Destiny: Fifty Years of Soviet-American Relations.* Boston: Beacon Press, 1985.

Charles Gati — *Hungary and the Soviet Bloc.* Durham, NC: Duke University Press, 1986.

Tom Gervasi — *The Myth of Soviet Military Supremacy.* New York: Harper & Row, 1986.

Ivan Gladky — *Social Programmes Benefit from Economic Restructuring.* Moscow: Novosti Press Agency, 1986.

Marshall I. Goldman — *USSR In Crisis: The Failure of the Economic System.* New York: W.W. Norton, 1983.

Lincoln Gordon, et al. — *Eroding Empire: Western Relations with Eastern Europe.* Washington, DC: The Brookings Institute, 1987.

Carola Hansson and Karin Liden — *Moscow Women.* New York: Pantheon Books, 1983.

Václav Havel, et al. — *The Power of the Powerless: Citizens Against the State in Central-Eastern Europe.* Armonk, NY: M.E. Sharpe, Inc., 1985.

Gustav Herling — *A World Apart: The Journal of a Gulag Survivor.* New York: Arbor House, 1986.

Erik P. Hoffmann and Robbin F. Laird — *The Politics of Economic Modernization in the Soviet Union.* Ithaca, NY: Cornell University Press, 1982.

Jerry F. Hough — *The Struggle for the Third World.* Washington, DC: The Brookings Institute, 1986.

Wojciech Jaruzelski — *Selected Speeches.* Oxford, England: Pergamon Press, 1985.

Basile Kerblay — *Modern Soviet Society.* New York: Pantheon Books, 1983.

Robbin F. Laird and Erik P. Hoffmann, eds. — *Soviet Foreign Policy in a Changing World.* New York: Aldine Publishing Co., 1986.

David Lane — *Soviet Economy & Society.* New York: New York University Press, 1985.

Michael Ledeen — *Grave New World: The Superpower Crisis of the 1980s.* New York: Oxford University Press, 1985.

John Lenczowski — *Soviet Perceptions of U.S. Foreign Policy: A Study of Ideology, Power, and Consensus.* Ithaca, NY: Cornell University Press, 1982.

Wolfgang Leonhard — *The Kremlin and the West: A Realistic Approach.* New York: W.W. Norton, 1986.

Martin McCauley and Stephen Carter, eds. — *Leadership and Succession in the Soviet Union, Eastern Europe, and China.* Armonk, NY: M.E. Sharpe, Inc., 1986.

Adam Michnik — *Letters from Prison and Other Essays.* Berkeley: University of California Press, 1986.

Andrew Nagorski — *Reluctant Farewell: An American Reporter's Candid Look Inside the Soviet Union.* New York: New Republic Books, 1987.

Joseph S. Nye Jr., ed. — *The Making of America's Soviet Policy.* New Haven, CT: Yale University Press, 1984.

Richard Pipes — *Survival Is Not Enough.* New York: Simon & Schuster, 1984.

Peter Rutland — *The Myth of the Plan: Lessons of Soviet Planning Experience.* Peru, IL: Open Court Publishing Co., 1986.

Arkady N. Shevchenko — *Breaking with Moscow.* New York: Alfred A. Knopf, 1985.

245

Konstantin Simis	*USSR: The Corrupt Society.* New York: Simon & Schuster, 1982.
Vladimir Solovyov and Elena Klepikova	*Behind the High Kremlin Walls.* New York: Dodd, Mead & Co., 1986.
Aleksandr Solzhenitsyn	*The Mortal Danger: How Misconceptions About Russia Imperil America.* New York: Harper & Row, 1980.
E.P. Thompson	*The Heavy Dancers.* New York: Pantheon Books, 1985.
Nikolai A. Tikhonov	*Soviet Economy: Achievements, Problems, Prospects.* Moscow: Novosti Press Agency, 1983.
Vladimir Voinovich	*The Anti-Soviet Soviet Union.* San Diego: Harcourt Brace Jovanovich, 1985.
Michael Voslensky	*Nomenklatura: The Soviet Ruling Class, An Insider's Report.* New York: Doubleday & Co., 1984.
Martin Walker	*The Waking Giant: Gorbachev's Russia.* New York: Pantheon Books, 1986.
Warsaw Treaty Member States	*Documents of the Meeting of the Political Committee.* Moscow: Novosti Press Agency, 1987.
Vadim Zagladin	*Our Aim: Universal International Security.* Moscow: Novosti Press Agency, 1986.
Adam Zwass	*The Economies of Eastern Europe.* Armonk, NY: M.E. Sharpe, Inc., 1984.

Appendix of Periodicals

Many periodicals which focus on the Soviet Union are not widely available. Below is a list of some useful publications and information about where to obtain them.

New Politics
New Politics Associates
PO Box 98
Brooklyn, NY 11231

A quarterly socialist journal.

New Times
Imported Publications
320 W. Ohio St.
Chicago, IL 60610

A weekly newsmagazine published in the USSR.

People's Daily World
USPS 146920
239 W. 23rd St.
New York, NY 10011

The official newspaper of the Communist Party, USA.

Political Affairs
235 W. 23rd St.
New York, NY 10011

The monthly theoretical journal of the Communist Party, USA.

Soviet Life
Subscription Department
1706 18th St. NW
Washington, DC 20009

A monthly photo, feature, and newsmagazine published by the USSR Embassy.

Soviet Military Review
Imported Publications
320 W. Ohio St.
Chicago, IL 60610

A monthly newsmagazine published in the USSR.

World Marxist Review
Progress Books
71 Bathurst St.
Toronto, Ontario, Canada, M5V 2P6

A monthly theoretical journal sponsored by Communist parties from around the world.

Index

Abalkin, Leonid, 151
Abram, Morris B., 107
Afghanistan
 Soviet involvement in , 37, 43
Aganbegian, Abel, 134
agriculture, Soviet, 142
 as dismal, 129-130
 as good, 125
Andropov, Yuri, 19
Armacost, Michael H., 40
arms control
 and human rights
  should be linked, 91, 92
  should not be linked, 79-85
Ash, Timothy Garton, 192
Ashby, Timothy, 42
Aspaturian, Vernon V., 38

Beichman, Arnold, 142
Benson, Steve, 21
Bettelheim, Charles, 130
Bialer, Seweryn, 154
Bonner, Yelena, 107
Bonofsky, Phillip, 112
Brezhnev, Leonid, 154
Brimelow, Peter, 154
Bukovsky, Vladimir, 220, 225
Bunce, Valerie, 178

Caribbean
 as US border, 43-44
 Soviet involvement in, 46
Caribbean Basin Initiative, 45
Castro, Fidel, 47, 55
Center for Defense Information, 50
Central America, 44, 45
Chesterton, G.K., 198
China
 compared to Soviet Union, 142,
  144-145
 relations with Soviet Union, 20-21,
  51-53
communism
 as inherently flawed, 133, 142
 failure of, 220
  as inherent, 133, 142
 in Eastern Europe, 196
 see also socialism
Council for Mutual Economic
 Assistance (CMEA), 185
 criticism of
  as invalid, 189-190
Courter, Jim, 19
Crowe, J.D., 222
Cuba

as Soviet proxy, 38, 45-48
 myth of, 54
intelligence agencies of, 46
Czechoslovakia, 177

Davidow, Mike, 199
DeOre, Bill, 132
Dobbins, Jim, 99

Eastern Europe
 and disarmament, 168
 exports to US, 185-186
 modeled after Soviet socialism,
  165-170
  as inhibiting growth, 171-175
 relationship with Soviet Union
  as colonialist, 37-38
  as cooperative, 169
  as stifling, 174
  economic dependence, 180-181,
   183
   as cooperative, 184-191
   as harmful, 176-183
   impact on Soviet Union, 178-179
   is a myth, 189-190
  political and economic links,
   181-182
 see also Poland
economy, Soviet
 and technological advances, 138
 as healthy, 127
  myth of, 128-133
 as improving, 134-139
  myth of, 140-146
 compared to Japan, 136
 compared to US, 123, 145-146
 crisis in
  as caused by bureaucracy, 130-131,
   141
  as caused by military
   expenditures, 132-133
 growth rate of, 135
 national income, 136, 137
 restructuring of
  as authentic, 214-215
  myth of, 154-159
  expanding trade, 152
  need for, 124-125
   worker incentives, 152-153
    as counterproductive, 131-132
  opposed by US, 150
 stagnation of
  as caused by closed system, 156-157
El Salvador, 39
Ellison, Herbert J., 176

European Economic Community (EEC), 187

Fox, Florence, 108

Gaddis, John Lewis, 81
Ganin, Vladimir, 184
Garner, Bill, 46
glasnost
  as authentic, 211-217, 231-236
  con, 87-88, 222-223, 225-230
  as unrealistic, 218-224
  impact on foreign policy, 224
  longevity of, 228-229
Gorbachev, Mikhail, 69, 87, 147, 211
  and Soviet system
    can change, 235-236
    cannot change, 221
  differences from previous leaders, 219-220
  reforms insufficient, 157-159
Gorshkov, Sergei, 45
Gramm, Boris, 109
Grenada, 40
  Cuban involvement in, 48
  Soviet involvement marginal, 57
  US involvement, 53-54
Gurevich, A., 110

Harrington, Ollie, 27, 126
Hejdánek, Ladislav, 171
Helsinki Final Act
  Soviet violations of, 90-91, 104
  US must keep a priority, 92
Hewett, Ed A., 156
Higginbotham, Jay, 83
Horowitz, David, 44
Hughes, John, 158
human rights, Soviet
  and arms control
    should be linked, 91, 92
    should not be linked, 79-85
  as guaranteed, 63-69
  as undermined, 70-78
  censorship, 233
  free education, 66
    myth of, 73-75
  free housing, 65-66
  free medical care, 65
    myth of, 71-73
  gender differences, 98
  political prisoners, 89-90
  violations
    as US propaganda, 30-31
    should be opposed, 86-92
    should be tolerated, 79-85
    US should pressure, 91-92, 104-105

International Convenants on Human Rights and Soviet Legislation, 67
Irvine, Arnold, 78

Jacobson, Julius, 231
Japan, 22-23
Jaruzelski, Wojciech, 201, 203
Jews, Soviet
  are repressed, 101-107
    as US propaganda, 108-114
  discrimination against, 75

Kadar, Janos, 169
Kallaugher, Kevin, 173, 229
Kazinov, Leonid, 63
Kennedy, Paul, 140
Khrushchev, Nikita, 100
Kobrin, Mikhail, 138
Kobyakov, Gennady, 122
Kuritsyn, Yuri, 34
Kutzik, Alfred, 112
Kuznetsov, Vladlen, 29

Latin America
  economic crisis of, 45
  Soviet involvement in
    as expanding, 42-49
    as not expanding, 50-57
  US involvement in, 35
Lenin, Vladimir, 66, 78
  tenets of, 35
Locher, Dick, 180
Lowe, Marty, 213
Luers, William H., 48, 235
Lyutov, Ivan, 167

MacNelly, Jeff, 103
manifest destiny, 30
Milosz, Czeslaw, 194, 196
Minard, Lawrence, 154

Natorf, Wlodzimierz, 186
Nicaragua
  Soviet involvement in, 40, 44
    as insignificant, 55-57
Nikolenko, A., 110
Nomenklatura, 76, 196-197
  as anti-semitic, 102
nuclear-free zones
  in Eastern Europe, 168
nuclear war
  preventing, 79-85

Orzechowski, Marian, 165

Perle, Richard N., 36
Pesky, Alan D., 105
Pett, Joel, 74
Pevnev, Yuri, 190
Pfaltzgraff, Robert L. Jr., 218
Pilon, Roger, 101

Pisarevsky, Gennady, 65, 124, 136
Poland, 170
  agricultural output of, 202
  and World War II, 200, 204
  disarmament efforts, 168
  economy of, 200
  human rights in, 201
  national income of, 201-202
  pre-war conditions of
    as negative, 201
  relationship with the Soviet Union,
    186
    as cooperative, 167, 199-205
    as invasive, 177, 192-198
    as liberation, 202-203
    West should reserve judgment,
      84-85
Polish-Soviet Friendship Society, 203,
  204
Pravda, 19

Reagan, Ronald, 106-107
  on Soviet human rights, 88
Renkas, Yaroslav, 63
Revel, Jean-François, 23
revolutions, 44
  as intrinsically good, 33-35
Rood, Harold, 17
Ryabtsev, E., 148

Sakharov, Andrei, 87, 107, 222
  opinion of glasnost, 233
  release of
    as propaganda, 87-88, 228
Schifter, Richard, 76
Sedov, Nikolai, 32
Shcharansky, Anatoly, 88-89, 107
Shelton, Sally, 55
Shevardnadze, Eduard, 89
Shevchenko, Yuri, 153
Simis, Konstantin, 70
socialism
  as peaceful, 28
  guarantees social equality, 66-67, 69
  Soviet
    as model for Eastern Europe,
      165-170
      fallacy of, 171-175
    supports revolution, 34-35
  see also communism
Sokolovsky, V.W., 18
Solzhenitsyn, Aleksandr, 83-84, 128, 227
Sontag, Susan, 196
Soviet
  citizens
    average income of, 76-77
      as rising, 127
    guaranteed full employment, 136

economy see economy, Soviet
human rights see human rights, Soviet
influence
  as decreasing worldwide, 51-52
intervention
  as humanitarian, 32-35
  as self-serving, 36-41
involvement, 18
  in Cuba, 53-55
  in Latin America
    as expanding, 42-49
    as not expanding, 50-57
  in Nicaragua, 40, 44
    as not extensive, 55-57
  in Vietnam, 20-21
Jews
  are allowed to emigrate, 112
  are not repressed, 108-114
  are repressed, 101-107
  arrests of, 103-104
  as highly educated, 110
  discrimination against, 75
  involvement in government, 109-110
military, 18, 37, 219
propaganda, 39
system
  as corrupt, 70-78
women
  and equal employment
    opportunity, 94, 98-99
  and state-subsidized day care, 95
  have full equality, 93-96
    myth of, 97-100
  involvement in politics, 96
    myth of, 100
Soviet Union
  and anti-US propaganda, 105-106
  as a threat to the US, 37
  as expansionist, 17-24, 40, 43
    myth of, 25-31
  as moving toward democracy, 148,
    217
  as peaceloving, 26-31
    con, 18-24
  as unchangeable, 78
  compared to China, 142, 144-145
  computer technology, 157-158
  demographics of, 143-144
  economic statistics, 123
  government of
    lacks public support, 83
    has helped Poland, 199-205
    has suppressed Poland, 192-198
  improvements in economic
    structure, 235-236
  in Eastern Europe
    as expansionist, 173-174

250

exports to, 188-189
harms Eastern European
economies, 176-183
con, 184-189
poverty in, 76-77, 82
restructuring of
as cosmetic, 225-230
myth of, 232-236
as impossible, 218-224
internal opposition to
as selfish, 215-216
is occurring, 212-217
socialism
as model for Eastern Europe,
165-170
fallacy of, 171-175
threatens US, 37
see also communism
Stalinism
as cause of economic stagnation,
154-159
Strauss, Franz Josef, 29
Suez Canal, 19-20
Sukhoruchenkova, Galina, 93
Sychev, Vyacheslav, 184

Talbott, Strobe, 72
Talyzin, N.V., 125
Tsoppi, Victor, 138
Tsypkin, Mikhail, 86

United States
as expansionist, 28-31
as moral dictator, 81-85
as preparing for war, 26-27
democracy
guarantees freedom, 38-39
guarantees human rights, 106-107
involvement
in El Salvador, 39
in Grenada, 40
poor labor conditions of, 68
poverty in, 67
response to glasnost, 150
social problems of, 106

Von Laue, Theodore H., 79
Voznesensky, Andrei, 232

Warsaw Treaty, 166
aids cooperation, 169
prevents war, 167
Wasserman, Dan, 52
Wick, Charles Z., 227
Willis, David K., 97
World War II
and Soviet interference in Poland
as negative, 193-194
as positive, 200

impact on Soviet/Eastern European
relations
as negative, 172
as positive, 166, 167, 169
Wright, Dick, 90

Yalta, 193-194, 195

Zabavskaya, Lyudmila, 93
Zamkovi, Vladimir, 25
Zwass, Adam, 182